ROUTLEDGE LIBRARY EDITIONS:
EARLY WESTERN RESPONSES
TO SOVIET RUSSIA

Volume 10

BOLSHEVISM IN PERSPECTIVE

BOLSHEVISM IN PERSPECTIVE

J. DE V. LODER

Routledge
Taylor & Francis Group
LONDON AND NEW YORK

First published in 1931 by George Allen & Unwin Ltd

This edition first published in 2018
by Routledge
2 Park Square, Milton Park, Abingdon, Oxon OX14 4RN

and by Routledge
711 Third Avenue, New York, NY 10017

Routledge is an imprint of the Taylor & Francis Group, an informa business

British Library Cataloguing in Publication Data
A catalogue record for this book is available from the British Library

ISBN: 978-1-138-04993-2 (Set)
ISBN: 978-1-315-11072-1 (Set) (ebk)
ISBN: 978-1-138-07019-6 (Volume 10) (hbk)
ISBN: 978-1-138-07034-9 (Volume 10) (pbk)
ISBN: 978-1-315-11510-8 (Volume 10) (ebk)

Publisher's Note
The publisher has gone to great lengths to ensure the quality of this reprint but points out that some imperfections in the original copies may be apparent.

BOLSHEVISM
IN PERSPECTIVE

by

J. de V. LODER

LONDON
GEORGE ALLEN & UNWIN LTD
MUSEUM STREET

FIRST PUBLISHED IN 1931

PRINTED IN GREAT BRITAIN BY
UNWIN BROTHERS LTD., WOKING

PREFACE

This book is the result of two visits to Russia, in the autumn of 1929 and 1930, of a combined duration of four months. On the first occasion I was accompanied by my wife. On the second occasion my companion was Mr. L. E. Hubbard, who had been in business in Moscow before the war. His experience of pre-revolutionary conditions and his command of the language were invaluable for arriving at a balanced appreciation of the situation.

So many personal impressions of Soviet Russia have been published that I have hesitated to add to the number. I am also conscious that, in spite of having travelled nearly 15,000 miles through the country, and having talked to many of the best-informed persons both in Moscow and elsewhere, I cannot claim to write with authority. But records of personal observations and the studies of specialists are apt to lack perspective. I have, therefore, felt justified in attempting to present a picture in which actual problems are set in an historical background.

Such an attempt is especially necessary because the Russian Revolution occurred at a time when public attention was absorbed by the war. The Revolution was seen, first of all, as an incident of the war. Its early development was considered primarily as it affected the fortunes of the Allies or the Central Powers. Subsequently, the fear of world revolution provoked an unreasoning hostility, which to some extent still prevails to-day. The result has been to distort the image of the Revolution as it is reflected in the Western mind, a distortion which is paralleled in Russia by the tendency to regard the war as if its primary importance was as a prelude to the revolution.

My first endeavour has been to depict the Revolution in

truer proportions, but I am necessarily handicapped because the time has not yet come when a final appreciation can be made. How did the Revolution happen? How did the Bolsheviks get power? How have they managed to keep it? These are questions which can and must be answered, but as the story nears the present day it loses definiteness in contact with unsettled issues. The situation is still so fluid that the Revolution cannot yet be regarded as finished. The reader must not be disappointed if a climax and a *dénouement* are missing.

The second part of the book turns from historical narrative to direct observation. It is personal and particular. What is the present condition of the country? What does it look like after fourteen years of Soviet Government? What impression do the people make? What is life like under Bolshevism? What progress is the Government making with its plans? These are questions for the answers to which I have relied on personal experience or on information acquired on the spot.

Part III is more general. It deals with Bolshevism as a working system. I have attempted to indicate the nature of the challenge which Bolshevism is making to orthodox Western Civilization, and to indicate possible lines of future development. I have not striven after colourless impartiality. My main object has been to give those to whom Bolshevism is instinctively repulsive grounds for opposition based on reason rather on emotion or prejudice. If an open conflict is inevitable we must go into it with our eyes open. If a conflict may still be avoided it will be because, understanding Bolshevism, and knowing where we stand ourselves, we shall not allow the two sides to drift into a position from which there is no issue.

Some paragraphs of Parts II and III have formed part of articles in the *Sunday Times*, *Daily Telegraph*, *Manchester*

Guardian Commercial, and *Europaeische Revue*. One of the posters reproduced has already appeared in the *Graphic*. The editors of these papers have kindly allowed me to incorporate this material. The photographs were all taken by Mr. Hubbard or myself.

My thanks are particularly due to Mr. Noel Skelton and Count Constantine Benckendorff for their criticisms and suggestions. I should also like to acknowledge the courtesy of the Soviet authorities to an admitted opponent.

J. DE V. L.

CONTENTS

PART III

BOLSHEVISM IN ACTION

ILLUSTRATIONS

MAP

PART I

THE REVOLUTION IN OUTLINE

CHAPTER I

THE AUTOCRACY IN DECAY

Revolution, like war, is never wholly unexpected, however paralysing the shock of the actual outbreak. In Russia the political sky had been darkening for nearly a century before the final catastrophe. Because Russia was remote from the rest of Europe, a mediæval and feudal autocracy long remained impervious to the influences which worked such profound changes among Western peoples. Peter the Great had tried, at the end of the seventeenth century, to put Russia on the same plane of development as Western and Central Europe, but the assimilation was so superficial that the country was not swept along with other nations into the current of new ideas which gathered force during the next hundred years. During the nineteenth century Russia was almost as little affected by the political, social, and economic movements of the times as Turkey. One the spiritual, the other the territorial heir of the Byzantines, both retained the forms of Government of another age. New wine could not ferment in these old bottles without bursting them, and to the very last the Tzars conceded no limitation in principle of their autocratic powers. Liberal ideas sometimes attracted and sometimes repelled successive monarchs, but changed nothing of the reality of their personal rule. A few classes such as the clergy, the nobility, and the Cossacks received privileges in order to make them the willing instruments of Government, but even they had no rights which were not the personal gift of the sovereign. It has always been the practice of autocrats to emphasize the common subjection of their liegemen by choosing their servants without regard to their social status. A surprising number of the distinguished figures of the last generation under Tzarism, especially in the army, were of humble origin, but this is only an illustration of the arbitrariness of the system. While in most countries monarchy was changing from an actual to a symbolic expression of power, in Russia the character of the Tzar remained the decisive factor of each reign.

Alexander I (1801–1825), educated in an atmosphere of eighteenth-century "enlightenment," aspired to be the generous father of his people, but his ideas did not go beyond a youthful fascination for the up-to-date despotism of Napoleon, followed by a more mature and conservative enthusiasm, which found expression in the idealistic side of the Holy Alliance.

Nicholas I (1825–1855) had no intention of allowing his position to be undermined by such romantic nonsense. "Enlightenment" was effectively discouraged with the suppression of the Decabrist conspiracy in the year of his accession, and he merely used the Polish revolt of 1831 as an opportunity for teaching rebels a lesson, and for withdrawing such autonomy as the Poles previously possessed.

Alexander II (1855–1881) might have canalized into constitutional channels the unrest, which by now was acquiring the force of a popular movement, if he had combined with his liberal instincts the determination and ability of a great leader. Unfortunately, while he succeeded in raising popular expectations, he remained bound to the traditional outlook of the privileged classes which surrounded the throne. He emancipated the serfs in 1861; he reformed the courts of justice; he inaugurated popular responsibility in local government by the creation of elective provincial councils, or *zemstvos* (1864), and municipalities (1870); but, when these measures did not yield the anticipated results, he had no answer save repression to the clamour of a disappointed people. The fault was on both sides. They had expected too much and he had given too little, or rather he had merely appeared to make concessions when a striking constructive policy was necessary. He fell to the bomb of an assassin, having loosened the foundations of the autocracy by destroying the feudal bonds which held the system together, but without having laid new foundations for a democratic state.

Under Alexander III (1881–1894) the structure of the Empire became at once more rigid and more brittle. Efforts to force heterogeneous peoples into a Russian mould were redoubled. The effects of the reforms of the previous reign were stifled. All political agitation was driven underground. The future was mortgaged for a superficial display of unity and strength.

Nicholas II (1894–1917) succeeded to a heritage bound to him mainly by a mixture of fear and traditional loyalty. He himself was not a person to inspire either of these emotions. Had he been the determined, relentless despot, which the title of Tzar of all the Russias evokes in imagination, he might have rightly earned the name of "Bloody Nicholas," applied to him in revolutionary jargon, but he would never have been so tamely swept away. Separated as he was from his subjects by a ceremonial gulf which testified to an almost superhuman authority, the Tzar was made to appear as the embodiment of a legend, whatever his characteristics as a man. The will of the autocrat was indissolubly associated with the acts done in his name. Nor can Nicholas II escape responsibility for them. Yet those acts were in no real sense his. He was dominated by his beautiful and imperious consort, Alexandra Feodorovna, Princess of Hesse, who pushed him along a path diametrically opposed to the inclinations of his gentle, simple nature.

With the limited outlook of a mediocre intelligence he accepted without question the conception of his position which had been presented to him since childhood, and with the obstinacy of a weak character he refused to listen to any different interpretation of his duties. Being convinced of the rightness of the autocratic principle, he did whatever his wife and his ministers, who thought likewise, told him was necessary to safeguard that principle. He knew nothing of what was passing through the minds of his subjects except through official reports, but he conscientiously believed that he was ruling them for their own good. Pity is the sentiment which he will surely inspire in history, but his contemporaries can hardly be blamed if they regarded him with hatred and contempt. There was massed against him the accumulated resentment of generations of sufferers under tyranny and the fury of minds thwarted in the expression of ideas which were the ordinary legal tender of political controversy in other lands.

Russia had long provided a fertile soil for the planting of revolutionary doctrine. Western Europe had felt the full impact of the upheaval in ideas represented by the French Revolution. The effect in Russia was little more than to set a few people thinking. Western Europe was too busy with problems of Liberal democracy, which were the practical outcome of that upheaval, to pay much attention to the following out of the theories whence they were derived. In Russia there was at first little opportunity for political action, and the spirit of the times had to find the best expression it could in intellectual ferment. Hence arose the great literary period of Pushkin, Lermontov, Herzen, Gogol, Turgeniev, Dostoievsky, and Tolstoy, all of whom were revolutionary in spirit, if not in the restricted political sense. Hence, also, the interest displayed in Socialism, which, while it appeared to most people in Western Europe at that time as the ravings of a few Utopian agitators, seemed to the Russian intellectuals to provide just the definite basis they required for the construction of a new order. The system of Karl Marx was particularly likely to attract them, because it combined features which would make a natural appeal to the Russian mind with other features which would just fill the gaps in the Russian powers of reasoning. Marxism was universal, inevitable, and certain. The Russian mind would respond immediately to universality, a glorious mystical vision of the whole; it would comprehend inevitability with its fatalistic appreciation of relentless force, it would cling to a dogmatic certainty which it could never achieve of itself.

The first modern Russian revolutionaries were not, however, consciously Marxists, though it so happens that they produced the type of revolutionary which foreigners have particularly identified with Russia, namely, the Nihilist. The rise of this movement dates from the early days of Alexander II's reign, just after the Crimean War, when Liberal ideas were more in favour in Russia than perhaps they ever were before or after. The name was first used by Turgeniev in 1862 in his novel *Fathers and Sons*. The movement began among students who adopted extreme views against all social order, renouncing God, the family, and property, and calling attention to themselves by extravagances of behaviour. In some ways it resembled, in political form, the sectarian religious movements which are common in Russia. The idea was to go about among the people, and, as schoolmasters, artisans, midwives, and so on, to preach surreptitiously the advent of a new age through the dissolution of all social bonds.

The Government dealt severely with these agitators. Terrorism was their reply. A "Society for the Liberation of the People" was founded in 1869, but the *Narodniki*, as its members were called, were always loosely organized. Although *Narodniki* were responsible for nearly all the political assassinations carried out or attempted during the succeeding half-century, individuals and groups often acted independently. Contact with foreign revolutionaries caused the *Narodniki* gradually to assimilate much of the doctrinal outlook of European Socialism. They were the forerunners of the Social Revolutionary Party, which played a dominating part in the early months of the Revolution. The Social Revolutionaries inherited the agrarian traditions and decentralized methods of the *Narodniki*. Both these tendencies had important consequences during the struggle for power against the Bolsheviks. The Left Social Revolutionaries, in particular, showed their Nihilist affinities by always drifting into opposition. They supported the Provisional Government against the Tzar, then the Bolsheviks against the Provisional Government, and finally turned against the Bolsheviks themselves.

Starting somewhat later, but ultimately to prove of decisive importance, were the Social Democrats, a purely Marxian party, developing, as might be expected, in an urban and industrial atmosphere. The particular form in which Marx elaborated his theories was meant to appeal to industrial communities, and, until a nucleus of modern industrial enterprises had grown up in Russia, his *Communist Manifesto* of 1847 and *Das Kapital* could hardly be expected to have much effect. The Social Democratic movement was made possible by the rapid growth of Russian industry in the eighties and nineties, and by some of its peculiar features. Owing to the predominance of foreign capital the growth of the native industrial middle class did not correspond to the growth of the industrial labouring class. The high proportion of large factories, moreover, favoured class-conscious solidarity.

The first prominent Russian Social Democrat was Plekhanov, who in 1885 was responsible for a "Programme for the Emancipation of Labour," which, however, went no farther than advocating the realization of the Socialist State by agitation for a constitution followed by gradual evolution. The "Russian Social-Democratic Working Men's Party" was not founded till 1898. Here Plekhanov's group, and a group which advocated working through local industrial organizations such as Trade Unions, were defeated by those who favoured a compact centralized party organization. This idea had already been put forward by Lenin, then a young man of twenty-eight, and at the time in exile in Siberia for his political activities. On his release in 1900 he went abroad and soon became one of the leaders of the party, the headquarters of which had also been driven out of Russia.[1] In 1903, the party split at a conference held in London. The actual point at issue concerned the conditions of membership. The majority, or *bolshevik* section, led by Lenin, insisted on restricting the party to a disciplined fighting machine of absolutely trustworthy adherents, and repudiated any compromise with the bourgeois parties. The minority, or *menshevik* section, led by Martov, were not so insistent on the paramountcy of the class war. They were prepared to accept recruits from any source, and even to modify the programme if it meant

[1] Nicolai Lenin was an assumed "party" name. His real name was Vladimir Ilytch Ulianov. He was born at Simbirsk in 1870. His father was a small landowner and a director of elementary education. His elder brother was executed in 1887 for complicity in a plot to assassinate the Tzar, Alexander III. He married a fellow revolutionary worker, Nadezhda Constantinova Krupskaya, in 1897, but had no children. By a curious coincidence, the headmaster of the high school at Simbirsk, where he received part of his education, was Kerensky's father.

acquiring more influence. Trotsky,[1] who was present at the Conference, but who adopted an independent attitude, which he retained until he definitely joined the Bolsheviks in August 1917, speaks of the "hard" and "soft" groups, a sufficiently accurate indication of the temperamental differences at the bottom of the dispute. The two sections henceforward worked separately, though both still claimed the name of Social Democrats.

A great deal has been made of the part played by Jews in the revolutionary movement, but it is not necessary to seek occult reasons for this. The inferior social status of the Jews under the Tzarist régime disposed them to revolutionary sentiments, their racial characteristics to the urban, internationalist outlook of the Social Democrats. There was, moreover, a spiritual link represented by Russian Orthodox Apocalyptic and Jewish Messianism. These factors were emphasized by more practical considerations. The "October" Revolution found the Bolsheviks eager to secure the services of Jews to replace the vanished Russian officials; the Jews were no less eager to provide for their own safety by taking service under the new régime. The special tolerance secured by the Jews in the early years of the Bolshevik rule depended on three interdependent factors, first their indispensability, secondly their tradition of mutual protection, thirdly their ability to represent anti-semitism as Tzarist and therefore counter-revolutionary. Jewish influence in the directing circles of the Bolshevik Party has steadily declined since the Revolution, in proportion as the party has become more nationalistic in its outlook. The Jewish element among the Bolshevik leaders was represented by Trotsky (Bronstein), Kamenev (Rosenbaum), Zinoviev, Sverdlov, and Litvinov. The

[1] Trotsky's real name was Leon Davidovich Bronstein. He was born in 1877. His father was a well-to-do Jewish farmer near Elizavetgrad in South Russia.

rest, including Lenin, Chicherin, Rykov, Lunacharsky, and Krassin, were nearly all pure Russians. Dzerzinsky and Stalin (Djugashvili) were Russian subjects, the former being a Pole and the latter a Georgian. Radek was originally an Austrian Jew and Rakovsky a Rumanian subject.

The first open conflict between the Tzarist Government and organized revolutionary forces came in 1905. The Russo-Japanese War had revealed the rottenness of the whole military and civil administration. The indignation of all classes was aroused. The national humiliation found expression in widespread agitation for constitutional reform. In December 1904 the Tzar promised that something would be done, but rejected proposals for even a consultative popular assembly. On January 22, 1905, a demonstration of St. Petersburg workers was dispersed by troops with considerable loss of life. This was by no means the first time such measures had been used, but the incident at once acquired symbolic importance, and "Bloody Sunday" stands out as a prominent date in the revolutionary calendar. In March 1905 the Tzar yielded to the pressure for a national assembly. A flood of political controversy was unloosed. The whole country was seething with excitement. The land hunger of the peasants expressed itself in agrarian disturbances. The industrial workers also began to assert their political claims by "direct action." Part of the Black Sea Fleet mutinied. The suggested constitution of the National Assembly, when it was published in August, only added fuel to the flames. On October 30th the Tzar issued his celebrated decree granting more liberal reforms, but this did not prevent revolutionary outbreaks, which were only put down after troops had fired into the mobs and barricades had been stormed. During November and December—the so-called "days of freedom"—the fate of the Government hung in the balance. It was at this time that the word *soviet*, which simply means "council," first acquired its revolutionary significance from the St. Petersburg Council of Workers' Deputies. This body, formed of representatives from factories under the direction of Socialist leaders, among whom Trotsky was prominent, controlled the insurrection in the capital, and announced itself ready, if necessary, to take over political power in the country. But the time was not yet. The army was still loyal, and most people were prepared to give the Tzar's constitutional experiment a trial. The revolution was defeated in 1905, but the revolutionaries had had experience from which they profited while they continued to plan for the future.

The years which elapsed between the disturbances of 1905 and the outbreak of war in 1914 have truthfully been called a period of reaction, but, although conservative forces had the upper hand, there was never a time in Russian history when more sincere efforts were made to save the country from the consequences of the inadaptability of the autocracy.

The failure of direct action discredited the revolutionary parties. The Bolsheviks, especially, lost ground which they did not regain until the revolution of 1917 had been in progress some months. The moderate bourgeoisie were alarmed at the glimpse they had had of what revolution might mean. The supporters of autocracy were able to take advantage of these circumstances to whittle down concessions which had only been grudgingly made; and, unfortunately, the new Parliamentary Assembly played into their hands by indulging in a great deal of wild talk. The first two Dumas, dominated by Liberal and Radical groups, were dissolved in 1906 and 1907 after short lives. The franchise was doctored in order to strengthen the parties of the Right, and in this way a tolerably pliable Assembly was secured.

At the same time an attempt was begun to build up such a propertied middle class as had proved so stabilizing an influence in the democracies of Western Europe, but was practically non-existent outside a few big towns in Russia. The object of Stolypin's land reforms was to create a class of well-to-do peasant proprietors, who could join with the old-established landlords in controlling local government. Schemes of industrial development were also set on foot, and it was hoped that by this means the number of people with a financial interest in the preservation of order would be increased.

Whether, given a sufficiently long period of peace and prosperity, this policy would have succeeded is a debatable point. The difficulties were immense. The land reforms were disliked by the poorer peasants because they strengthened the rich peasant, or *kulak*, at the expense of the village community, or *mir*. The "Slavophile" intelligentzia opposed them as alien to the Russian mentality, and indeed there was much in the argument that it was impossible suddenly to inculcate a conception of private property as a stake in the country among people in such a primitive state of social organization. The Socialists, of course, regarded the whole proceeding as rank Capitalism. Nor would it have been easy to create a class of Russian industrialists. Russian industry had always depended on foreign capital and management. There was little chance of stimulating the rapid growth of native enterprise.

But the final stumbling-block to the development of Russia in a democratic direction lay in the refusal of the autocracy to recognize the necessity of such a course. The Tzar and his more intimate advisers never accepted constitutional government as a praiseworthy ideal. There were many progressive members of the ruling class who wanted to save the monarchy by persuading it to take the lead in reform, but even when such persons obtained important administrative positions they were always in danger of dismissal if they were suspected of becoming politically unreliable.

There were but meagre grounds for the optimism of those who expected to see the establishment of the Duma lead to a Government chosen by Parliament. The official tendency was all the other way. The Duma had been accepted as a regrettable necessity to prevent revolution. It had little responsibility. Ministers were still appointed on the Tzar's personal authority, and he could still exercise full legislative and executive powers on his own responsibility. Thus the Duma was prevented even from being a truly representative safety valve. Similarly, in the provinces, the activities of the *zemstvos* and municipalities were systematically checked.

As time went on the Tzar succeeded in alienating an ever-increasing proportion of his subjects. The professional and commercial intelligentzia, the moderate politicians, and the small country gentry, all elements fundamentally disposed to seek a peaceful solution of political difficulties, were snubbed and bullied until they resigned themselves to the inevitable. And all the time a subterranean murmur indicated that other interests, which had nothing to lose by the disintegration of the existing order, were causing the masses to stir uneasily in anticipation of an upheaval which they believed could not be long delayed. It is hard to believe that at this stage any bridge could have been formed to unite the Tzar and his people. The war provided the last chance, and, at the same time, destroyed it.

This is not the place to discuss the degree of Russia's responsibility for the war, but it can hardly be doubted that the Government were thankful for the opportunity of diverting attention from internal politics. The initial effect of the outbreak of hostilities was indeed remarkable. An almost unanimous enthusiasm for the national cause swept the country. Strikers, who had been tearing up tramlines in the capital a few days earlier, joined in patriotic demonstrations. Ninety-six per cent. of those called to the colours responded.

It was not long, however, before this mood began to change. The war had hardly been in progress a year when symptoms of unsteadiness began to manifest themselves. Thenceforward the situation deteriorated steadily until catastrophe overwhelmed the country.

Russia was in no condition to stand the strain of a prolonged conflict. With the entry of Turkey on the side of the Central Powers, she was almost isolated from the other Allies. The only avenues of communication left open were through the White Sea ports, icebound in winter, or along the Trans-Siberian Railway round three-quarters of the globe. Russia was largely dependent on imports for manufactured goods. Her industries were quite inadequate, either to cope with the demands of the population, or to supply the army with the immense quantities of material required by modern warfare. These difficulties were aggravated by the incompetence and corruption of the administration. During 1916 it became daily clearer that the whole economic structure of the country was breaking down. The improvident mobilization of skilled workers was impeding production. The prohibition of vodka, by cutting off a third of the revenue from taxation, and eliminating an important medium of exchange between town and country just when the peasant was finding that he could buy little with the price of his grain, had serious results. The railways were disorganized. Food began to run short, and during the winter of 1916 bread queues were as much a feature of the city streets as they have been under revolutionary conditions.

More serious still was the deterioration of morale, both military and political. The defeats of 1915, when the Russians were thrown out of Galicia, lost Poland, and retreated hundreds of miles all along their Western front, were sufficiently depressing in themselves, but the revelation of the Government's incapacity brought home by these events did far more damage. The demand for Ministers who would command the confidence of the country, by which was meant responsible Parliamentary Government, became insistent. The army itself was no longer the blindly loyal servant of the Tzar. Casualties had weakened the old officer caste, which guarded the military tradition. Soldiers and civilians alike shared the common despair of achieving victory under the existing system. Disabled men returned to their villages with stories of the lack of the most elementary equipment, even rifles, at the front. The victualling of the army had been largely taken over by semi-official bodies such as the Union of Zemstvos and Municipalities. The peasantry saw no sense in putting up with such sacrifices for a cause they did not really feel was theirs. The more educated classes saw the country drifting helplessly to ruin.

No one was impressed when the Tzar personally assumed the supreme command. On the contrary, it was only felt that further opportunities for intrigue had been afforded at the one centre where they were most harmful. The prestige of the dynasty was falling fast. Tales of what were known as the "dark forces" spread abroad and developed into a tangle of monstrous fable, much of it false, but reflecting the justifiable concern at the rottenness of the heart of the Empire. The relations of Rasputin with the Court, the Empress's intrigues, and the pro-German sentiments attributed to her, the suspicion of treachery aroused by the appointment of a series of unpopular Ministers, these and many other factors contributed to an uneasy tension which by the end of 1916 was being openly spoken of as the prelude to revolution.

It may or may not be true that official circles were preparing to negotiate a separate peace in the hope of saving the throne. It was even alleged that the food shortage had been deliberately aggravated and disorder encouraged in order to make the further prosecution of the war impossible. The important thing is that, true or false, nothing was too bad to be believed. It is often not facts but what people believe to be facts that determine the course of events. All the pent-up grievances of the people, their political subjection, their economic difficulties, their privations, their war weariness, their patriotic humiliation, came to be concentrated in hatred, contempt, and, at the very least, exasperation, with the Tzar and the system for which he stood. Everywhere groups were meeting to consider what steps could be taken. Members of the Duma thundered, officers conspired, the mob growled. It might be said that there was scarcely a soul in Russia at the beginning of 1917 who was not a revolutionary of some sort. The Government was as if paralysed. People went about apprehensively wondering what spark would fire the explosion.

CHAPTER II

THE "FEBRUARY" REVOLUTION

On Monday, March 12,[1] 1917, Petrograd awoke to the knowledge that the blow had fallen. There had been food riots during the previous few days. Stores had been looted. Troops had been called out, but were known to be unwilling to fire on the mobs. Armed police had been posted in strategic positions, at the bridges, in Government buildings, on the roofs of houses, and had been responsible for most of the shooting. The Government was felt to be letting the situation get out of its control. The population of a great city takes a little time to realize that something has happened to suspend the routine of daily life, but on that Monday morning the streets were deserted save for patrols, and knots of anxious citizens discussing the news. Cabs and trams had disappeared. Shops were closing. Sporadic firing could be heard from various quarters.

The decisive action which turned riot into revolution had been taken by the Duma. On March 11th Rodzianko, the President, had telegraphed to the Tzar at the *Stavka* (General Headquarters) at Mohilev, appealing for the appointment of a Ministry in which the country could have confidence. Anarchy, he said, reigned in the capital, and the existing Government was powerless. The answer came at midnight in the form of an order indefinitely adjourning the Duma. A conference of party leaders had at once been summoned and decided that the Duma would

[1] February 28th, old style. All dates are given according to the modern (Gregorian) calendar, which is thirteen days ahead of the old (Julian) calendar. The titles "February" and "October" Revolutions have been kept because it is thus that they are familiarly known. The Bolsheviks adopted the Gregorian calendar as from February 1, 1918.

continue its meetings as a private body. A "Committee of the Imperial Duma for the Establishment of Order in Petrograd and for Intercourse with Institutions and Persons," representative of all the principal parties, was set up. It included Rodzianko, the President, Miliukov, the leader of the Kadets, and Kerensky, the Labour leader, among its members.[1]

Meanwhile mutiny had broken out among the Petrograd garrison. Some regiments had disarmed their officers, and a number who resisted had been killed. Other units were divided as to whether they should march against the mutineers or join them. Many soldiers were to be seen helping civilians to clear out the police posts, for the animus of the population was almost solely directed against policemen and military officers, who embodied the old régime for them, and against whom they exacted a pitiless vengeance for past tyrannies. The worst scenes of violence took place among the naval units at Kronstadt, but, all

[1] Apart from the extreme Conservatives, who automatically disappeared with the outbreak of revolution, the most important groups in the Fourth Duma were:—

1. The "Octobrists," led by Gouchkov, and to whom Rodzianko belonged. Their programme was the fulfilment of the Tzar's decree of October 30, 1905, which had never been properly implemented.
2. The Constitutional Democrats, called Kadets after the initials of their name. They were a bourgeois party of liberal reformers, and had been considered dangerously radical during the First and Second Dumas. They now represented the bulk of the progressive section of the educated classes. Their leader was Miliukov.
3. The Populist Socialists, commonly known as *Trudoviki*, or Labourites. They were moderate Socialists, and formed the Left Wing in the Duma. Kerensky was their leader. He was also a member of the Social-Revolutionary party, which, like the Social-Democratic Mensheviks and Bolsheviks, were not represented in sufficient numbers to form separate Parliamentary groups.

As the Revolution proceeded, the dividing-line between the moderate parties faded. The supporters of the Provisional Government were drawn from all the above, and eventually included the Right Wing Social-Revolutionaries and some Mensheviks. The Bolsheviks got the support of the rest of the Mensheviks and the Left Wing Social-Revolutionaries.

things considered, the Revolution was accomplished with comparatively small loss of life. The total of those killed during the disturbances immediately preceding and following March 12th is usually given as not more than a thousand.

On the afternoon of the 12th deputations from units of the garrison and labour organizations began to appear before the Duma, proclaiming their adherence to the revolution. The capital rallied to the new authority with scarcely a struggle. The Ministers of the old Government were placed under arrest, rather to save them from the mob than because they were thought dangerous. The Petrograd Soviet of Workers' Deputies, which had played such a large part in the disturbances of 1905, re-emerged as the champion of the working classes, which were scarcely represented in the Duma. It established its headquarters in the same building as the Duma, the Tauride Palace. The majority of its members were Social-Revolutionaries and Mensheviks. The Bolsheviks were an insignificant fraction. In the exaltation of the first hours of the newly won freedom it was thought that all classes would co-operate in establishing the new régime, but such hopes were to be shattered almost as soon as they were expressed.

The first and most urgent problem was the attitude to be adopted towards the dynasty. The Soviet was republican, the Duma still largely monarchist. The Temporary Committee was inclined to favour a Regency under the Tzar's brother, Michael, but it soon became clear that the existing temper of popular opinion would not stand a Romanov on the throne. After some anxious hours of uncertainty as to whether loyal troops might not be on the march to Petrograd, news from the front indicated that there would be no resistance to the deposition of the Tzar. Nicholas, on hearing of the revolt, had set out from General Headquarters to join his family at Tsarkoe Selo. His train was intercepted, and at Pskov, on March 15th, he signed the abdication on behalf of himself and his son, nominating the Grand Duke Michael as his successor. Almost simultaneously the Temporary Committee of the Duma was appointing a Provisional Government to prepare the way for the summoning of a Constituent Assembly. The Grand Duke was persuaded not to accept the throne unless it was offered to him by the express wish of the people. Any difficulty with the monarchists was thus settled. The Tzar himself was shortly after taken to Tsarkoe Selo, where the Imperial family remained under guard until they were removed to Tobolsk in July.

The Provisional Government was headed by Prince Lvov, a much respected mediocrity, who had been President of the Union of Zemstvos. One of the Tzar's last acts had been to designate him as a President of the Council of Ministers likely to be acceptable to the Duma. Miliukov was Foreign Minister, Gouchkov, War Minister, and Kerensky, Minister of Justice. It was a broad-based Liberal Government. Kerensky was the only Socialist member, and he had had to take office on his own responsibility, after the Petrograd Soviet, of which he was a vice-President, had refused to participate officially in it.

The Duma and the Soviet now stood to each other in something like the relation of Government and Opposition. The Duma was Liberal, the Soviet Socialist. But although they met in the same building, and were constantly in touch with one another, they remained separate bodies. Neither was disposed to forgo its independence. Since the Duma had refused to assert its official existence, and was moreover not representative of the masses, the Soviet considered that the Duma had no more authority as a revolutionary body than itself. There arose in this way, from the very beginning of the Revolution, a division of power, which ultimately brought to disaster all efforts to find a generally acceptable foundation for a new system of government. On the very day the Revolution started the Soviet had established a militia of its own, equipped with arms looted from the Arsenal, which eventually became the nucleus of the Red Guard. On March 14th it had issued its celebrated Order No. 1 directing the formation of Soviets in all naval and military units, which were to send representatives to headquarters. Instructions were also given that, while discipline must be preserved, compliments were no longer to be paid to officers off parade. On March 21st the garrison of Petrograd took the vital decision of placing itself at the disposal of the Soviet. The Duma was unable to make any effective reply. As a body it faded into the background, until it was finally dissolved by Kerensky in October, leaving the Provisional Government to shoulder all the responsibility of ruling the country without any organized support beyond what the Soviet would grant it.

The lack of cohesion among the more politically educated class made it impossible to stem the steady drift to the Left. The amnesty granted to political prisoners and exiles turned loose numbers of clever but irresponsible agitators. The Germans, who were naturally delighted to help stir up trouble, even gave facilities for the passage of a number of exiled revolutionaries from Switzerland. Lenin was amongst them, and arrived in Petrograd early in April.[1] A week or so later Trotsky appeared from

[1] Lenin was in Cracow at the outbreak of war. He and Zinoviev were arrested by the Austrians as enemy subjects, but soon released as "defeatists," and allowed to go to Switzerland. Here Lenin worked till 1917 in an endeavour to mobilize international Socialist opinion against the war. On his return to Russia he found the Bolsheviks inclined to accept coalition with the more moderate Socialist parties. He at once set himself to fight the spirit of compromise among his own followers. His extreme views created a sensation, and it required all his personal authority to get them adopted by the party. His main point was to insist that the seizure of power by the proletariat must

America, after having been detained at Halifax until the British authorities made sure that the Provisional Government had no objection to his admission. The masses, ignorant, excited, and feeling their power for the first time, were easy prey for whoever offered them the most attractive prospects. It was inevitable that some play should be given to the natural ebullience of the time, but the Provisional Government took an altogether too complacent view of its power.

The Provisional Government was faced with two major tasks, the first to stabilize the internal situation, the second to carry on the war. Each by itself would have strained all its resources; together they were more than it could manage.

The Revolution had been accepted in the provinces with as little resistance as in the capital. The administrative

precede the making of a "democratic" peace, and that therefore the bourgeois Provisional Government must be opposed. He also rejected Parliamentary in favour of Soviet democracy. This was the antithesis of the Menshevik and *S-R* policy. These parties believed in exerting pressure from below, leaving nominal power in the hands of bourgeois Ministers under conventional forms of government. According to them a "democratic" peace involved continuing the war in order to defend the Revolution against German imperialism.

The outbreak of the Revolution found Lenin in Zurich. Permission to return to Russia through Allied territory had been refused. There was more chance of the Germans giving facilities to well-known "defeatists." A Swiss Socialist, Fritz Platten, arranged with the German Legation at Berne that a party of Russian revolutionaries should be allowed to cross Germany into Sweden, with no questions asked, on condition that they communicated with no one during the journey except through Platten himself. The party consisted of about thirty persons, mostly Bolsheviks, including Lenin and his wife, Zinoviev, and Radek. The basis of the agreement with the Germans was, nominally, an exchange of internees. As the Provisional Government was understood to have decided to treat people returning to Russia through Germany as having had relations with the enemy, most of the non-Bolsheviks refused to travel in this way. Actually, no difficulties were raised at the Russian frontier. This is the basis of the famous "sealed waggon" story. Platten subsequently published a pamphlet, *Die Reise Lenins durch Deutschland* (Berlin, 1924), with contributions from Lenin, Krupskaya, Radek, and Zinoviev, describing the whole proceeding.

machinery of the old régime simply ceased to function. Unfortunately, it was not easy to replace it. One of the most remarkable features of the Revolution was the spontaneous appearance and rapid growth of the Soviet movement all over the country. Towns, villages, factories, and garrisons immediately began electing committees, which proceeded to assume the functions of local government according to their own lights. Few of them were very extreme, but most were socialistically inclined, and nearly all were in the hands of inexperienced, ignorant people. The result was naturally chaotic. The chief trouble was that it was almost impossible to make use of the better educated elements. Officers were tainted with monarchism, the *zemstvo* was identified with landlordism, anyone with the remotest connection with the old régime, including priests and schoolmasters, as well as actual officials, was regarded with suspicion. The masses had no confidence in those who were not of themselves. The peasants looked upon the Revolution mainly as an opportunity for seizing the land. The moment the hand of authority was removed they started dividing up the neighbouring estates. Sometimes the landlords suffered violence, but often they were left alone if they did not resist. In industrial districts the workers demanded a share in the management, and in many cases forced owners and technical experts to abandon the mines and factories. The envoys, or Commissars of the Provisional Government, seldom had the backing necessary to establish order in accordance with Ministerial decrees. Democracy was popularly interpreted as the right to form committees, and hold elections, regardless either of central co-ordination, or of fixed terms of office.

Abroad, the Revolution had been, on the whole, greeted with sympathy. The Central Powers, of course, hoped to profit by the disorder. The Allies hoped that the acquisition of political freedom would provide the national cause with fresh stimulus. Many people in Russia, indeed, supported the Revolution because they thought it would enable the war to be conducted with greater vigour. Events proved the German view to be the more correct of the two.

The condition of the army at the front, already bad, deteriorated still further with the relaxation of discipline and the diversion of attention to events in the rear. The Government was obliged to allow systematic "democratization." Order No. 1 was only the beginning of a process which struck at the authority of the Commanders, and brought politics into every detail of military administration. Hostilities practically ceased. The Germans wisely refrained from taking military advantage of the situation for fear of awakening the national spirit. On the contrary, they encouraged fraternization, and promised not to attack unless they were themselves attacked. The sudden suspension of the strain of war had a paralysing effect on the army's will to fight. Soldiers deserted in thousands, and many units resolved themselves into political meetings in permanent session. The attitude of a large section of the peasant rank and file is expressed in the following resolution of the 100th Division, which ran: "We do not want to die, especially just now, when we are getting land and freedom. To attack would be dangerous for us."

The first crisis in the Provisional Government came over the question of war aims and the expropriation of the landlords. Miliukov, the Foreign Minister, was still making declarations in very much the same tone as his Tzarist predecessors. The Soviet demanded the adoption of a policy of "Peace without annexations or indemnities." About the same time a Peasants' Congress demanded the nationalization of the land, but here again serious divergencies of views manifested themselves, this time on the subject of compensation. The resignation of Miliukov and his moderate colleagues resulted. Prince Lvov remained Prime Minister, but the Soviet sanctioned the filling of the vacant places with its own Socialist nominees. Kerensky became Minister for War. The Bolsheviks had voted against the co-operation of the Soviet with the Provisional Government and had organized a demonstration of protest, appealing for an immediate and, if necessary, a separate peace.

The Soviet now definitely dominated the Government, but in agreeing to active participation in it had also committed itself to the continuation of the war. This attitude was endorsed by the first All-Russian Congress of Soviets,[1] held in June, despite the strenuous efforts of the small Bolshevik minority, who marched up a detachment of sailors from Kronstadt. A reaction was passing over the country, and the moment seemed to have come for an effort to pull the army together. By no means all the troops had lost cohesion. Many resented dictation from regiments safely ensconced in the capital. Resistance to the foreign invader was still a powerful incentive. The country wanted peace, but not a peace of surrender.

The Government's efforts during May and June to restore discipline achieved some measure of success. Special shock troops and "battalions of death" were formed. On July 1st an offensive was launched on the Galician front. From the point of view of the Allies as a whole, the move was opportune. The transfer of German divisions to France was arrested at a critical time, when American troops had not yet arrived on the scene. From the Russian point of view the result was not so fortunate. After initial successes the Russians were thrown back in disorder.

[1] It contained 285 Social-Revolutionaries, 248 Mensheviks, 105 Bolsheviks, and 137 members of about ten other parties, mostly Socialist.

The Bolsheviks chose this moment to make a serious bid for power. The prestige of the Provisional Government was seriously shaken, and even the moderate majority in the Soviets was losing ground. Defeat in the field strengthened the clamour for peace. The food situation was bad. The commandeering of supplies, and the control of prices, annoyed the peasants. The financial situation had obliged the Government to call a halt to the raising of wages, and the industrial workers were grumbling. A revolt among the garrison and industrial population of Petrograd was organized in the middle of July. The object was to force the Soviet to overthrow the Government and take power into its own hands with the support of the extreme Left Groups. The slogans, "Peace, Bread and the Land" and "All Power to the Soviets," attracted wide popular support, but the partisans of the Government were still strong. The attempt at a *coup d'état* failed. Disorders were suppressed. Lenin escaped to a hiding-place in Finland. The Provisional Government, however, failed to take advantage of this opportunity of asserting itself, and lost its best chance of getting a really firm grip on the country.

The Government was not only in trouble with the Left but with the Right. As the Socialist extremists waxed stronger, the bourgeois and conservative elements were asking for stronger measures to be taken against them.

It had been intended to prosecute the Bolshevik leaders for treason on the grounds of having received financial assistance from German sources. They were thus to have been got out of the way, and their party discredited, without the apparent use of unrevolutionary methods of political repression. The case against them had not been completed at the time of the July insurrection, but some of the evidence was then prematurely made public, and the chance of obtaining conclusive proofs was thereby destroyed.

Kerensky has stated his moral conviction of their guilt,[1] while the Bolsheviks have, of course, totally denied the charge.[2] The truth or falsity of the accusation therefore remains uncertain, but legal confirmation of such transactions was hardly necessary to show that the Bolsheviks were acting contrary to the national war-time interests. They were clearly playing the enemy's game by preaching defeatism and pacifism, though their ultimate object was quite different. They did not care who won the war. They only wanted to throw Russia into chaos in order to seize power themselves. They hoped to see disorder spring up in other countries also, including Germany, and thus to inaugurate the world revolution.

The collapse of the prosecution enabled the Bolsheviks to allege a counter-revolutionary plot. The Government's failure to crush the Bolsheviks with every means in its power was on all sides interpreted as weakness, and was particularly exasperating to the groups of the Right. Trotsky and a few others were arrested, but soon released.

Up to this time the Government cannot be blamed for trying to unite all sections of opinion by compromise, but it was now hopeless to attempt to keep the middle of the road. There could be no question of joining up with the Bolsheviks, and it was therefore suicidal to antagonize one of the strongest centres of resistance to them. At the same time it must be remembered that even moderate Socialists were averse to any course that savoured of reaction, and that the apparent defeat of the Bolsheviks led to an underestimation of their strength.

As a result of these events Prince Lvov resigned on July 20th. Kerensky accepted the Premiership, but had some difficulty in forming a Government. Eventually his colleagues, though drawn from many sections of political

[1] *The Catastrophe*, chap. x.

[2] See Trotsky, *My Life*, chap. xxv.

opinion, took office as individuals rather than as representatives of their parties. His hold over the rank and file, both of the Right and the Moderate Left, was precarious.

After much delay, due to the difficulty of setting up the appropriate machinery and of explaining to a people unaccustomed to high politics the significance of the whole procedure, the meeting of the Constituent Assembly had been fixed for the middle of October. The events of July caused a postponement to be made till December. Meanwhile it was thought advisable to summon an All-Russian State Conference, to which organizations representing all kinds of interests and opinions might send delegates. The intention seems to have been to improvise an Assembly, which, now that the Duma had ceased to play any part, would counteract any tendency of the Soviets to swing towards the Bolsheviks. The Conference met in Moscow at the end of August, and much the most significant feature of it was the emergence of General Kornilov, who had replaced Brussilov as Commander-in-Chief after the recent offensive, as the champion of the Right. Kornilov had been agitating for some time for military reforms to prevent the army from going absolutely to pieces, and certain elements had been toying with the idea of a military dictatorship.[1]

The events which immediately followed the Moscow Conference are not very clear, but there seems to have been a conspiracy on the part of certain officers to overthrow the Provisional Government and to make Kornilov

[1] Kornilov, a Siberian Cossack by birth, was a Divisional Commander in August 1914 and a Corps Commander in March 1917. On the outbreak of Revolution he was appointed Military Commandant in Petrograd. It was he who had officially to place the Empress under arrest. He was made Commander-in-Chief of the South-West front in July and Supreme Commander-in-Chief in August. He was noted for personal bravery, but his impetuosity several times compromised the troops under his command. His capture by the Austrians and dramatic escape helped to create a Kornilov legend.

dictator. It had been decided to move the capital to Moscow because of the proximity of the German forces to Petrograd. The Commander-in-Chief was asked to send reliable troops to cover the move, which the Bolsheviks were representing as a betrayal of the population, accusing Kerensky at the same time of becoming counter-revolutionary. Kornilov despatched General Krimov with a force whose real task was to stage a *coup d'état*. But when the troops learnt what was in the wind they refused to enter the city. This happened during the second week in September. The Bolsheviks gave the incident as proof that the Provisional Government was working hand in hand with reactionaries. Whatever the truth may have been, the effect was a final breach between the Provisional Government and the Right, and a big swing over to the Bolsheviks among the garrison and populace in the capital. On September 16th the elections to the Petrograd Soviet gave the Bolsheviks a majority for the first time. Trotsky became its President. The enrolment of a Red Guard, which soon numbered 10,000 men, was begun. Meanwhile the Government had broken up, and Kerensky was attempting to rule at the head of a Directorate of five members. His position was desperate, and the possibility of Bolshevik rule had become imminent.

CHAPTER III

THE "OCTOBER" REVOLUTION

In the eight months between the "February" and "October" Revolutions Russia jumped two centuries of political history. From the rule of a monarch whose type belongs to the eighteenth century she passed to the domination of the most extreme socialistic doctrines known to the twentieth. It has been impossible to follow the process except in bare outline. There is still no generally agreed interpretation even of the main facts. The kaleidoscopic march of events, the motives and characters of the chief actors, the emotions and arguments which affected opinion, still await analysis at the hands of someone ready to give his life to the task of sifting the vast mass of available material. The same can be said for the period with which we have still to deal, the period which saw the Bolsheviks seize power, and keep it, against all logical expectation, despite all efforts to dislodge them. But some intelligible conception of what actually happened must be formed if the advent of the Soviet State is to be understood.

A multitude of threads formed the tangle of issues out of which the crisis was developing in October 1917. There was the war, impelling some to think of national defence as a primary matter, and others to be overwhelmed by a desire for peace. There was the sudden removal of the hand of authority from a people accustomed to unquestioning obedience. There was the conflicting momentum of ambitions and cravings, which were almost as numerous as there were beings to express them. There was the faith of the ignorant masses in a better world thrust into their grasp. There was the fever of the peasant to possess the land. There was the greed of life's failures seizing the chance of satisfying their envy. There was the vindictiveness of the victims of oppression. There was the idealism of intellectuals, skilful in the weaving of words, but inexpert at dealing with facts. There was the former ruling classes' horror of disorder and attachment to possessions. There was the inevitable antithesis between performance and promise, which always tends to discredit the Government in power. There was the common inclination in times of stress for the mass of people to huddle together in apathetic uncertainty while power passes to extremists who know their own minds. These were some of the many factors which, acting upon each other, produced inertia, and reduced government by reason to impotence.

Someone had to cut the knot. Kerensky, a lawyer by training, a gifted orator, an astute politician, a persuader, but not a commander of men, had lost prestige, partly because his character no longer gave confidence, and partly because the Provisional Government had been eight months in office without solving the country's main problems. It is profitless to try and apportion praise or blame. Even if every act of the Provisional Government were to be justified, and all allowances are made for its difficulties, the fact remains that by the autumn of 1917 nobody was prepared to defend it. The attempt to superimpose a military dictatorship had failed. Kornilov was a brave and capable soldier, but no statesman. The *coup* was ill-prepared, and in any case it was too much identified with the old régime to make a popular appeal at this juncture. The Bolsheviks had become, by a process of elimination, if by nothing else, the only possible alternative.

Unlike the other political parties, the Bolsheviks knew what they wanted and had a leader who knew how to get it for them. Circumstances favoured them, but they cannot be denied the credit of having taken the line which split the Social-Democratic party in 1903, and which made it possible for them to take their opportunity when it came.

The Bolsheviks may have dreamed of such an opportunity, but they can hardly, in the lean years of exile and underground scheming, have expected it. Had the Revolution not coincided with the war, events might well have taken quite a different course. The army might have supported the Revolution, but it would not have been in the condition in which March 1917 found it. The Revolution would probably have been, what Marxian theory indicated it should be, a bourgeois revolution. Indeed, so obsessed were Socialists of all kinds with the belief in a period of bourgeois democracy as a necessary stage preliminary to the proletarian revolution, that even many Bolsheviks refused to admit that their hour had come.

The Bolsheviks have been described as "Socialists in earnest." Not only did they believe in the full Marxian gospel contained in the *Communist Manifesto* of 1847 and in *Das Kapital*, not only did they believe in history as a perpetual class struggle, in the State as an instrument of class domination, and in the seizure of power by the workers as a necessary step to the millennium of the Communist classless State, but they did not shrink from facing the logical consequences of an attempt to fulfil their programme. For this they had Lenin to thank. Other Social-Democratic parties had relegated the Marxian objectives to the limbo of distant ideals, and had been content to make a place for themselves in practical politics as extreme reformers. Lenin had consistently rejected all compromise with bourgeois Capitalism on the perfectly sound grounds that it was foolish to help improve and strengthen a system which had to be totally destroyed. Revolution by force would alone, he considered, produce the conditions for the successful establishment of the dictatorship of the proletariat. Nor did he believe that, given a successful revolution, Communism and Capitalism could exist permanently side by side. The world would only be safe for Communism when the whole world was Communist. The Communist State must work towards universality through World Revolution, or ultimately perish. The Bolshevik party was accordingly organized not with a view to winning votes at elections, but as a disciplined phalanx to be hurled into the revolutionary struggle, to smash the enemy's defences, and to be a rallying point for the mass of indeterminate opinion.

None of the Bolsheviks was a deep or original thinker. Their theoretical writings are mostly commentaries and expositions of the Marxian thesis. They accepted their fundamental ideas ready-made from abroad. The distinctive characteristic of Bolshevism lies in the practical interpretation which Lenin was able to give these ideas. This is not to say that Lenin was merely an opportunist, but only that, with a definite goal in view, he knew how to harness the means to the end. Stalin has declared that Lenin made concrete the theory and tactics of the proletarian revolution and of the proletarian dictatorship. Marx had not defined how the proletarian revolution was made, nor what the proletariat was to do when it got power. The missing chapters, as Kamenev put it, "were written by Lenin, not only in books, but in life."

The problems Lenin set himself when the Russian Revolution broke out were simply these: how to seize power, and how to hold it. He was not primarily concerned with the fate of Russia as a nation, nor with providing freedom, justice, and well-being for the Russian people. These things were important only in their bearing on the main issue of Bolshevik domination. There must be an

"LONG LIVE THE SOVIETS!"—A POSTER DEPICTING THE TRIUMPH OF THE RED REVOLUTION OVER THE PANIC-STRICKEN CROWD OF CAPITALISTS, OFFICERS AND PRIESTS, WHILE, IN THE BACKGROUND, IMPERIALIST FINANCE LETS LOOSE INTERNECINE STRIFE

independent Russian State to take over, therefore the Germans must be prevented from overrunning the country. He must have the widest possible measure of popular support, therefore he must champion popular clamour and discredit the Provisional Government.

In the autumn of 1917 Lenin realized that the decisive moment had come. The Bolsheviks were riding on the crest of a wave, while everyone else was in the trough. Many of his colleagues did not share his views. Lenin's hardest struggle in bringing about the "October" Revolution was inside his own party. Kamenev, Zinoviev, and Rykov were the principal members of the opposition to a bid for power. They argued that the Bourgeois Revolution was not yet over, that the peasants would not support a proletarian dictatorship, and that if the Bolsheviks had to rely on force they would get beaten. They wanted to wait, and act only if the Bolsheviks had a majority in the Constituent Assembly. Trotsky, as usual, held a somewhat independent position. On the main issue of seizing power he was with Lenin, but he agreed with the opposition that the peasants would be hostile. This did not disturb him, however, because he was more confident of the imminence of revolution in other countries. Lenin replied to all this that it was now or never. They must act while the feeling aroused by the Kornilov *putsch* was strong. They had a majority in the Petrograd Soviet and probably in the Congress of Soviets about to assemble. This was as good an indication as any that the country was behind them. A *fait accompli* would bring over many waverers. He seems to have believed that the opposition of the peasants would not be formidable; but although, like Trotsky, he imagined World Revolution to be near, he thought the *smychka*, or alliance between workers and peasants, vital for the consolidation of the revolution at home while it was developing abroad. This point of view became extremely important later when he preferred to conciliate the peasants with the New Economic Policy rather than risk collapse through their hostility.

All the germs of the subsequent dissensions within the party are discernible during the discussions of these critical days. The sequel showed that there was something in each point of view. The peasants did prove intractable. Government by force did become necessary. On the other hand the World Revolution failed to materialize and the preservation of the *smychka* did play a vital part in saving the revolution in Russia.

Lenin's first preoccupation was to get a move on, but he was also anxious not to give the impression that power was being seized by a minority. The immediate difficulty was solved by winning a majority in the Soviets. Subsequently it was necessary to invoke the theory that the Communist Party could act for the whole proletariat. The facts of minority rule, of peasant hostility, and of the use of force against others than the bourgeoisie, were explained by the survival of bourgeois ideology and counter-revolutionary propaganda among the masses, who were thus unable to realize what they really wanted. A minority dictatorship of the party became the effective synonym for a majority dictatorship of the proletariat.

The decision to attempt the seizure of power was taken by the Central Committee of the Bolshevik party on October 23rd, Zinoviev and Kamenev alone voting against it. On October 25th the Petrograd Soviet voted the formation of a War Revolutionary Committee, "the staff for seizing power," as it was described, although the proposal had been defeated in the Executive Committee by the Social-Revolutionaries and Mensheviks. This body was something more than just a Committee of the Soviet. It was the embryo of a new Government. Headed by Trotsky, and including a number of Bolshevik sympathizers in touch with Government Departments and the troops at the front, it controlled the armed forces and munitions at the disposal of the Soviet in the Petrograd military district. Headquarters were established in the Smolny Institute, formerly a Convent School for the daughters of the nobility, and from here the decisive events of the next fortnight were planned and directed.

The Committee's first step was to appoint Commissars at all strategic points, barracks, railway stations, telegraph offices, and telephone exchanges. The next was to secure the formal support of as many units of the garrison as possible. There seems to have been no concealment of these measures. The Provisional Government was powerless. They made half-hearted attempts to arrest the Bolshevik leaders, but they had no force on which to depend. When they tried to suppress the Bolshevik newspapers, the printing works were at once re-started under the protection of Red Guards. On November 5th the Committee issued instructions that no orders were to be executed without being countersigned by a Soviet Commissar. The cruiser *Aurora* was brought up from Kronstadt and anchored outside the Winter Palace, where Kerensky had his headquarters.

The uprising had been planned for November 7th, no doubt because the Second All-Russian Congress of Soviets was due to meet on that day. At 2 a.m. the Central Telephone Exchange was seized, and by daybreak Bolshevik troops and Red Guards had occupied the main centres of communication and administration. They met with very little resistance. At 10 a.m. the War Revolutionary Committee issued a proclamation declaring the overthrow of the Provisional Government and assuming control in the name of the

Soviet. At noon the session of the Council of the Republic or Pre-Parliament was closed by a detachment of sailors.

Meanwhile, the members of the Provisional Government had shut themselves up in the Winter Palace, but except for the detachments of the Military Cadet Corps, the troops on guard were not dependable. The Cossacks remained neutral, and the Women's Battalion offered little resistance. G.H.Q. at the front had been wired for reinforcements, and Kerensky himself had motored off early in the morning to meet them. They never materialized. Before evening all the approaches to the Palace had been blocked by Bolshevik forces. At 9 p.m. the *Aurora* and the guns of the Peter and Paul fortress opened on the Palace, but apparently most of the ammunition used was blank. Only three or four live shells struck the building. At 11 p.m. the attack closed in. The gates were rammed with motor lorries, and the remains of the defence retreated, fighting from room to room. Most of the loss of life and damage was caused during the next few hours. At 2 a.m. on the 8th a room was discovered containing sixteen Ministers, who were marched off under arrest.

Meanwhile the Second Congress of Soviets had met at 10.45 p.m. It included 362 Bolsheviks out of its 562 members. The Congress was asked to endorse the actions of the War Revolutionary Committee, whereupon the Mensheviks and the Right Social-Revolutionaries left the Chamber. In the early hours of the morning the Congress formally took over the government of the country.

There was at first little need for the Bolsheviks to adopt drastic measures of terrorism and repression. Moscow was won after a few troublous days and some street fighting. Kerensky collected a handful of troops under General Krasnov at Pskov, but, having advanced as far as Tsarkoe Selo, they melted away before the "Red" defences. Kerensky escaped with difficulty, and managed to get out of the country. In the northern and central European provinces the local Soviets mostly accepted the new authority, but except in a few urban and industrial centres the Bolsheviks were not strong outside this area.

The first acts of the new Government were such as any reader of Lenin's pronouncements might have anticipated. The following are among the Acts endorsed by the Third Congress of Soviets in January 1918. All State property, including the railways, was transferred to the people. The private ownership of land was abolished. The principle of self-determination for the non-Russian peoples was re-affirmed. Banks were nationalized. Business secrecy was suppressed. All the financial and international obligations of the Tzarist and Provisional Government were repudiated. The secret war treaties between the Allies were published. A universal appeal for the cessation of hostilities was made.

The Bolsheviks found that it was not only for the sake of their pledges but as a matter of dire necessity that they had to sue for peace. The front was finally crumbling. The soldiers, utterly demoralized by propaganda, were deserting, whole regiments at a time, and hurrying home in fear of missing the distribution of the land. The enemy was free to advance as it willed, and it was only the fear of arousing the spirit of national defence that deterred the Germans from occupying Petrograd.

A fortnight after seizing power the Bolsheviks issued an appeal to stop the war on a basis of no annexations and no indemnities. When these overtures remained unanswered they announced their intention of concluding a separate armistice. Encouraged by the mutiny in the German fleet in September and by news of disaffection in the French army to exaggerate the war weariness of other belligerent nations, they were genuinely disappointed when foreign peoples paid so little attention to what was heralded as the beginning of the World Revolution. On November 27th the first Bolshevik *parlementaires* crossed the lines. On December 3rd, Krilenko, the newly appointed Bolshevik Commander-in-Chief, arrived at General Headquarters accompanied by a bodyguard of sailors. General Dukhonin, the Chief of Staff, refused to acknowledge the new authority. He was shot down and his body thrown into the street. On the same day negotiations with the enemy opened at Brest-Litovsk; on the 15th an armistice was signed. On the 23rd the Peace Conference began.

The Germans and Austrians were startled by the audacity of the terms offered by the Bolsheviks. They found themselves being harangued as if the Russians and not they were the victors. But the Bolsheviks both wanted to make an impression and to delay the proceedings as long as possible. In the first place, here was a platform whence they could speak to the world, and they entertained hopes that they might still rouse public opinion in the belligerent countries to their support by appealing to the masses over the heads of their Governments. In the second place, they knew the Central Powers wanted peace quickly so as to be able to transfer forces to other fronts, and hoped they might exact better terms by fighting every point. In the third place, they were divided amongst themselves about the policy they were pursuing. Lenin was in favour of signing a definite peace treaty. Trotsky thought that a Government which was setting out to wage war against Capitalism all over the world could not consistently sign treaties with capitalist Governments. They were afraid on the one hand of being swept away if the Germans and Austrians advanced, while they ran the danger of appearing humbugs if they yielded to anything but *force majeure*. The more the Bolsheviks wriggled the firmer the Central Powers became. The Bolsheviks were naturally unwilling to allow the western territories to escape their grasp. Their adherence to the principle of self-determination was somewhat embarrassing, but they thought that by pressing for evacuation by the Germans on behalf of the local populations they might raise a party to support union with the Soviet State. The Germans merely replied that as these lands had already declared for separation from Russia they could not be included in the undertaking to evacuate Russia, which they were prepared to give. At Christmas the Conference was adjourned to give the Bolsheviks a chance of making up their minds. Meanwhile, probably at German instigation, the Ukraine put in a claim to negotiate as a separate State, and by the time the Bolsheviks returned Ukrainian grain was already on its way to Germany and Austria. They now made the peculiar suggestion that the war should be declared over, that there should be no more fighting, but that there should be no actual treaty. It was an ingenious attempt of the Bolsheviks to have their cake and eat it, but the Central Powers were naturally not going to leave matters thus unsettled. The negotiations trailed on, and in the interval important events took place in Petrograd.

It must not be supposed that even in Russia proper there was anything like a general feeling in favour of the Bolsheviks. The prevailing attitude was passive and apathetic. There was no inclination to go back on the fundamentals of the Revolution, but there was no enthusiasm for any of the candidates for power. Two months of Bolshevik rule had already dissipated some illusions, but none of the other parties disposed of sufficient force to command respect. Many hopes were still centred on the Constituent Assembly, which, after another postponement, was now due to meet on January 18th. It was commonly supposed that the Bolsheviks would never be able to establish themselves permanently, and popular opinion, with characteristic ingenuousness, was inclined to ascribe to the Constituent Assembly an almost supernatural omnipotence. The Bolsheviks were alive to their danger, for they hardly expected to have a majority; but they dared not intervene, since they had themselves used the failure to convene the Assembly as a stick with which to beat the Provisional Government. The election returns soon made it clear that there would be an anti-Bolshevik majority in the Assembly. The anti-Bolshevik parties, and particularly the Social-Revolutionaries, the strongest of them, raised their heads once more. Strenuous canvassing began for the support of the units of the Petrograd garrison. An anti-Bolshevik newspaper was started, and for some time held its own. The cry was "rally to the defence of the Constituent Assembly," but it appeared that while the masses were quite willing to see the Constituent Assembly depose the Bolsheviks, they did not propose to take any active steps in the matter themselves. The chief weakness of the Social-Revolutionaries lay in the fact that they hesitated to adopt the methods for which they condemned the Bolsheviks. A small group actually devised plans to assassinate or kidnap the Bolshevik leaders, and might have carried them out had they not been restrained by their own chiefs. Thus, although they must have known that the Bolsheviks meant to keep in the saddle by force if necessary, the anti-Bolshevik parties went into the struggle with their hands tied. On the day of the meeting of the Assembly they organized imposing demonstrations, but their supporters were urged not to carry arms, whereas the Bolsheviks had armed patrols everywhere.

The Assembly began by electing Chernov, a Left Social-Revolutionary, as President, but rejected a Bolshevik motion to approve a "Declaration of the Rights of the

Labouring and Working People," which had been passed by the Petrograd Soviet. The Bolsheviks thereupon left the Chamber. They had, however, managed to fill the galleries with their supporters, and their exit was the signal for an outbreak of hooliganism, which made it impossible to proceed with business, and gave an excuse for the entry of parties of Red Guards into the hall. The President was told that if the session continued there would be trouble, whereupon the delegates, deeming discretion the better part of valour, filed out of the building amid the jeers of the mob. Needless to say, they were never allowed to reassemble.

The populace, having been quite willing to abide by a trial of strength, swung over to the victors. What could be the good of the much-vaunted Constituent Assembly, they said, if it could not defend itself? Once again the Bolsheviks had triumphed by superior organization and tactics. The situation had been a dangerous one for them. At no other time would it have been easier for the prognostications of that large number who maintained that Bolshevism was too exotic a growth to last to have been justified. Thereafter they had to be reckoned with much more seriously. To crown their opponent's defeat the Third Congress of Soviets, which, in anticipation of these events, had been summoned to meet on the same day, ratified the "Declaration of the Rights of the Labouring and Working People," and a resolution proposing a federal structure for the new order. Upon these acts was founded the Constitution of the Russian Socialist Federation of Soviet Republics, which was ratified by the Fifth Congress six months later.

Although they had strengthened their position at home the Bolsheviks were in no better position to resist the Central Powers at Brest-Litovsk. Exasperated by delays, the German and Austrian Commanders terminated the Armistice on February 16th and began to advance. On the

19th the Bolsheviks capitulated.[1] On March 3rd the Treaty of Brest-Litovsk was signed, and shortly afterwards ratified by the Fourth Congress of Soviets. Russia was out of the Great War at last, but at what a price! Finland, the Baltic Provinces, Poland, Lithuania, White Russia, and the Ukraine were surrendered to the Germans to carry out their plan of a string of buffer states under their protection. Parts of the Caucasus were ceded to Turkey. Agreement to financial payments and commercial preferences was extorted. The Bolsheviks squirmed and called down curses on the heads of German "imperialists." They even, for one moment, dallied with the idea of turning to the Allies for help. How strange if Allied intervention had actually come about through the Bolsheviks themselves!

[1] It was the threat of the German advance which determined the Bolsheviks to move the centre of Government to Moscow. The change of capital took effect on March 12, 1918.

CHAPTER IV

THE CIVIL WAR

The Brest-Litovsk negotiations gave the final impetus to the disintegration of the Russian Empire. The bonds which had previously united it were already much weakened. The Tzar was gone, and the non-Russian peoples had little inclination to submit to upstart Russian demagogues. There was a natural reaction against the centralized system of the past. Poland and the Baltic lands were in German occupation. These and other outlying territories were very sceptical about the social changes in progress. Finland was breaking away. The Ukraine had already demanded a federal status. The Cossacks of the Don, the Kuban and the Terek were organizing themselves under local leaders. In the Caucasus, which might be called the Balkans of the Middle East, the Georgians, Armenians, Tartars, and other peoples were quarrelling among themselves and with the Turks, who were threatening to make good in this quarter what they had lost to the Allies elsewhere. Bessarabia was preparing to unite itself with Rumania. Autonomist movements in Siberia and the Far East were bringing into existence innumerable Congresses, Assemblies, and Committees, which, in that vast area, had much difficulty in finding out what the others were doing, and were often at loggerheads round the personality of some local leader. With the advent of the Bolsheviks any semblance of restraint disappeared. Every divergent interest, economic, political, and racial, took its own course, and in several cases found outside support from the Allies or the Central Powers as the exigencies and opportunities of the war directed.

The three years, 1918, 1919, and 1920, were the period of civil war and foreign intervention. Every town and province was divided in its allegiance. The adherents of different political creeds, the partisans of various political and military leaders, fought each other up and down the country, though chiefly along the main lines of railway and river communication. Territory changed hands with bewildering frequency. Local Governments rose and fell almost from day to day.

Broadly speaking, the conflict resolves itself into a struggle between Reds and Whites, and from this point of view can be roughly divided into three phases. The first, up to the end of the European War in November 1918, covers the occupation of the Ukraine and Trans-Caucasia by the Central Powers, the formation of various counter-revolutionary centres, and the almost complete encirclement of the area under Bolshevik control. The second, up to the late autumn of 1919, is the decisive phase, marking the peak of the White efforts, the fluctuations of Allied intervention, and the turn of the tide in favour of the Reds. The third, up to the end of 1920, covers the final collapse of the counter-revolution and the Bolshevik war with Poland.

With the official cessation of hostilities between the Bolsheviks and the Central Powers, the Russian armies disbanded. Part rallied to the Bolsheviks to form the nucleus of the Red Army. Part drifted home, either individually or in bands, scouring the countryside and bringing political disturbance to the remotest villages. News that General Kaledin[1] was heading a military movement in the country of the Don Cossacks drew some units and many officers, among them important commanders[2] such as Generals

[1] An Army Commander in 1917.

[2] Out of forty Army Commanders, Fleet Commanders, and Chiefs of Staff,

Kornilov,[1] Alexeiev,[2] and Denikin,[3] to that region. Detachments of non-Russian troops, Finns, Esthonians, Letts, Lithuanians, and Poles tried to work their way westwards, where, behind the German lines, it was understood that their compatriots had self-determined their separation from Russia. A Czech Army Corps, formed from Slav prisoners and deserters from the Austrian army, stood on the Galician front, uncertain what to do.

The Treaty of Brest-Litovsk required the withdrawal of the Bolsheviks into Great Russia proper. The Germans and Austrians advanced as the Bolsheviks retired. In the North they occupied Reval, Pskov, and everything West of the Petrograd-Vitebsk-Gomel railway. In Finland the anti-Bolshevik Government was obliged to accept German assistance. Petrograd had long been at the enemy's mercy, but they had no wish to drive those with whom they had concluded so satisfactory a peace to desperation. They only wanted to make sure of preventing the Allied detachments at Murmansk from descending on the city from the North. In the South the Ukrainian Rada, which had declared its independence in January 1918, conveniently called in the Central Powers to help them resist Bolshevik attacks. The result was the occupation of the whole of the Ukraine by Austro-German forces. This gave the Central Powers command of the Black Sea and access both to the South Russian wheat belt and the Donetz coal-fields. The Rada,

Denikin (*The Russian Turmoil*, p. 148) gives nineteen as serving with anti-Bolshevik organizations, nine as serving with the Bolsheviks, and fourteen as having "retired from the struggle" after 1918.

[1] Kornilov had been arrested after his abortive *coup d'état*, but escaped in the confusion of the Bolshevik revolution.

[2] Chief of the General Staff under the Tzar, August 1915 to March 1917; then Supreme Commander-in-Chief till June, when Brussilov succeeded him.

[3] Commanded a Brigade in August 1914 and a Corps in March 1917. He was Chief of Staff to Alexeiev, commanded the Western Front during the offensive of July 1917, and the South-Western Front at the time of the Kornilov *putsch*. He also was arrested and escaped.

having exhibited restlessness under this high-handed treatment, and having even shown signs of making contact with the Allies in the small corner of Rumania which was still in their hands, was replaced by the more amenable dictatorship of the Hetman Skoropadski.[1]

Meanwhile the Volunteer Army, consisting mostly of ex-officers, had been formed by Kornilov and Alexeiev on the Don, to fight the Bolsheviks. In February 1918 its strength was only about 4,000. It remained independent of any Government, as it disapproved of the Don Cossacks' inclination to trim their sails to the Germans,[2] and only gradually acquired influence over the Cossacks of the Kuban. Kornilov was killed in an attack on Ekaterinodar in April, and the command devolved on Deniken. Alexeiev, until his death in October 1918, directed the political side of affairs. During the summer the army maintained itself with fluctuating fortunes between the rivers Don and Kuban.

The Bolshevik forces in this part of the world were mainly recruited from soldiers returning from the Caucasus front. A Bolshevik-Armenian Government existed in Baku. Daghestan and the Caspian Coast were in Bolshevik hands and formed the link with the Reds on the lower Volga, and thence with Moscow. In Trans-Caucasia, however, the chief influence was nationalistic. A Trans-Caucasian Assembly proclaimed independence in April 1918, but the principal peoples, the Georgians, Armenians, and Azerbaidjan Tartars, almost immediately split up into separate states. The occasion for disagreement was the advance of the Turks, who had been assigned the districts of Kars and

[1] An Army Corps Commander in 1917.

[2] Kaledin was defeated by the Bolsheviks early in 1918, and committed suicide. He was succeeded by General Krasnov, who later published his revolutionary reminiscences in fictional form under the title, *From Double Eagle to Red Flag.*

Batoum[1] by the Brest-Litovsk Treaty. They were further planning to seize the pipe-line to the Caspian together with the oil-fields. The Tartars, being Moslems, were disposed to side with the Turks. The Georgians were for resistance, and for helping the Armenians, who were already suffering cruelly at the hands of both Turks and Tartars. They decided to call in the Germans, who were not on the best of terms with their Turkish Allies, and wanted the oil themselves. A German force was consequently sent across the Black Sea and occupied Tiflis in June. The Turks and Tartars were at the same time attacking Baku, where Russians and Armenians of every political complexion were joining in the defence. A small British force[2] was despatched to their assistance from Persia with the object of keeping the oil-fields out of enemy hands. It was unable to cope with the situation, and, on its withdrawal in September, the city fell amid sack and massacre. This indeterminate situation continued till the Armistice.

Meanwhile, the Czech Army Corps, which was left stranded on the south-western front, was making history. Retreating before the German advance into the Ukraine, the Czechs began negotiations with the Bolsheviks for facilities to reach Western Europe. Their intention was to get transferred to the allied front in France. The Bolsheviks would have been glad to be rid of them, as they showed no signs of going Red, and were much the most formidable armed force left in Russia. At first their transportation to Archangel was suggested, but this move presented considerable difficulties, and though a few detachments found their way to this port, the Corps as a whole preferred to undertake the 5,000-mile journey by the Trans-Siberian

[1] These districts were a Turkish "irridenta." They had been ceded to Russia after the Russo-Turkish War of 1878.

[2] See *The Adventures of Dunsterforce*, by Major-General L. C. Dunsterville (Arnold, 1920).

Railway to Vladivostock, where Allied ships were expected to pick them up.

At this time Siberia was in hopeless confusion. Bolshevik and anti-Bolshevik centres alternated along the railway line. The industrial centres in the Urals were mostly Bolshevik, but farther South General Dutov had formed a White group of Orenburg Cossacks. A moderate socialist Government carried on a precarious existence round about Omsk. Irkutsk was a strong Red centre, so was most of the country along the Amur railway. At Chita, near the junction of the Chinese Eastern Railway, one Semenov, Ataman of the Siberian Cossacks, and an influential person, through his Buryat mother, with the peoples on the Mongolian frontier, established the headquarters of an independent band of marauders. At Kharbin in Manchuria General Khorvat claimed to represent anti-Bolshevik interests. Returned soldiers, released political exiles, members of the Duma and Constituent Assembly, with other refugees from the West, joined up with one or other of these self-constituted authorities. Dotted all over the country were half a million prisoners of war, mostly Germans and Hungarians, who were entitled to repatriation by the Treaty of Brest-Litovsk and were trying to work their way westwards.

The Czechs' eastward journey was thus fraught with difficulties. They had agreed to surrender a proportion of their arms, but, however conciliatory Moscow might be, conflicts with local bodies, who objected to the disorganization of their particular military and supply arrangements, were inevitable. Relations between the Czechs and the prisoners of war could hardly be friendly, for the former were travelling to the Allied front and the others were hoping to regain the armies of the Central Powers. "Incidents" multiplied, and the Bolsheviks now demanded the total disarmament of the Czechs. They refused to comply, and at the same time it occurred to someone that they might be the means of restoring the Allied eastern front.

In May 1918 the situation was that 14,000 Czechs had reached Vladivostock, but had found no ships there to take them away. Some 30,000 more were strung out along the railway with their rearguard at Penza. The eastward movement was checked and then reversed. Between June and August 1918 the Czechs, seizing arms and munitions wherever they found them, established themselves all along the Trans-Siberian Railway, and formed a line from Ekaterinburg[1] in the Urals to Kazan[2] on the Volga and down that river to Samara. They were now definitely anti-Bolshevik, and placed themselves at the disposal of a democratic Government which had sprung up in Samara. Local White levies were joining up, and the left flank was covered by the support of the Ural and Orenburg Cossacks. Allied troops had been landed at Vladivostock. Their instructions were to help the Czechs and safeguard Allied interests generally, but not to interfere in internal conflicts.

Yet another anti-Bolshevik front was in course of formation in the North during these summer months of 1918. Communications with Russia had been maintained by the western Allies during the war by the sea route round the North Cape. In 1916 a small British force was established at Murmansk, whence a railway was being built to

[1] It was when the Czechs were approaching Ekaterinburg in July that the Tzar and the Imperial Family, who had been removed thither from Tobolsk in April, were shot by the retreating Reds.

[2] At Kazan the reserve of the State Bank, amounting to 650 million gold and 100 million paper roubles, fell into White hands. This treasure had been removed from Petrograd by the Bank officials, who remained in charge of it throughout its subsequent romantic peregrinations. It is strange that this vast sum should have remained virtually intact until it was handed over to the "Political Centre" at Irkutsk at the beginning of 1920 on the fall of Admiral Kolchak.

Petrograd for the conveyance of supplies destined for the Russian armies. Farther East along the Arctic coast large depots of munitions had been accumulated at Archangel. In the spring of 1918 the Bolsheviks began to remove these munitions, not to fight the Germans, but for use against the internal enemy. In February, the Allied Embassies, having been withdrawn from Petrograd in consequence of the decision not to recognize the Bolshevik Government, moved to Vologda in anticipation of being taken off from Archangel when the ice melted. On August 2nd they arrived in the town, to find that the anti-Bolshevik elements had got the upper hand and that British troops were being landed. It was feared at the time not only that the Bolsheviks would carry off the munitions, but that the Germans might be tempted to seize them. The British found themselves committed to the support of a Provisional Government of North-West Russia—in loose touch with the Samara Government, and later with Kolchak's Government—which they soon discovered was incompetent, riddled with internal dissensions, and objectionable to the population. British and American troops, whose primary business was simply to guard and remove Allied stores, were in fact obliged to hold a wide front against the Bolsheviks because the Provisional Government, while claiming protection as a loyal ally, was incapable of organizing its own defence. Before long they were occupying all the country west of the Dvina and north of the 62nd parallel.

By the late summer of 1918, it appeared that Moscow was about to be completely encircled. Up till now the difficulties of the Bolsheviks had been largely internal. In the summer of 1918 the Social Revolutionary[1] party was raising its

[1] It is important to realize that the Social-Revolutionaries were as hostile to the Whites as to the Reds. The Left Social-Revolutionaries co-operated

head. Savinkov, a former adherent of the Provisional Government, had organized a secret anti-Bolshevik organization. He was supposed to be in touch with the Allies. Reverting to the old Nihilist revolutionary technique, the plan was to kill the Bolshevik leaders, and to provoke an insurrection, which would enable the Czechs from the East and the British from the North to advance on Moscow. Only the first part of the scheme ever came to anything. In order to embroil the Bolsheviks with the Germans, Count Mirbach, their Ambassador, and General von Eichorn, the commander of the army of occupation in Kiev, were assassinated. In August, Lenin was shot at and wounded, and Uritzky, the President of the "Cheka," was killed.

This conspiracy was made the justification for a campaign against foreign intervention,[1] and for the beginning of ruthless measures against internal political opponents. So far there had been no general political proscriptions. The bourgeoisie had been subjected to a strict control, somewhat akin to that appropriate to "enemy aliens," but except locally and in the civil war zones no concerted attack had been made on them. Now a regular class war was declared with the deliberate intention of cowing opposition. Mass executions and the relentless extermination of the bourgeoisie became the order of the day. The "Red Terror" had set in.

Having crushed the internal enemy, the Bolsheviks turned on the external foe. Just as the anti-Bolshevik

with the Bolsheviks up to the Treaty of Brest-Litovsk. Thereafter the party as a whole opposed the Bolsheviks on the grounds that hostilities should have been continued as a revolutionary war such as the French revolutionaries had waged.

[1] It was while resisting a raid on the British Embassy in Petrograd in order to obtain information implicating the Allies that Captain Crombie, the British Naval Attaché, was killed.

organizations were becoming menacing the Red Army was beginning to take some sort of shape. For this the Bolsheviks had to thank Trotsky's indefatigable energy, remarkable organizing ability, ruthless determination, and inspiring oratory. Being at peace with the Central Powers, they had little to fear from the West and South, though they much resented what they regarded as the Austro-German invasion. Denikin's Volunteer Army was not yet formidable. Allied intervention from the North had only just begun. Nevertheless the situation on the Volga had become critical. Trotsky has graphically described the weeks during which he dared not move his special train from the bridgehead opposite Kazan for fear the wavering front should break. He calls the defence of Sviyazhsk the Valmy of the "October" Revolution. The situation was saved. The Czechs were repulsed. A counter-attack was launched. By the middle of October, Kazan, Simbirsk, and Samara had been retaken. The line of the Volga was never again so seriously threatened.

The Czech defeat was not solely due to the superior numbers brought against them. Those internal difficulties which eventually wrecked the White prospects in Siberia were already beginning. The Czechs themselves had been drawn into the struggle partly by accident and partly to please the Allies. Their relations with local governments were often strained. They were disgusted at the lack of cohesion and determination among the better classes, who seemed quite willing to let them do the fighting, while contributing little support themselves. Largely through their agency a number of local governments were induced to coalesce into what was known as the Omsk Directorate. The War Minister was Admiral Kolchak.[1] In the middle of

[1] Admiral Kolchak had been in command of the Baltic Fleet at the time of the Revolution. Although a popular officer, he was a strict disciplinarian, and

November Kolchak overthrew the Directorate and proclaimed himself Dictator. In this action he had some support from the Allied Missions, but the Czechs, who held very liberal political views, considered him reactionary. Thenceforward their support of the Whites became half-hearted. The proclamation of the new Czecho-Slovak State in Prague at the end of October turned their thoughts once more towards home. Moreover, they felt that if the Allies really wanted the eastern front reformed they should have done something more than send a few battalions to Vladivostock.

It is as difficult to convey an adequate idea of the military conditions of the Civil War campaigns as it is to disentangle the policies of the various parties concerned. The armies began by being little more than improvised formations, many of which did not rise above the level of guerilla bands. The disbanded soldiers usually kept their arms and equipment, but, at first, the organization of commissariat, transport, and the supply of munitions was exceedingly difficult for all sides. Units lived from hand to mouth. The importance of operations as often as not consisted in the seizure of stocks of provisions and war stores lying at railway stations occupied by the enemy. The chief fighting followed the main lines of communication, and particularly the railways. The railway officials often worked the lines for both sides. Armoured trains played a specially prominent part. These moving fortresses, acting very much on the initiative of their commanders, resembled a modern version of the baronial castle in mediæval warfare. There is nothing that can really be called a strategic plan in any of the

he resigned rather than accept the sailors' committees authorized by Kerensky. He went to America, and was then offered employment by the British in the Middle East. On his way there he was diverted to China, where he helped to organize anti-Bolshevik forces in Manchuria, and whence he subsequently went to Siberia.

movements during 1918. The Reds had the advantages of interior lines, of the possession of the munition factories in the neighbourhood of Petrograd and Moscow, and of the control of the navy. The Whites were better provided with experienced senior officers, their troops were more amenable to discipline, and, in the Czechs, they had the support of the only really cohesive force in the country. These distinctions, however, tended gradually to even themselves out. The Reds found able commanders, the Whites enlarged their areas of occupation sufficiently to be largely self-supporting. The discipline of the Red Army improved, that of the Whites did not. Both sides resorted to "conscription," which was often tantamount to press-gang methods. Both sides filled their ranks from prisoners, who were given the alternative of joining up or being shot. Quarter was neither given nor expected. What were called atrocities by one side were called reprisals by the other. Humane commanders were seldom able to restrain the ferocity of the rank and file.

The bitterness and hatred engendered by the struggle increased as it proceeded. The non-combatant population suffered from all hands. It was dangerous to welcome anybody When a town or a district changed hands, the supporters of the defeated party had little mercy to look for. Destruction of property and requisitions hit all alike. In Red territory the poor peasants and workers were set on to attack the *kulak* and the bourgeois. In White territory the age-long feud between the Cossacks and the peasants led to endless trouble. In these circumstances the mass of the population inclined to be hostile to all types of government. They had little sympathy with Communism, but the White military leaders were too much identified with the old régime to command general confidence, while the moderate socialist parties ruled singularly ineffectively.

It would be futile to speculate on the outcome of the struggle had there been no foreign intervention. The fact that the Revolution occurred in the middle of the war made it impossible for any of the belligerent countries to stand absolutely aloof. The policy both of the Central Powers and of the Allies was primarily dictated not by their attitude towards the Revolution but by the exigencies of the war. As far as the internal Russian conflict is concerned, it may be said that the Reds benefited just as much by German policy between the "October" Revolution and the Armistice as the Whites did from Allied assistance after the Armistice. The Germans could at any time have swept the Bolsheviks away, and this was a line much favoured among the German army itself. But the German Government were probably deterred by the same considerations which later prevented the Allies from intervening effectively on behalf of the Whites, namely disinclination to get entangled in an adventure whose cost in life and money would probably have created difficulties at home, and which would, if successful, have saddled them with heavy responsibility for the régime ultimately established in Russia. The Treaty of Brest-Litovsk again helped the Bolsheviks just as much as the Germans. While it certainly gave an impetus to the White movements, which considered the prosecution of the war just as important as their domestic political objectives, it also safeguarded the Bolsheviks from interference along the greater part of their front.

The Armistice wrought a complete change in the situation. The Treaty of Brest-Litovsk was repudiated. The Germans and Austrians were obliged to withdraw, not only from the Ukraine and White Russia, but from the Baltic countries and Poland. The Turks were ordered out of the Caucasus. The Black Sea was opened to the Allied fleets.

The Germans had prevented the formation of strong governments in the territories they had occupied for fear lest their own plans should be impeded. Therefore, when the evacuation began, the Reds had little difficulty in taking their places. Appeals were made to the Allies by anti-Bolshevik organizations to re-establish the "cordon" in order to give them time to put themselves in a state of defence. The Allies refused to do this, but, taking into consideration the fact that many had taken up arms because they thought they were helping the Allied cause, they were allowed to draw on Allied war stores.

The policy of the Allies was not to interfere beyond this point in the purely Russian conflict, but they thought themselves entitled to support the self-determination of the non-Russian peoples. British troops were landed at Batoum to clear the Turks out of Trans-Caucasia, and to uphold the independence of Georgia, Armenia, and Azerbaidjan. On the Baltic the Esthonians threw back the Bolsheviks with White Russian help, but disagreements prevented the formation of a common anti-Bolshevik front. The Whites established themselves outside Esthonian territory, and came to be known as the North-Western Army. In Latvia the Allies authorized the Germans to suspend their evacuation, while the Bolshevik invasion was stemmed and Riga recaptured from them. In Poland the French began the organization of a national army at the beginning of 1919.

The situation in South Russia requires separate and fuller treatment. Chaos reigned in the Ukraine during the winter of 1918. Partisans of Skoropadski, the Bolsheviks, Petlura, a moderate socialist leader, and the Whites, fought each other indiscriminately. Finally, by the end of the year, Petlura, who was also the champion of Ukrainian separatism, was momentarily triumphant. Meanwhile,

Denikin had gained notable successes in the Kuban. By September the strength of the Volunteer Army had risen to 40,000 and the beginnings of a civil administration were coming into existence in co-operation with the various Cossack Governments.

Allied influence was exerted from two points. The country East of the Crimea was counted a British sphere under General Milne in Constantinople. West of the Crimea was counted a French sphere under General Berthelot at Bucharest. Not a little confusion and friction resulted from this division of authority. The French saw in an independent Ukraine, associated, perhaps, with Poland, and under their influence, a potential counterpoise to Russia. They were, therefore, disposed to support Petlura, and in December 1918 several French and Greek divisions were landed at Odessa. In January 1919, however, the Red Army overwhelmed Petlura and took Kiev. A little later a Red offensive against Krasnov's Don Cossack army gained the important Donetz industrial region and threw the Whites back on Rostov. On the other hand Denikin, who was now receiving supplies from the British, was continuing his successes, and by the middle of February had cleared the Bolsheviks out of the northern Caucasus, reaching the Caspian and cutting them off from both the Baku and Grosny oil-fields.

The Whites in Odessa appealed now to Denikin for help. The Franco-Greek forces were under instructions not to get engaged against the Bolsheviks, who were advancing on the city. Some idea of the confusion that prevailed is indicated by Denikin's statement that in the neighbouring port of Nicolaiev there were at this time five competing authorities, a Town Council adhering to the old Provisional Government, a Commissariat of Petlura's Ukrainian Directorate, a Bolshevik Workers' and Soldiers' Soviet, a German Garrison Soldiers' Council, and a French Commandant of the Allied forces. Denikin was appointed Commander-in-Chief of the White forces in South Russia, but at the moment the title was more or less nominal. He could do little with his existing resources so far from his base. At the beginning of April the Allies evacuated Odessa, which was promptly occupied by the Reds, with the now familiar accompaniment of massacre and rapine.

Meanwhile the Red offensive on the Don had been checked. The Volunteer Army, swelled by the incorporation of other White forces, and with its rear safe at last, was preparing to advance.

Had the various White fronts been able to co-operate effectively at this juncture, victory might have been theirs in 1919, despite the internal weakness of all the White Governments. The Red armies were badly scattered, and harassed by insurrections in the newly occupied territories. The White armies were now well equipped and standing on their own ground. But the importance of co-operation was only exceeded by its difficulty. Communication between Kolchak in the centre, Denikin on his left, and the scattered North and North-Western groups on his right, was never properly established.

Kolchak claimed a vague supremacy for his so-called All-Russian Government, but as a matter of fact he was hardly master in his own house, or rather his mastery was only secured by measures which alienated a large proportion of the Siberian population. He had launched an offensive in the middle of March, which nearly reached the Volga once more, but had been thrown back almost to its starting-point by the end of May.

The pressure on Kolchak was relieved by the removal of Red troops to oppose Denikin's advance. The Volunteer Army was sweeping all before it. Tzaritzin on the lower

Volga and Ekaterinoslav in the Ukraine fell to him towards the end of June, Kharkov in July. In the western Ukraine Denikin found Petlura, whom the Whites detested for his separatist tendencies, operating with the Poles, who had for some months been surreptitiously encroaching beyond their ethnographic boundaries. Kiev was occupied. A Red counter-attack towards Kharkov in August was repulsed. By the middle of October the line ran from Tzaritzin to Kiev through Voronezh, Orel, and Chernigov. Cavalry patrols were approaching Tula, an important armament centre, not 200 miles from Moscow.

The North-West army was also moving. General Yudenich on the Esthonian border had organized a dash on Petrograd. He was supported by a British naval demonstration in the Gulf of Finland. Within seven miles of the city the Red defence stood firm on the Pulkovo heights. The Whites wavered. Fresh Red troops came up. By the end of October Yudenich's army was being chased over the Esthonian frontier and disarmed.

This failure coincided with the exhaustion of Denikin's effort. Although his army had doubled in numbers during the advance, the reliable parts of it could not cope with the demands made on them. The new recruits were untrained, and the Cossacks were giving trouble because they were anxious about what might be happening at home. Moreover, the communications were being harassed, as those of the Bolsheviks had been early in the year, by independent guerilla bands. Such "partisan" leaders as Makhno and Grigoriev are said to have had, at times, as many as 20,000 men under their orders. The rapidity of the advance had precluded the possibility of setting up any civil administration. The mass of the population had remained apathetic. In the hour of success, political differences, which had been repressed when existence was at stake, broke out again. The Volunteer Army fell back before Red attacks. The retreat became a rout. In December the Whites, now little more than a rabble, were back behind the Don, whence they had started six months previously. The Cossacks rallied for a while to the defence of their home country, but in the spring of 1920 the last resistance collapsed. Denikin, with the remnants of his army, save for a portion which had taken refuge in the Crimea, was evacuated, with Allied assistance, to Constantinople.

On the other fronts also the tide had definitely turned. The Allied forces in the North had been withdrawn in September, and the Archangel Government, left to its own resources, was crumbling. In Siberia, Kolchak was being involved in disasters even more overwhelming than those which were overtaking Denikin.

The defeat of the White offensive in the Urals in the spring was followed by a steady deterioration of the Siberian army. The breach between the "Supreme Ruler" and the Czechs widened. The latter gradually withdrew from the front and concentrated on guarding the Trans-Siberian Railway West of Irkutsk. Instructions from their home Government later reinforced the inclination to confine their activities within the limits set to the Japanese and other Allied troops, who had charge of the line between Lake Baikal and Vladivostock. Kolchak's own troops proved of little value unaided, while his arbitrary methods of civil administration provoked growing hostility. Corruption was rife. While the front was starved, the rear made itself thoroughly comfortable. The spirit of patriotic self-sacrifice failed among just those classes who should have inspired it. When the Red attacks were more strongly pressed, the retreat degenerated into flight. Omsk was abandoned in November, and thenceforward indescribable confusion prevailed. The Czechs remained the only disciplined force, but their primary concern was to extricate themselves from the tangle, not to save the Whites. The climax came when Kolchak ordered Semenov to destroy the tunnels, through which the railway passes the end of Lake Baikal, in order to prevent their evacuation. The plan was frustrated, but the Czechs now refused to lift a finger even to ensure Kolchak's personal safety. This was in December, when the Reds had already reached Tomsk. Revolts against the "Supreme Ruler" were in progress everywhere. A Social-Revolutionary Government, usually referred to as the "Political Centre," had been set up at Irkutsk. Kolchak fell into their hands, and was summarily shot on February 7, 1920.

The Bolsheviks did not advance east of Lake Baikal. Following the White collapse, the Allied forces, including the Czechs, were gradually evacuated. For two years longer a Far Eastern Republic maintained a precarious existence with Japanese support.

The collapse of the White movements was sudden, complete and final, but, though the issue of the Civil War was decided, the Red Army still had some fighting before it.

Just as the Bolsheviks were consummating their victory a diversion arose from a different quarter. Poland, having been confirmed in its independence by the Paris Peace Conference, was effervescing with nationalist sentiment. During 1919 she had taken advantage of Bolshevik pre-occupation elsewhere to extend her ill-defined eastern frontier. Negotiations for a permanent settlement had been started,[1] but, contrary to Allied advice, the Poles insisted on making extravagant demands. Not only did they stand out for something far exceeding their ethnographical claims, but they required an indemnity, for which they

[1] The Armistice arranged in September 1919 had released Bolshevik troops for service against the Whites at a critical moment.

proposed to occupy Smolensk as a guarantee. If there is any nation against whom all Russians will combine regardless of politics it is the Polish. The Bolsheviks had the country behind them in refusing these terms. Having made an agreement with Petlura, the dispossessed nationalist dictator of the Ukraine, the Poles proceeded to assert their claims by force. By the end of May 1920 they had occupied Kiev, Minsk, and Vilna. Then they were driven back by a Bolshevik counter-attack, and, by the middle of August, had retreated to the outskirts of Warsaw. So far the principal Allied Powers had observed the frigid aloofness of spurned advisers; but they were not prepared to see Poland entirely absorbed into the Bolshevik sphere of influence, and an essential buffer between the Russian and German Communists removed. A French General, Weygand, was called to the rescue. Fortunately the Red Army had outrun itself. With expert stiffening the Poles rallied, and this time it was the Russians who retreated precipitately. An armistice was arranged on October 11th, and by the Treaty of Riga, signed in March 1921, the present eastern frontier of Poland, less than her ambitions, but more than her ethnographical rights, was settled.

Meanwhile the last White flicker had been extinguished. Under cover of the Polish War, General Wrangel had mustered the part of Deniken's army which had been left in the Crimea. He had occupied some coastal districts. He had held out through the summer. In the autumn the Red Army, relieved of anxiety by the Polish armistice, had concentrated upon him, and he had succumbed. In November 1920 his beaten regiments went to join the hundred thousand refugees already in the Turkish capital.

Sufficient indication has already been given of the circumstances which made the Bolshevik victory possible. Its primary cause, however, was the lack of unity among the anti-Bolshevik elements. No one of them succeeded in dominating the others, and their views were too divergent to be covered, save transiently, by a common programme. How could the peasants be expected to enthuse for people who talked about restoring the land to its former owners? To them this meant going back on the whole Revolution. How could Liberals and moderate Socialists be expected to put up for long with the dictatorship of Generals brought up to regard politicians and Parliaments as so many time-wasters? The principles of the Revolution again seemed at stake. How could the military leaders tolerate the dismemberment of the Empire when the unity of the Fatherland was one of their most cherished ideals? Georgians, Ukrainians and Letts were as much Russian to them as Indians, French-Canadians, and Irish are British to us. The temperamental gulfs between the peasant, bourgeois, and military minds remained unbridged. No outstanding figure emerged to assume the undisputed championship of the common cause.

To the anti-Bolshevik elements mentioned above some might be disposed to add the new border States and foreign Powers. It was certainly not to the interest of any of these that the Reds should win, but neither was it their business to dictate what sort of Government should rule Russia. The new States were too busy with their own affairs to think of joining an anti-Bolshevik crusade. They thought first of consolidating their own independence, and the denial of their right of self-determination by the Whites did not arouse eagerness to assist them. The reasons which restrained the Germans from active intervention have already been given. What the Central Powers might have done while the war was still in progress was much harder for the Allies to justify after the Armistice. It is true that the fear of World Revolution provided a new motive for intervention. Moreover, the civilized world had been profoundly shocked by the "Red Terror," and by the repudiation of financial and other international obligations. But the armies and public opinion demanded demobilization, not the beginning of a new war. The prevalent anti-Bolshevik sentiment, stimulated as it was by Russian *émigrés* and diplomats of the old régime, condoned the breaches of neutrality to which the gift of supplies and presence of Allied troops in Russia led, but it was felt that if the Whites could not win without the help of foreign armies they deserved little sympathy.

The compromise arrived at, though less entangling than downright intervention, was nevertheless no real compromise at all, but simply the result of vacillations between two opposite policies. Sometimes those who favoured intervention, sometimes those who favoured withdrawal, were in the ascendant in the Cabinets of Europe and at the Peace Conference. There was enough intervention to give the Bolsheviks a patriotic cry; there was not enough to ensure White victory. In order to isolate the rest of the world from the contamination of Bolshevism, a *cordon sanitaire* was established, which was, in effect, an economic blockade. At the same time the Prinkipo Conference was being arranged in the futile hope of finding common ground for negotiations between all parties in the soothingly remote atmosphere of this delectable island in the Sea of Marmora. In truth, foreign Governments never really grasped the meaning of the Russian Revolution, and they were not infrequently misled by information which they were unable to appreciate in its proper perspective.

By the end of 1920 the attempt to suppress the Bolsheviks by force had come to an end. Both internally and externally a new phase of the Revolution was about to open.

CHAPTER V

RECONSTRUCTION

By the end of 1920 Bolshevik rule was in a fair way to being established in most of what is now Soviet territory. There was at any rate no serious obstacle, now that neither White nor foreign armies were any longer a military danger, to the consolidation of Bolshevik power wherever the Red Army could gain a footing. The Bolsheviks had reconciled themselves to the loss of Finland, the Baltic States, and Poland because they were not prepared to provoke foreign intervention on a large scale. They had no intention of sacrificing the political and economic advantages which the domination of the rest of the former Russian Empire would give them. Most of European Russia and Siberia was already in their hands, but they still had to deal with peoples whose independence they had already recognized in principle, while the Far-Eastern Republic, parts of Central Asia and Trans-Caucasia, were still beyond their grasp.

The Russian Federation of Socialist Soviet Republics, commonly referred to as the R.S.F.S.R., had been formed early in 1918. As its territory expanded, new units composed of non-Russian national groups were added to it, though the autonomy of the constituent parts was very limited. A more serious problem arose when it came to dealing with peoples who already had an organized existence of their own. Some way had to be devised of respecting the principle of self-determination and at the same time ensuring the effective control of Moscow. These apparently contradictory aims could, however, be adjusted on the theory that since the Communist social order was to be established universally, the validity of the right of self-determination must depend on the acceptance of Communism. The R.S.F.S.R., as the only original and authoritative Communist State, therefore affirmed in effect that while any people might proclaim its independence, this should not stand in the way of any measures that might be taken to bring it into the Communist system.

The effect of this policy was the construction by the end of 1922 of the political entity officially known as the Union of Socialist Soviet Republics.[1] The procedure in every case where an independent State had been set up was approximately the same. First, an excuse had to be found for military occupation. This was seldom difficult. After the defeat of the White armies and the withdrawal of foreign troops, Red forces could always intervene in support of a Communist rising. The bourgeois Governments in the Ukraine, the Caucasus, and the Far East were left practically defenceless; neither had the Emir of Bokhara the means to resist a disciplined army. The next step was to set up a Soviet Government, and to conclude with it a treaty of military and economic alliance, which left effective control in the hands of the Government of the R.S.F.S.R. in Moscow.

The Russian Empire was being reconstituted in a new form, with wider and more dangerous ambitions than it had ever had under any Tzar, but strikingly similar in many aspects of its foreign policy. For the old-fashioned territorial imperialism of the Tzars had been substituted the imperialism of a new social order. There was just the same desire to acquire influence in China, in Afghanistan, and in Persia, to threaten India, and to meddle with the internal affairs of European States. The only difference was that Russian expansion was said to be blocked by Capitalism

[1] Commonly referred to as the U.S.S.R., or the Soviet Union. See Appendix for a description of its present political organization.

instead of by Slavophobia, and that the objects of Russian solicitude were no longer Slavs and members of the Orthodox Church, but Communists.

A fundamental and startling transformation had nevertheless been achieved, though at a cost such as even the Bolsheviks can scarcely have reckoned upon. With the *naïveté* which characterized so many of their early actions, they had seriously hoped that the abolition of private rights in property, and the subjection of the individual, body and soul, to the ends of an impersonal social theory, might have been smoothly accomplished. They even expected those whom they were expropriating and dragooning to play their parts in the spirit of detached curiosity with which a member of the audience goes on to the stage to assist in the performance of a conjuring trick. Their reading of Russian psychology was indeed not so wide of the mark as might be supposed. They depended at first almost entirely, as they still do very largely, on the co-operation of bourgeois officials, technicians and intellectuals, who were just as much fascinated as terrorized, and they rightly counted on the opposition of the peasants being almost entirely negative. What they quite failed to realize was that even such a primitive organism as the Russian could not be destroyed without devastating consequences. The year 1921 brought the reckoning for playing fast and loose with every instinct of human nature.

In order to avoid breaks in the narrative no mention has been made of the progressive modification of the economic system since the initial measures of the Third Congress of Soviets taken soon after the "October" Revolution. Lenin's policy of effecting the change from private to public ownership in industry by gradual stages was accelerated by circumstances, until the Government found itself saddled with a task quite beyond its powers. The danger of too abrupt a transition was foreseen but not avoided. In the first place there was the eagerness of the rank and file of the party to forge ahead. In the second place there was the necessity of putting an end to the chaos produced through the taking over of factories by the direct action of works Soviets. In the third place there was the refusal of owners and managers to carry on under the new conditions.

The Banks were nationalized in December 1917, shipping in January 1918, and large-scale industry (concerns with a capital of over 1,000,000 roubles) in June 1918. So far the process was reasonably orderly, and in many cases the change did not mean a very substantial difference from the system of war-time control which already existed. A Supreme Economic Council was created in December 1917, which took over the machinery of the War Industries Committee, and added departments as various industries were trustified. Former owners were required to stay on as managers, and local control was exercised through the Trade Unions by means of factory Soviets.

The reaction of the military and political situation on economic organization was a tightening of central control. The exigencies of the Civil War and the necessity of "disciplining" the bourgeoisie both hastened the direct taking over of industry by the Government. There resulted a system which came to be known as "War Communism," and which lasted until the introduction of the New Economic Policy ("Nep") in 1921. One feature of "War Communism," the forcible mobilization of labour, was primarily a war measure, while another, the abolition of money, happened almost automatically with the collapse of the value of the currency to vanishing point. It is again an illustration of the naïve self-confidence of these incredible people that they should have taken on direct responsibility for the entire processes of production, distribution, and exchange in the area under their rule, and this without administrative experience, on the morrow of a violent political convulsion, and in the midst of a struggle for very existence. It is not surprising that they failed. The mystery is how they survived at all.

There is some difference of opinion as to whether "War Communism" was the result of the force of circumstances or of a deliberate attempt to introduce Communism at a stroke. The first view is used to uphold the contention that "Nep" was only a tactical move, a return to the original programme of introducing Communism by stages. The second view is used to show that "Nep" marked the decisive defeat of Communism as an immediate goal. The whole controversy seems to be based on a false antithesis. Both views are true as far as they go. The Bolsheviks underestimated the difficulties of putting Communism into practice, but they had intended to avoid alarming the peasants by not rushing things. In fact, unforeseen difficulties forced them to outrun their programme. The attempt to introduce practical Communism was nevertheless made. "Nep" was unquestionably an acknowledgment of defeat, but there is no conclusive evidence to show whether that defeat was due to the particular difficulties of the time or to the inherent unsoundness of Communism. People will give different answers according to whether they believe in Communism or not. It cannot yet be said that the defeat was decisive with any more confidence than it could have been said in 1915 that the battle of the Marne had made it impossible for the Germans to win the war.

Although the military tide had turned in favour of the Reds, the condition of the country by the beginning of 1920 was appalling. It was just about as much as the Bolsheviks could do to keep the army going. The railways were in such a condition that they could hardly minister to military needs, let alone keep the towns supplied. It was almost fortunate that, owing to the peasants' refusal to grow anything beyond what they needed themselves, there were few supplies to transport, and that the urban population was simply melting away to the villages. Some cities lost over half their inhabitants in this way. Industry was virtually at a standstill. Trotsky, who was head of the War Revolutionary Committee all through this period, has told us that he realized that "War Communism" would have to be dropped and some element of personal incentive reintroduced. He suggested the substitution of a grain tax for the food levy, but was overruled by Lenin and the Central Executive. He then declared that the only alternative was to carry "War Communism" to its logical extremity. Labour armies were created in February 1920, and managed to achieve some increase in production. Eight months later the mobilization for labour of all male citizens born in the years 1886, 1887, and 1888 was decreed, and this was followed by the allocation of sewing work to all women between the ages of fifteen and forty-five. In November even the smallest industries were nationalized. But these were simply measures for squeezing the orange dry, and ended in arousing the hostility of the Trade Unions, because Trotsky wanted to abolish their independent position and put them under military discipline.

The results of this policy were serious. Workers and peasants had been estranged from each other, and both were in revolt against the agents of the Government. During 1920 there were strikes in 70 per cent. of state enterprises and risings in several country districts. More significant still was a mutiny of sailors at Kronstadt, which had to be put down by force. Famine was threatening, and in fact during 1921 reached terrible proportions, especially in the Volga area.[1]

Millions died, and yet more millions would have died but for the work of the Society of Friends and of the American relief organization under Dr. Nansen. The Bolsheviks owed much at this time to the efforts of those whom they never ceased declaring to be their enemies.

Everybody was clear that something must be done, but there was a great variety of opinion as to the form action should take. The decision was vital, because, for the first time, the new régime was being called upon to legislate for peace-time conditions. There were some, like Trotsky, who were for putting the country on a permanent basis of highly centralized and almost military organization; others were for reverting to the original structure of loosely knit local Soviets. Between these extremes there were many shades of opinion. Lenin, however, saw that the absolutely essential thing was to restore equilibrium between town and country. The agricultural basis of Russian life was a fact that could not be ignored. The peasant must be induced to grow food and a demand must be created for the products of industry. The New Economic Policy, which, after much resistance from the Left Wing, was accepted by the Party Congress in June 1921, achieved these objects by substituting a tax in kind for the system of requisitions, and by relaxing the State trade monopoly. A free market was opened for peasant produce, and private persons were permitted to lease small industries. Individual incentive was restored, and the burden on the economic administrative machine was lightened. A new stabilized currency was introduced

[1] Novels like Gladkov's *Ciment* and Nevierov's *Tashkent* give an idea of conditions at this time. Both of these are obtainable in English translations. A number of French translations of similar works have been published by the *Nouvelle Revue Française*.

in 1922. The way was also opened to relations with foreign countries.

Whether the New Economic Policy be considered a strategic retreat from Communism or merely a tactical retirement, its effect was instantaneous and far-reaching. The next six years are a period of steady economic recovery. Although it is impossible to speak of anything like prosperity and plenty, yet conditions were more tolerable than they had been since before the Revolution started. The progress of reconstruction was slow because, in the first place, what we call the Soviet system was feeling its way along uncharted courses, and because, in the second place, foreign countries were only willing to contribute very slender financial assistance.

During this period there were also some important political changes. Lenin had a stroke in May 1922, and although he recovered sufficiently by the autumn to keep control of affairs for a few months more, he was still a very sick man. In the spring of 1923 he had another seizure, and on January 21, 1924, he died. Who was to succeed him? None of the other revolutionary leaders approached him in authority. Trotsky, the most brilliant of them, and the most popular in the country, held views which were already looked upon with disfavour in many quarters. He was the exponent of the theory of "permanent revolution," according to which things must not be allowed to settle down, but, through the maintenance of a relentless class war at home, and the constant stirring up of trouble abroad, must be kept moving towards the World Revolution, without which Communism could not ultimately succeed. From a theoretical point of view there was much to be said for Trotsky's contention, but the world situation had changed since the days when he was doing wonders of inspiration and organization between 1917 and 1920.

By 1924 the tide of revolution had receded in foreign countries, while at home there was a reaction against the more violent manifestation of the revolutionary spirit. The more empirical and opportunist point of view was represented by Stalin, whom Trotsky once called "the outstanding mediocrity of the party." The strength of his position lay in his mastery of the Communist party machine. His primary aim was to make Communist rule safe in Russia. Trotsky's following was largely personal, but he had many of the older generation of Bolsheviks on his side. For a time after Lenin's death Stalin, Zinoviev, and Kamenev formed a kind of triumvirate. Then the internationalism of the two latter tainted them with Trotskyism, against which Stalin was directing all the forces of propaganda over which he had control. In January 1925 Trotsky was forced to give up the War Office, but he kept up the fight for three years more. Finally, at the Fifteenth Party Congress, at the end of 1927, the expulsion of the Opposition was decreed. Trotsky himself was exiled to Central Asia, whence, after trying to reconstruct his party underground, he was deported to Turkey in January 1929. One by one other well-known leaders also dropped out. Joffé, Krassin, Dzerzhinsky died. Zinoviev, Kamenev, Bukharin, and, more recently, Lunacharsky and Rykov, have faded into the background. This change of personnel is an important factor in considering the present situation.

Meanwhile, to return to economic matters, the signs of capitalist recrudescence under the influence of "Nep" were not without having a disturbing effect on the Communist leaders. A new sort of profiteer, the "Nepman," was arising in the towns, while in the country the peasants showed no signs of taking any more kindly to Socialism. The Government, however, was very much stronger in 1927 than it was in 1920. Schemes for industrializing the country were being worked out, and it was decided that a big push towards general collectivization should be made all along the line. The Five Year Plan was launched in 1928. Following "War Communism" and "Nep" the country now entered upon a third phase of Communist development, which might be termed "State Capitalism." The atmosphere of stress has returned with the throttling of private trade, the coercion of the peasants, and the privations which the effort to effect a vast and rapid increase of industrial production has entailed.

The new régime has not yet found its final form, but the transformation of the Russian Empire into the Union of Socialist Soviet Republics has quite definite implications.

What do the words "Union," "Soviet," and "Socialist" imply? Enough has already been said about Bolshevism to indicate that it is an attempt to realize a contradiction in terms. Class distinctions, and with them all distinctions involving the relations of rulers and ruled, master and servant, or any social, economic, and political superiority and inferiority, are to be abolished; but this is said to be possible only through the dictatorship of one class, which shall be so comprehensive that no other shall remain to challenge it. Force, in fact, is to be abolished by force. Two conflicting tendencies are, therefore, constantly apparent in all the actions of the Bolsheviks. On the one hand, they are all for independence, voluntary co-operation, and allowing everyone to behave as he likes. On the other hand, they insist that nothing shall be permitted which is inconsistent with the dictatorship of the proletariat. The difficulty of reconciling these two positions runs through the whole process of the formation of the new institutions. There is to be self-determination, but everyone is to be made to choose the same path. There must be centralized unity of control, but for all that local autonomy is to be aimed at. The dilemma appears in the federal problem or the problem of nationalities, which is represented by the word "Union." It appears in the problem of administration or of contact with the people, which is represented by the word "Soviet." It appears in the problem of who shall wield power, which is represented by the word "Socialist."

PART II

ROUND THE SOVIET UNION

CHAPTER VI

THE INCIDENTALS OF TRAVEL

Many parts of the world have experienced troublous times since the war. Most of Central and Eastern Europe has known extreme poverty and famine. Revolutions have taken place in many countries. But nowhere has the crisis been so prolonged, nowhere has society been so fundamentally disturbed as in Russia.

The events narrated in the preceding chapters have resulted in the isolation of a population of a hundred and fifty millions, occupying a sixth of the earth's surface. For fourteen years a persistent attempt has been made to inoculate this substantial fraction of the human race with a philosophy of life which runs counter to the most widely accepted beliefs of civilized peoples. The World War, the Civil War, and the Polish War have long been ended, but the class war still rages. The Soviet Union is formally at peace with its neighbours, but it still issues calls to social revolution within their territories. No more baffling enigma puzzles the world than the fate of the Communist experiment. No graver menace threatens the dominant civilizations of our age than the possibility of its success. It is of the first importance to know what is actually happening behind the Soviet frontier, where so momentous a drama is being enacted.

The following chapters describe the state of the country as I found it during my visits in the autumn of 1929 and 1930. Besides Leningrad and Moscow, where I stayed about three weeks on each occasion, my journeys in the provinces took me twice to Kharkov, the Caucasus, and parts of the Black Sea coast. In 1929 I spent a few days in

Odessa and Kiev. In 1930 I saw something of the Urals, Siberia, the Volga, and the Kuban.

I must confess to a thrill of not altogether pleasurable anticipation on approaching the Soviet frontier for the first time. Two such obvious bourgeois as my wife and myself might, I thought, be made to feel their inferiority by the proletarian dictatorship.

The train that had brought us through Berlin and Warsaw across the endless East European plain reached the Polish frontier station of Stolpce at dusk on a September evening. After a long wait and much bustle of officials and business with passports, the train moved slowly on. An interval, and the light from the carriage windows showed up a line of barbed-wire entanglements. A moment later the red-and-white striped Polish boundary post appeared beside the track. Next door to it was the all-red Soviet boundary post. We passed another line of entanglements. Beside them stood a sentry in the pointed cloth helmet and long full great-coat of the Red Army. A moment later we drew alongside the brightly lighted platform at Negoreloye, the Russian frontier station.

The Customs is a large room fitted up in the usual way. Pictures of Lenin, Stalin, and other Bolshevik leaders hang on the walls. Red flags are stuck round them. Above, are long strips of red bunting, inscribed with appropriate texts in white letters: "Workers of the World Unite"; "He who works not eats not," and so on. Everything proceeded very leisurely but methodically. There was none of the usual hectic atmosphere at a frontier station. For a long time no one took any interest in our luggage. Meanwhile, there was money to be changed, and sleeper reservations to be confirmed. Finally, our bags were very thoroughly examined, but all our belongings were replaced with care. To our relief everyone was charming. The Soviet Authorities are alive to the importance of first impressions. Occasional glances at fellow-travellers seemed to show that native proletarians are shown less consideration.

On my second visit I began my experience of Soviet conditions at London Bridge. A line of Soviet steamers plies between London and Leningrad, and the five days' journey affords an instructive example of Bolshevism decked out for export.

Our ship, the *Sibir* (3,700 tons gross), was a product of the Five Year Plan, built in Leningrad. The engines were from the Russian Diesel Works, and so far as I could see the only foreign articles on board were the davits and some of the instruments, which were English. A hypercritical eye might have detected the indifferent quality of some of the fittings, such as joinery, doors, locks, and port fastenings, but on the whole the passenger accommodation was excellent. Everything was done to make one feel at home, and to make sure that one should land in a frame of mind to see Soviet institutions through rosy spectacles.

At first sight there was nothing conspicuously Sovietic to be noticed except the flag, and the hammer and sickle crest on the crockery. But those who expected something striking of a Soviet ship were not to be disappointed. The great sensation was the discovery that the third mate was a woman. As her hair was cropped, and she wore trousers, she was not noticed at first. Passengers were encouraged to go all over the ship, not excluding the bridge, where they were even allowed to handle the charts. I have not noticed that such latitude is permitted on other Soviet ships; on those on the Black Sea routes, for instance.

The captain was a character. He was an "old Bolshevik," that is to say he belonged to the Party before the Revolution. He once edited a Communist newspaper in Australia, where he was imprisoned for sedition. Anyone less like one's conception of a revolutionary it would, nevertheless, be hard to meet. He was a large, slow-moving man, with a typical peasant cast of face, very well read, and with an excellent sense of humour. His only apparent Communistic idiosyncrasy was a refusal to wear uniform. He always went about in an old tweed suit and a rather grimy cap. The most remarkable of his performances, however, was as interpreter in a political debate got up one evening between some members of the British Labour Party and the crew. He translated every speech from English into Russian, and vice versa, as the debate proceeded, almost verbatim, and extraordinarily accurately. The Labourites had to defend themselves against some severe attacks, with a party of British Communists sniping from the flank.

The captain is apparently supreme at sea, but his orders can be challenged by the ship's Soviet before the proper authorities on shore. The crew was rather numerous, as an eight-hour day necessitated three complete shifts. Each department—the engine-room, the stewards, etc.—was organized into what is called an *artel*, which apportioned the work among its own members. There was a Lenin corner aft, with the usual statuette, red flags, Marxian texts, and posters. This was used as a club-room, where the crew also attended lectures, and were even given English lessons. Everything in fact seemed too good to be true, but as propaganda it was well done.

It is often suggested that travellers to Russia are so carefully shepherded that they cannot get a true impression of conditions in the country. This is an exaggeration. There is no obligation to have a guide or to follow a particular itinerary. No restriction of any kind was placed on my movements during either of my visits. The only limits to investigation are one's knowledge of the language, and the physical difficulties of travelling in a country where accommodation and transport are restricted and primitive off the main avenues of communication.

Nevertheless, conditions of travel are not the same as in the countries most commonly frequented by tourists. Parties of more than three or four people are bound to be looked after. Unless special arrangements were made in these cases, seats in trains, rooms in hotels, motor-cars for expeditions, or even food and drink, would be impossible to obtain. The authorities can hardly be blamed if they endeavour to show only that which is likely to create the most favourable impression.

Criticism appears to be welcomed, so long as it is not what is called "hostile," or unfair-minded. Responsible officials are genuinely interested in the reasons for a visitor's antipathy to their system. I was never conscious of having been watched myself, but if this sometimes happens, and if, as certainly happens, correspondence is read, one of the chief motives is the collection of candid opinions. Should anything compromising for a Russian be discovered in this way, advantage is taken of the information, but the foreigner need have no fears. I suppose he might be ordered to leave the country, but probably the worst that would befall him would be the refusal of another visa.

"Intourist," the State tourist agency, supplied a document for my 1930 journey which we called "the magic paper." It was a circular introduction, which not only procured access to all kinds of officials, but was the means of obtaining the best available lodging, food, and transport. There was no need to stand in queues or waste time with the many vexatious formalities which a Russian has to put up with. It is naturally as well to refrain from using exceptional privileges as much as possible, but, in a country where every citizen's actions are strictly controlled, some sort of special passport is necessary. When a foreigner is in difficulties he should go straight to the G.P.U.,[1] who have the power and the will to do anything for him in reason.

It is remarkable that the preferential treatment accorded to foreigners should arouse so little resentment. It must be exceedingly annoying to see strangers eating food which you cannot obtain yourself, and ushered into shops and theatres and trains while you have to wait your turn with a hundred others. This tolerant attitude may be partly due to the traditional obligations of hospitality which prevail in less highly developed countries, and partly to the association of foreigners with the technical assistance from abroad, which is doing so much for economic reconstruction. The large parties of tourists which descend on Moscow and Leningrad for a few hectic days seem in danger of compromising the foreigner's popularity. I once saw a large and not very amiable crowd outside the Hôtel d'Europe, in Leningrad, watching the passengers off one of the liners which tour the northern capitals. There was a good deal of resentment at these well-dressed, prosperous people being given a sumptuous lunch, and having most of the motor transport of the city mobilized to take them sightseeing. It seemed a somewhat curious inversion of thought to display ill-will against the tourists, who were only taking advantage of, and paying for, what the Authorities offered. It would have been more reasonable to blame the Authorities for conditions of life so obviously inferior to those to which the foreign visitors were accustomed.

Many people seem to think it dangerous to travel in Russia. Actually, public order is as well kept as in any other country, and I have, personally, never met with incivility from officials. I was once arrested by an over-

[1] Political Police—generally known by these initials, pronounced "gay-pay-oo." O.G.P.U., or "Ogpu," is seldom used in Russia.

zealous policeman, or "militiaman" as he should be called, since the word "policeman," with its flavour of Tzarist oppression, is no longer used, for taking photographs in one of the public markets in Moscow. The militiaman thought I should have had a permit. He was wrong, and the officer in charge of the police station released me at once. It was some time, however, before I could leave the building, since everyone wanted to ask questions about conditions in England. Much the same thing happened in Tiflis, where a soldier, or, as I should say, a "red army-ist," for the word "soldier" suffers from the same taboo as "policeman," arrested my companion for photographing a building which turned out to be a barracks.

In spite of persistent anti-British propaganda, the fact of being an Englishman was never a source of trouble. On the contrary, an Englishman receives the more consideration for being a rarer specimen than an American or a German. He may perhaps be regarded as one of a rather dangerous species, but this merely excites curiosity and provides opportunity for discussion such as every Russian loves.

Prices are high for the foreigner who has to change his money into roubles at the official rate, which is arbitrarily kept near par. On the other hand, there is so little to buy that expenses do not aggregate much more than the cost of a journey in most other countries. Everything is cheaper in the provinces than in Leningrad or Moscow, but the quality of food and accommodation is correspondingly lower.

Food is a serious preoccupation to the traveller. In Moscow and Leningrad the hotels used by foreigners provide adequate and palatable fare. There is usually at least one tolerable, but expensive, co-operative restaurant in big towns. Elsewhere meat is a luxury. Cabbage soup, *kasha* (buckwheat porridge), bitter black rye bread, and tea are staples of a diet which soon become extremely monotonous. Eggs and white bread are generally obtainable on the private market. Nearly all wine and spirits are prohibitively dear, vodka is plentiful, but the good brands are expensive. Beer is comparatively cheap, but is quite expensive enough considering its poor quality. Tea is the universal beverage, and never seems to be lacking, though lemons to put in it, according to the Russian custom, were rare in 1929, and were quite unobtainable in 1930. Coffee is nearly always synthetic and nasty. An excellent mineral water called Narzan is usually obtainable.

Centres frequented by tourists, and places where foreign technicians are employed, are usually better supplied. At Stalingrad, in 1930, there was an "Intourist" agent who produced gargantuan feasts, or so they seemed after nearly a week on the Volga, where neither the steamer nor the towns could rise above subsistence rations. There was a noticeably greater difficulty in obtaining supplies in 1930 than in 1929. For the seven weeks' tour of the provinces which I made in 1930, "Intourist" in Moscow sold us a sackful of various tinned foods which came in extremely useful. They were nearly all articles manufactured for export, such as biscuits, sardines, cheese, and salt fish, of excellent quality, but unobtainable by the native population. Cigarettes, which could be bought at any street corner in 1929, were strictly rationed in 1930, and the foreigner is again obliged to buy export brands from special stores. The G.P.U. have special shops through which resident foreigners are supplied.

The ordinary Russian habit is to have one main meal in the day, generally between three and five in the afternoon. The usual office hours are from 9 a.m. till 4 p.m. without a luncheon interval, but punctuated with many glasses of tea. This is a sensible arrangement, as the early dinner leaves a long clear evening. In the old days elaborate suppers, prolonged half through the night, were a great feature of gay life in the large towns, but nothing of the kind exists now.

Russian hotels are not so bad as might be expected. Until recently even the first-class hotels in the biggest towns had been allowed to fall into a depressing state of faded grandeur, but a little judicious expenditure on paint and plumbing is gradually improving matters.

The accommodation assigned to my wife and myself at the Hôtel d'Europe at Leningrad in 1929 is worth describing, though it should soon be a thing of the past. It was a large suite. There was an enormous sitting-room with nineteen chairs in a row round the walls, all showing signs of former magnificence, covered in striped green satin, now very threadbare. A huge elaborate gilt clock that did not go stood on the mantelpiece. Dark brown striped wallpaper, much faded, ran up to the immensely high ceiling. There were no curtains or blinds, and no carpet. The bedroom had the same dingy walls, eight tapestry chairs with corded fringes, a cupboard without a key or handle, and two rather rickety iron bedsteads. There was a bathroom, but the water was seldom hot, and the plug in the wash-basin was missing. The windows had never been opened since they were sealed up for the winter of 1917, and the only ventilation was a hole right through the outside wall into the street, opened and closed with a brass shutter.

In the provinces, where something much worse might be anticipated, the standard of cleanliness was at least as good as anywhere in Eastern Europe. This is not much of a compliment, I admit, but indicates tolerable conditions. Here again things are getting better every year, especially in the growing industrial towns, where new hotel buildings are everywhere being erected. In some places the best rooms are reserved for foreigners. At Sverdlovsk, a Russian engineer we had met on the train was actually refused accommodation, although one of these rooms was empty and he was prepared to pay the price.

The most satisfactory of the traveller's various temporary habitations are the trains. A broad gauge and a leisurely gait contribute to the comfort of long journeys. Communism notwithstanding, there are several classes of accommodation. They are not, however, called first, second, and third, but "international," "hard," and "soft." "International" means the old cars of the Wagon-Lit Company, which are well kept, clean, and roomy, with assiduous attendants who can produce tea and biscuits at any time. "Soft" means the old first and second class carriages, which usually provide sleeping room for four people, and roughly correspond to our third class sleepers. "Hard" means the old third and fourth class carriages, which have bare wooden seats. "International" cars are only attached to a few expresses on the most important lines, but what the traveller loses in comfort by a "soft" or "hard" carriage he makes up by coming into contact with more people. Although railway fares are low, few people can afford a berth in the "international," unless travelling at the public expense.

The increasing strain which the Five Year Plan is putting on the railway system made itself noticed by the deterioration of the train services between 1929 and 1930. On my first visit the trains ran well to time. On my second visit they were constantly hours late, and the breakdown of locomotives and rolling stock, as well as the congestion of traffic, were continually causing delays. The main line from Moscow via Kharkov and Rostov to the Caucasus seemed the worst affected.

Russian railway stations are always interesting and

TOP: A MARKET AT A RAILWAY STATION

BOTTOM: A HALT ON THE TRANS-SIBERIAN LINE. PASSENGERS DRAWING HOT WATER FROM THE *KIPYATOK*

frequently entertaining. There is always a crowd of prospective passengers. An instinctive restlessness seems to impel the Russian to travel. He does not merely go to a specific place for a specific purpose, he migrates. He becomes a nomad on wheels. Perhaps he hears conditions are better in the Caucasus than in Siberia. When he has saved his fare he packs up his household possessions, envelops them in a mattress, attaches a few pots and pans, and, with his family, goes to the station to await a train. As often as not he arrives there without knowing anything except the general direction he means to follow. He is, at any rate, quite oblivious of the existence of a time-table, which he probably could not read, and is quite content to wait several days for a place on a train. The result is that every railway station in Russia looks like a camp. Every corner is piled with luggage, round which whole families lie and sit. It is often difficult to push through the throng, or, at night, to pick one's way over sleeping bodies. I never tired of observing the variety of types and costumes and the queer assortments of baggage.

An enamelled teapot or billy-can is an absolutely essential article of equipment. At every station there is a *kipyatok*, where boiling water can be obtained from a tap. Whenever the train stops, every passenger dashes out and lines up with his can. The scene is so characteristic that it stays in my mind as symbolic of Russian travel.

CHAPTER VII

LIFE IN THE CAPITALS

The former capital of the Russian Empire, and the present capital of the Soviet Union stand for much that is central in the movement which gives the country its chief present interest. Moreover, most travellers get their first impressions from one or the other, and, whithersoever their subsequent journeyings may lead them, Moscow, at any rate, must remain the pivot of their experiences.

The Revolution brought home to Europe the fact that Peter the Great's "window looking out onto Europe" was a shop-window, concealing behind a modern frontage a structure of another age and continent, a structure so insecurely buttressed with make-shift props that a bad storm was sure to bring it to the ground. The hurricane blew, the light from the throne was extinguished. Tzar, courtiers, decorated officials, uniformed guardsmen, liveried flunkeys, dashing equipages and glittering mansions lost their illusions of reality like actors when the curtain goes down before the footlights. The empty shell of St. Petersburg became Leningrad. The centre of Russian life moved to Moscow. The population of the former capital dwindled by two-thirds. The broad streets and quays were empty. The paint upon the buildings discoloured, the plaster flaked off. For five or six years travellers spoke of a city of the dead. It seemed as if it might sink into the marshes upon which Peter's freakish genius planted it. Then life began to flow back, but neither the same stream nor in the same measure. The factories hummed once more, the port awoke to deal with the reviving timber trade, the inhabitants drifted back until the population nearly reached its former level. Streets were repaired and buildings repainted. The "window looking out onto Europe" has been reopened, but an atmosphere of decay and listlessness remains.

For two hundred years Russia posed as a "Western" State, and St. Petersburg was the stage on which this bluff was acted, a spaciously planned baroque city with wide avenues, tree-lined canals, vast squares, triumphal arches, commemorative columns, ornate palaces, and monumental churches; a magnificent enough setting, and one which still pleases the eye, incongruous as it now appears. Anything less in keeping with the Soviet régime was hard to imagine. One wanders about gazing in astonishment at the beautiful Admiralty building, its yellow-ochre walls picked out with white and surmounted by a slender gilded spire, at the rose-tinted stucco front of the Winter Palace, at the huge polished red-granite columns of St. Isaac's, and one is surprised to see them being carefully restored to their pristine freshness. The Soviet Government is not going to waste good scenery, even though the play has been rewritten and the cast changed.

Nothing of all this seems part of present-day life. Along the interminable length of the Nevsky—no one uses the new official name, the Prospect of the 25th of October—a shabby throng jostles on the pavement, stands in queues outside its poorly garnished shops, and piles into the trams which clang ceaselessly up and down the street. There is some animation here, and in the industrial suburbs, but most of the side streets in the centre of the city are almost deserted. Whole rows of shops stand dismally closed, with rusting shutters and half-obliterated signs. A dilapidated cab clattering over the cobbles in an empty square recalls the prints of eighteenth-century London. The convalescence of what is still a great commercial city proceeds slowly and lackadaisically. Grass sprouts along rows of drain-pipes where repairs have been delayed. Streets that were being picked up in the autumn of 1929 were not yet relaid when I saw them again in the summer of 1930. Some foreigners say they would rather live in Leningrad than in Moscow, but this must be chiefly because the Finnish frontier is only an hour away, or perhaps because, everything notwithstanding, Leningrad is still more European than any other place in Russia. For me Leningrad is too sad. It has not yet remade a personalty, if one can use such an expression about a city, in harmony with its new position.

The ghosts of the past still linger. More than anywhere they linger at the late Tzar's home at Tsarkoe Selo. The Alexander Palace, as it is called, to distinguish it from Catherine the Great's rococo palace, which matches the fashionable fantasies of so many other rules of the day, is an unpretentious white country house in the style of the English Regency. The rooms used by the Imperial Family have been left untouched, as they were on the day the Revolution broke out. They were furnished and decorated soon after Nicholas II's accession in the late nineties, and bear the stamp of the generation. They might still be inhabited. Photographs and knick-knacks remain on the tables, with toys, games, and sewing-baskets set down as they were last used. War-maps, showing the situation at the beginning of 1917, are spread out on the billiard-table. The children's bedrooms contain their personal belongings, books and clothes. The Tzarevich's medicines and surgical appliances still occupy their accustomed places.

Moscow belongs to a different world. It is as decidedly the cradle of the future as Leningrad is the mausoleum of the past. The atmosphere is charged with dynamic force. The feeling that nothing is worth while gives place to a pervading sense of vitality and activity. Life beats a much quicker *tempo*. The traffic moves faster; people go about their business more briskly. Here is a place, one feels, where something is happening.

"Motion" best expresses the atmosphere of Moscow. For fourteen years it has been the centre of stirring events, but, besides this, it throbs with the essential restlessness of the whole country. Leningrad represents an official policy; Moscow represents a people in the making. It is a shoal thrown up on the boundless Eurasian plains by the ebb and flow of the tides of wandering humanity. It is peculiarly shapeless, as if civilization had not yet hardened its outline. It has the fluidity of a desert city like Marakesh, the malleability of a permanent camp like Pekin. There is a primeval Moscow out of which two other Moscows rise, the Byzantine Moscow of the Tzars and the Communist Moscow of the Revolution.

New forces are attempting to bind the shifting sands. A new city of asphalt, steel, and concrete is encroaching on the sprawling, dishevelled jumble of cobbled streets and undistinguished buildings, all reduced by recent vicissitudes to a uniform level of dilapidation. What a strange contrast is presented to the monuments of the older dispensation with their suggestion of fairyland! The Kremlin, a citadel of lofty rose-brick walls, crenellated and spire-turreted, above which clusters of golden domes twinkle irregularly, is such a palace as befits a legendary king. The fantastic, many-coloured church of St. Basil is wildly improbable. Autumn sunshine within monastery walls, no longer tenanted by religious devotees, but by houseless families or workers' clubs, still evokes an ethereal glamour. Gold are the domes of the white churches topped with spangled crosses; light golden brown are the shimmering leaves of the white-trunked birches, springing out of the grass among the tombstones; a faint mist gives the scene a lightness which makes it hardly real in spite of its brightness. Moscow is indeed a city of transformations.

Even more vivid than the contrast of churches and palaces with institutions and factories is the impression of the life in the Moscow streets. From my bedroom in the Grand Hotel I used to watch the stream which flows constantly through the double-arched gateway between the Red Square[1] and the Square of the Revolution. This is the famous Iversky Gate, where was formerly a very holy shrine, and near which is now cut in large letters in the wall of the offices of the Moscow Soviet the Marxian text, "Religion is Opium for the People." It would be the equivalent of watching the London crowds at the Westminster end of Whitehall. Beyond the gate lies the Red Square, where big political celebrations are held, a large bare rectangular open space outside the Kremlin walls, and adjoining the quarter where the Government offices are concentrated. On the nearer side are the Square of the Revolution and the neighbouring Sverdlovsk or Theatre Square. Up and down them passes an endless stream of crowded trams, fiercely ringing their bells to clear a way through the mass of hurrying pedestrians. All the principal thoroughfares teem with people.

To Western eyes the number of horse vehicles, and particularly of little ramshackle open cabs, is very striking. Motor traffic consists almost entirely of lorries. The few ordinary motors all belong to Government offices and trading organizations. In 1929 it was sometimes possible to hire a taxi. In 1930 they had almost all been commandeered for official use. Two Rolls-Royces, presumably used by big-wigs in the Kremlin, became familiar sights.

Amid the din of street noises the human stream flows dark and subdued. People do not look starving. Their

[1] This is not a revolutionary name. It has always been so called.

poor and shabby clothing is more conspicuous. Everybody dresses very much alike: the men in blue or brown blouses, breeches, jack-boots, and peaked caps; the women in loose bodices and skirts, with a handkerchief tied over their heads. The prevailing costume is thus sufficiently different from that of an ordinary Western city to attract the stranger's attention. The ordinary lounge suit is a rare sight, and so is a woman wearing a hat. Our most usual of costumes is as conspicuously foreign as a turban in Piccadilly. Women's attire has none of its accustomed individuality. The only article of clothing upon which the men exercise any taste for variety is headgear. Peaked caps predominate. The bowler and trilby are practically non-existent. But every shape and size of fur hat is affected. There is the small soft astrakhan cap of the more bourgeois-looking members of the official ranks; there is the fur-trimmed leather cap with upturned ear-caps much favoured by cab-drivers and others whose work lies in the streets; there is the more exotic Caucasian hat, a stiff circular crown of something like Persian lamb covered in with coloured cloth. More rarely there is the skull-cap of the Tatar, Kirghiz, or Buryat, and the shaggy sheepskin busby of the Turcoman or the "mountaineer" of Daghestan. Beards are more common than with us, and as shaving, even among the clean-shaven, seems to be practised intermittently rather than habitually, the effect of a Moscow crowd is shapeless and shaggy. In actual fact the Muscovite looks rougher than he really is. Individually he is a quiet, orderly, and kindly creature, courteous, curious, and talkative.

Social life has been completely disorganized, and what survives is on a very limited scale. There is neither the means nor the leisure for it. Everyone's spare time is largely taken up with obtaining the bare necessities of life. Shopping, with ration-cards, queues, and a shortage of almost every commodity, is an anxious and tedious business. Nothing could prevent Russians meeting together for discussion, but the grimness of present conditions is not conducive to conviviality. There is not even that official social life which oils the wheels of international relations in most capitals. The foreign representatives live in isolation. Even Commissars are too poor to entertain, while few Russians dare compromise themselves by too close an association with foreigners. To the depressing effects of penury is added the restraint necessitated by political caution.

Then suddenly one realizes that this revolution is a war, or rather a series of simultaneous wars: it is a war for economic existence, a war for the soul of the people, a war to turn the world upside-down. Small wonder that life appears hectic and overstrained. The stranger is bewildered at first. He feels as if he had stepped "Through the Looking-Glass." Yet such is the adaptability of human nature that nearly everyone has got used to topsy-turvydom. For some there is a starvation of the soul which exceeds physical privations, but even "former people," as survivors of the upper and middle classes are called, have often almost forgotten the old life. But sometimes when one is asked how life in Russia compares with that in other countries, and one speaks of abundance and freedom, a wistful look comes into the eyes of the questioner.

The theatres and cinemas provide the main opportunities, short of the vodka bottle, for relaxation from the constant tension of life under these conditions. Unfortunately, there are many partisans of the vodka remedy for "the blues." I saw more "drunks" in Russia than I have seen anywhere else for a long time. (I have never been to the United States.) There is a pretty little piece of official by-play going on about the drink question. The Finance Department gets a large revenue from the vodka tax, and encourages its consumption. The Health Department, on the other hand, is perpetually issuing anti-drink posters for display in factories. Messrs. Dilly and Dally are evidently much the same at the Kremlin as in Whitehall. But to return to theatres and cinemas—I suppose I need scarcely say that both are quite first-rate. From the realistic appeal of the Great Theatre to the highly abstract constructivism of Meyerhold there is a series of steps, but all the way through there is the same superlative technical standard, be it in dancing, singing, acting, instrumental performance, photography, or actual production. It cannot be said that the stage or the film has suffered in any way under the present régime. There is no lack of talent, and because it was one of the few channels through which the bourgeoisie could bring themselves into line with the new conditions, the artistic professions are crowded.

Some people are surprised to learn that the Bolsheviks have been at great pains to establish an artistic reputation. They are very sensitive to any suspicion of vandalism. It is true that you will hear some caustic comments on the Government's policy of preserving so much of what was prized as beautiful by bourgeois society. The fashion is to be very advanced artistically and only to recognize that which expresses the materialistic, mechanistic, and collectivist ideology of Communism. Nevertheless, largely owing to the influence of Lunacharsky, who was, however, deposed from the Commissariat of Education in 1929, the Government has refused to defer to extreme views. The Museums of Moscow and Leningrad are among the best in the world. They have been reinforced by the pick of former private collections. The gallery of modern French paintings in Moscow is unique, though, of course, it was not the Bolsheviks but private persons who originally collected them. There is, indeed, little that could be called really distinctive in revolutionary art. The most that can be said is that Communism and the national character colour the line of Western modernism which is being followed.

The most cheerful place in Moscow is the river on a summer's evening. The water is alive with rowing-boats and bathers. The vogue for sport, which is much encouraged by the Bolsheviks, here finds full scope. There is a stadium for watching aquatic games. There are boat-houses for rowing clubs. Eights and fours, sometimes manned by women, are a conspicuous sight. All the way down one bank, from the outskirts of the city to the Sparrow Hills, stretches Moscow's playground, the Park of Culture and Rest. Here a vast crowd congregates in the evening. There are tennis courts and pitches for the very popular game of net-ball. Provision is even made for instruction in bayonet and sabre fighting. There are shooting galleries where Sir Austen Chamberlain, M. Poincaré, and Mussolini are the targets of proletarian marksmanship, Several bands enliven the air with music. There is a circus. There are sand-pits and swings for the children. In fact, there is profitable entertainment for all.

Much of what has been said about Moscow applies in varying degree to other big towns, but Moscow remains the heart of Russia and of Sovietdom. Nowhere else can you find quite the same atmosphere of movement and purpose. Here is Bolshevism working at its best. There is little in the way of institutions, museums, theatres, and so on that can be seen to better advantage elsewhere. But it would be an error to judge all Soviet Russia by Moscow. The Soviet Union is like a pond into which a handful of stones has been thrown. The largest stone is Moscow. The most important provincial cities, many of them capitals of member-states of the Union, are smaller stones. The ripples represent the strength of Communist influence. They extend over a greater or less area, but the stone that is Moscow is the only one that sends ripples all over the pond. Moscow and Leningrad between them hold, it is said, at least a third of the total strength of the Bolshevik Party. The farther you get from the centre, the more strongly do the old traditions persist, and the intenser therefore are the contrasts.

CHAPTER VIII

GLIMPSES OF THE PROVINCES

(i) The Urals and Siberia

Eastwards from Moscow the Trans-Siberian Railway strikes across Asia, and, after covering over 5,000 miles, reaches Vladivostock on the Pacific Ocean. Between the Urals and Lake Baikal it passes through the geographical centre of the Soviet Union. A few years ago this region very nearly became its political centre, for the removal of the Government to Siberia, in the event of Moscow being threatened from the West or South, was at one time seriously contemplated. The day may come when its economic centre may have shifted in this direction, for the richest of its mineral deposits lie in the Urals and in the Kuznetzk Basin, while agricultural possibilities are still undeveloped, and the cotton of Turkestan is within easy reach.

The vision of what might be called a Russian Canada, since like Canada the effective area of exploitation is a horizontal strip of habitable country shading into vast expanses of arctic waste, has already fascinated the designers of the Soviet Economy. On a long view that part of the Five Year Plan which concerns it is one of the most important.[1]

Months rather than weeks would be needed thoroughly to investigate what is going on in this vast area. The Ural Administrative Region is 650,000 square miles in extent and has a population of nearly 7 millions. The Siberian Administrative Region covers 1,750,000 square miles, and

[1] The whole Siberian question in its widest sense is discussed in *Neu-Sibirien* by Georg Cleinow (Berlin, 1928).

has a population of about 8½ millions. It is true that most of these territories are virgin forest and frozen tundra, inhabited only by a few trappers, lumbermen, gold-diggers, and native tribes. Nevertheless, even the settled regions are large. Sverdlovsk, the capital of the Urals, is a day and a half's journey from Moscow. Novo-Sibirsk, the capital of Siberia, is as far beyond Sverdlovsk. The mining centres of Magnetogorsk and Kuznetzk are twenty-four hours from each of these places. The fortnight I was able to devote to this region in August 1930 only sufficed, therefore, for the most cursory survey.

The officials of the Ural and Siberian State Planning Commissions did their best to help. The "magic paper" from "Intourist" opened all doors. The difficulty, however, is not to get Russian officials to talk but to pin them down to facts. At Sverdlovsk two enthusiasts lectured for two hours about the Five Year Plan in the Urals, one taking up the tale when the other was out of breath. Most of what they said related to the future, and it was hard to discover exactly what was already accomplished. At Novo-Sibirsk an army of experts with maps and plans was mobilized. There was no lack of eagerness to impart information, but these notes are not solely derived from these sources.

The Urals have long been exploited industrially, but the development of their full economic possibilities on systematic and up-to-date lines is a recent undertaking. Gold, platinum, emeralds, and numerous semi-precious stones are found in important quantities. Asbestos is also now being mined in quantities which will soon rival Canadian production. But the future of this region depends chiefly on the growth of the iron and steel industry. Even if the forecasts of the Five Year Plan are not immediately realized, the Urals will surely become the biggest centre of Russian heavy industry before long. The plant now under construction at Magnetogorsk, which should be turning out 2½ million tons of steel annually by the end of 1932, will be the largest in the world. It is being erected by an American firm. The raw material comes from a mountain of solid magnetic iron-stone of excellent quality. These and other new works are still unfinished. An enormous tractor factory is being erected, also under American direction, at Cheliabinsk, to produce annually 50,000 machines of a composite type which has been evolved from the study of several foreign makes. So far, neither here nor elsewhere in the Urals, has there been any substantial production of finished articles.

The centre of Siberian industry lies many hundreds of miles to the East in the Kuznetzk Basin, between Novo-Sibirsk, the capital of the Siberian Region, and the Mongolian border. "Kuzbas," as it is called, is an enormous coalfield with other minerals, including iron, in proximity. The production of coal in 1930 was stated to have been 5,000,000 tons. In 1932 it should be 25,000,000 tons.

The development of this region is not so advanced as the Urals, but the possibilities are impressive. Novo-Sibirsk will one day be a place of considerable importance, both as an industrial centre and as the junction of the Trans-Siberian line with the line to Central Asia. The new "Turk-Sib" railway between Semipalatinsk and Alma Ata links Novo-Sibirsk with Tashkent. It was officially opened on May 1, 1930, but is still not fit for heavy traffic. The late Lord Curzon's observations, in his *Russia in Central Asia*, on the Trans-Caspian railway in 1889, some time after the official opening, are appropriate to this new line.

The development of Siberia and of the Urals are organically connected, but there has been considerable controversy about the plan to be followed. Just as Turkestan cotton is to be exchanged for Siberian grain, so Kuznetzk coal is to be exchanged for Ural iron. The point at issue has been the direction of new railways. The local administrations of the Urals, Siberia, and the Autonomous Republic of Kazakstan have views of their own, which do not always square with those of Moscow.

Agricultural development seems for the moment to be taking second place. The southern parts of the Ural Region and the western parts of the Siberian Region are, however, important grain-producing and dairying districts.

It is intended that the Siberian Region shall ultimately be divided into eighteen economic districts, each of which will specialize in some branch of industry and agriculture, and organize the rest of its production mainly for its own needs. Thus Kuznetzk will specialize in heavy industry, but will also try and feed the new towns which are springing up. Omsk will specialize in wheat, another district in dairy-farming, and so on. Within these economic districts there are to be what are called *Kombinat*, i.e. collective agricultural-industrial communities. This, we were told, is a new idea which has not yet been put into practice, but represents the next stage in socialization. To begin with, at any rate, the *Kombinat* would probably be on an agricultural basis. It would include a central *sovhoz*, or State farm, surrounding *kolhozi*, or collective farms, and agricultural industries such as the preparing of flax, the repairing of implements, and tanneries.

To reach these regions from Moscow there is the Trans-Siberian express. It is an unpretentious affair nowadays, consisting of a sleeping- and a dining-car, with two ordinary carriages at either end. On the platform, its destination, Vladivostock, is put up on a board as inconspicuously as if it were a suburb of Moscow. Russians have little sense of the drama of distance such as our little Western countries have given us.

Outside Moscow small *dacha* settlements are strung along the line in the woods. They are wooden houses, the week-end cottages of the formerly well-to-do. Now they are occupied by families of workers on holiday.

We travelled all the first day through a predominatingly forest region of beech, spruce, and pine, with large agricultural clearings. Sometimes the train passed along what is almost a tunnel between the trees; sometimes the line was flanked with fields and pastures dotted with villages of wooden houses. A good deal of the land looked as if it were under some form of large-scale farming, and there appeared to be new tracts of land being brought under cultivation. Towns were far apart, small, and built of wood.

It was very hot, although we were as far north as Aberdeen. The thermometer in our carriage registered over 90° Fahrenheit in the afternoon. There were few signs of life in the fields during the heat of the day, just an occasional peasant cart, and, every now and then, a red dot where a woman in coloured skirt or kerchief was working among the stooks, for the harvest was in full swing. Towards evening we passed into more open and undulating country. At each station groups of peasants were gathered on the platform, types with which everyone is familiar from pictures, the men in blouses and jack-boots or birch-bark sandals, the women, plain and flat-faced, with a kerchief over their heads.

We awoke on the second morning in what might have been the Black Forest—a region of pine-clad hills and pleasant valleys. Actually we were passing over the crest of the Urals, a range which scarcely deserves the prominent hatchings by which it is usually shown on the map. The average elevation is only about 1,500 feet, and the highest peak is under 5,000 feet. As mountains the Urals are a fraud, but I suppose they deserve some respect as the only hills of any kind between Berlin and the Altai, and they are certainly a welcome break in this monotonous landscape.

As we approached Sverdlovsk (formerly Ekaterinburg), the capital of the Ural Region, there were many signs of industrial activity. The main line was being doubled. Branch lines and sidings were being constructed in connection with the development of mining and metallurgical works. Train loads of new machinery, apparently of American and German origin, were standing in the station.

On the platform a booth displayed assortments of the semi-precious stones in which the Urals abound. Their names read like the description of the New Jerusalem in the Book of Revelation. Topazes, aquamarines, beryls, amethysts, tourmalines, chalcedonies, and chrysolites lay piled in little saucers, and there were ornaments of malachite, lapis-lazuli, nephrite, and jasper.

Sverdlovsk is a growing town of some 150,000 inhabitants, but in spite of many new buildings and an atmosphere of awakening industrial activity, it retains many of the characteristics of a sleepy Russian provincial town. Long, straight, broad, and ill-paved streets, lined with wooden houses, decorated with fretwork patterns round the windows and eaves, still give much of it the air of an overgrown village.

It was here that the Tzar and his family were imprisoned and shot. Along one side of a large, untidy, cobbled square, and facing a church which is now used as a school, there is a low whitewashed brick house, formerly the residence of a wealthy family. It was here that the Tzar and his family were brought from Tobolsk in April 1918 when the White forces, advancing from Siberia, approached that town. While it was occupied by the Imperial prisoners, the house was surrounded by a wooden stockade, which has since been removed. Apart from the actual place of execution, all signs of their tenancy have disappeared, but there is a series of photographs showing each room as it then was. There are also some photographs of Czech soldiers digging for remains of the victims in the neighbouring forest, where the bodies were burnt, and of one or two objects such as the cross of a decoration and a diamond pendant, which were among the things they found. The house is now a museum of the Revolution, with illustrations and relics of the growth of the revolutionary movement and of the civil war period.

A large painting by a local artist, who was, apparently, an eye-witness, depicts the handing over of the Imperial Family to the Ural Soviet on their arrival from Tobolsk. It was some three months later, when the continued successes of the Whites forced the Reds to evacuate Ekaterinburg, that the prisoners were executed. The decision was, it seems, taken by the Ural Soviet on its own responsibility and in some haste. They were equally afraid of the Tzar falling into the hands of the counter-revolutionaries and of withdrawing towards Moscow with so important a potential centre of disaffection in their charge. No compunction at making the Tzarina and the children share his fate seems to have touched them.

It is curious to find the whole episode treated just as a fact in the history of the Revolution, and with almost as much detachment as if the late Tzar were some figure as remote as Louis XVI or Charles I. There is no attempt either to conceal the facts or to make propaganda out of them. A framed copy of a local newspaper, the *Uralski Rabotni*, of July 18, 1918, testifies to the circumstances of the event as they were given to the world on the day after the execution, and that is all.

In the last room of the Museum there is a notice to the effect that as soon as ten or more people are assembled the attendant will show the way to the place where Nicholas Romanov was executed. On this particular occasion the attendant was a young girl, and our party, which consisted of a few workmen, two or three peasant women, and a rather bourgeois-looking couple, who probably belonged to the technical specialist class, followed her out of the house and round the front to a side door, which must have been a servants' entrance. As the house is built on a slight slope, this door gives access to a half-basement below the main ground-floor level. The room in which the execution took place opens off a hall-way. It is not more than twelve or fifteen feet square, whitewashed, with a low vaulted ceiling and a window high up in the outside wall just above the level of the street. In this confined space eleven people—the Tzar, the Tzarina, their five children, and four attendants—were herded together and shot.

The wall opposite the door has been stripped of plaster, exposing thick wooden boards. At intervals there are square recesses where the bullets have been cut out. These marks are all low, four feet or less from the ground. Someone asked why this was, and our guide explained that the victims had huddled crouching against the wall. A few holes in the floor boards indicate shots fired to finish some of them off. A more ghastly scene cannot be imagined. I went away much moved, the more so, perhaps, because of the stark matter-of-factness with which the scene is presented.[1]

From Sverdlovsk I visited a *sovhoz*, or State farm, which supplies the town with milk and vegetables. It was typical of the attempt to supply urban centres from the immediate neighbourhood. Officially, it is a dairy farm, and so comes under the Milk Trust, which appoints the manager. The

[1] The results of the official inquiry conducted by the Omsk Government during the White occupation are contained in *Enquête Judiciaire sur l'Assassinat de la Famille Impériale Russe* (Paris, 1924), by N. Sokolov.

man we saw might have been the factor of some small estate in the old days. At present the farm covers about 10,000 acres, of which about 3,500 are cultivated. There were 600 cows. Apart from vegetables for the town, all the crops were for winter feeding. Cattle have to be kept indoors seven months of the year in this climate. About thirty stallions were kept for the service of the neighbourhood, and, as an experiment, hundreds of rabbits of a blue-grey variety, described to us as "champagne," were being bred for meat and fur. During 1930 the farm was to be enlarged to 45,000 acres, of which 25,000 are forest, and the cows were to be increased to 3,000. We were told that the cows gave an average of 3,000 litres of milk a year each, with about 4 per cent. of fat. Some were a kind of Friesian, and others a red Dutch breed, both crossed with the local "Tagil." They made no butter or cheese here. We saw the herd being milked in the open. They were rather a poor-looking lot. The farm buildings were mostly new and quite well kept, but in no way exceptional. The nucleus of the farm used to belong to a monastery, and there seems little doubt that the land is being much better exploited than it was then. We did not see much modern machinery, but were told they had a few tractors and reapers. They lend this machinery to neighbouring collective farms. The fact that so much has to be done by hand no doubt accounts for the large number of hands. Four hundred people are employed in winter. At the time of my visit about 2,000 people were at work, but this included several hundreds employed on new buildings. There were said to be twelve similar farms in the Ural Region. Some of these export produce to other provinces and abroad.

On resuming the journey eastwards from Sverdlovsk the country soon became flat again, and more open than it had been hitherto. There was much more grassland. East of Tiumen there were places where the eye carried right to the horizon across an unbroken plain. The weather was cooler. The harvest was less far advanced.

East of Omsk the country becomes very bleak. The trees are stunted, there are large expanses of reed and marsh, the villages are many miles apart, and look miserably poor. It is curious that while flocks of ducks and geese are to be seen wherever there are houses, hardly any chickens seem to be kept. There is very little grain to be seen in this district, and not so many cattle as farther West. There are richer arable and dairy-farming districts to the South. Although it was the second week in August, hay was still being cut, and the wild flowers, which must have been a fine sight a month earlier, were nearly over.

We arrived at Novo-Sibirsk in the evening. We were told at first that the hotel was full up, but the "magic paper" from "Intourist" produced a room at once.

There was a co-operative restaurant round the corner, where, in spite of mixed company and a dreadful "fug," comparatively good food was obtainable—at a price. A young man at our table, coaxed into loquacity with a couple of cigarettes, held forth very bitterly against conditions of life. He could get nothing to smoke and his rations would not feed a dog, he said. He came to this restaurant when he could afford it, which was not often.

A foreigner is still so rare in these parts that we attracted considerable attention. Russians are, at the present time, avid for information about the outside world. They are not importunate, but take every opportunity of proximity in a restaurant or a train to be politely inquisitive. On one occasion, in Novo-Sibirsk, a man, who had evidently been following us for some time, overtook us in the street, and insisted on our walking at least a mile out of our way with him, while he discoursed nineteen to the dozen about what he claimed to be the real condition of things in Russia. He was an ardent Communist, and was apparently doing his good deed for the day by correcting any false impressions we might have.

Novo-Sibirsk is a town of about 125,000 inhabitants, on the River Ob, which, even 2,000 miles from the sea, is over half a mile wide. Every year a fleet of barges goes down to the sea during the short summer and meets a convoy of steamers from Europe, with which it exchanges cargoes. Novo-Sibirsk was formerly called Novo-Nikolaievsk, and began as a small railway centre some thirty-five years ago when the Trans-Siberian was being built. It has therefore no pretension to historical interest, and is looked upon as an upstart by such places as the neighbouring Tomsk, which regards itself as the intellectual centre of Siberia, with its University and its population descended from colonists and cultivated political exiles. In appearance Novo-Sibirsk is typical of a Russian provincial town. The majority of the houses are of wood; most of the streets are unpaved and lined with irregular avenues of birch. Among the people, the peasant type predominates. There are signs, however, that modern life is encroaching on the traditional environment. There are several factories in the centre of the town, and a score of modern buildings rise somewhat incongruously above the surrounding shacks.

The industrial pride of Novo-Sibirsk is the "Kombainstroi," large works which are being erected for the manufacture of combined harvesting and threshing machines, and which are to supply the U.S.S.R. with an output of 25,000 machines a year. According to the chief engineer, the whole undertaking is being planned and erected without foreign assistance. He himself had spent some time with the Freyne Co. of Chicago, who are granting the patent rights. Work on actual construction was only started in the spring of 1930, so that the skeletons of a few brick buildings are all there is to see.

The site of the works is on the other side of the River Ob, where a new industrial city has been planned. Other new factories, notably an assembly shop for the motor-cars from the Ford works at Nizhni-Novgorod, and a textile factory, are to be built there. The Five Year Plan includes the building of two new bridges across the river, but these have not yet been started, and everything has to cross by the one existing railway bridge or by boat. We were taken over in a launch, and drove the remaining couple of miles. The ferry (two huge barges under the charge of a tug) was full of peasant carts. The road was very rough indeed. It would have saved a good deal of effort to have started with making the bridges and some roads, but the Russians always seem anxious to begin with the roof and to have something to show as soon as possible. Building methods seemed antiquated by our standards. Bricks and mortar were being man-handled up ramps. A great many of the workers engaged in this were women. The bricks themselves were of poor quality, very sandy and brittle. At the same time, and although the *tempo* of the workers seemed slow, a good rate of progress must be maintained. We were told that the bricklayers build an average of 500 bricks a day, and that the maximum was 1,800. There is a shortage of building materials of all kinds, especially constructional steel. One of the buildings was being roofed with wood in order that it should be finished by the scheduled date.

The chief engineer strutted round with his thumbs in his waistcoat, as pleased as Punch with the whole concern. A lanky individual, who turned out to be the Secretary of the Committee which runs the weekly works newspaper, also attached himself to us, making lengthy notes of all our remarks. A very tolerable lunch was provided at the canteen, where we were introduced to the Secretary of the local Party Committee. When it transpired that I had been a Conservative M.P., the usual argument about debts, intervention, and capitalist unwillingness to give Russia financial help ensued, but all in the most friendly spirit.

Labour is short, and most of the workers have had to be taught their jobs on the spot. One of the first buildings to be finished is a school, with accommodation for 1,000 pupils, for training workmen in skilled jobs connected with the factory. The more intelligent will be sent on to technical institutes to train as qualified technicians and engineers. The workers were housed in good wooden huts and seemed well looked after. The Co-operative was better stocked than most Moscow shops. No one may buy anything until he has been three weeks at the works. It was found that people signed on for a few days simply in order to get access to these supplies. Blocks of communal houses (known as the socialized city) are being erected. Production is supposed to start in 1932, but what with the difficulty in getting material and labour, and the shortness of the open season, this seemed optimistic.

From Novo-Sibirsk my companion and I set out for Kuznetzk, 300 miles to the South. The journey took twenty-four hours, and I will relate its vicissitudes as an example of what sometimes happens when travelling in the remoter districts.

Lulled into false security by assurances that all arrangements for the trip had been made, and thinking that everything must be all right when our tickets were duly delivered to us at the hotel, we were congratulating ourselves on having got things made so easy for us. We were soon disillusioned. A motor was to have fetched us from the

TOP: FERRY OVER THE RIVER OB AT NOVO-SIBIRSK

BOTTOM: PEOPLE WAITING FOR A 'BUS IN THE PRINCIPAL SQUARE OF NOVO-SIBIRSK

hotel to catch our train, which was due to leave at 1.30 at night. One o'clock came, but no car; 1.10, and still no car; so we took an *izvoshchik*, which was luckily standing in the street, piled ourselves into it, and clattered off at full speed, swaying dangerously as we bumped along the ill-paved streets. We reached the station with five minutes to spare, but there were no porters at that time of night. Humping our luggage, which was just about all we could manage, we staggered through the station, picking our way among peasants sleeping thick on the floor.

The train was standing away from the main platform in a sea of mud. We splashed our way, panting, to our carriage, and heaved our bags on board. It was then we discovered that our tickets were for "hard" instead of "soft" seats. There was just time to get the supplementary vouchers at the ticket office as the train started late. We were lucky enough to get a four-berth compartment to ourselves in the "soft" coach.

We awoke next morning to face a wet and dreary landscape. We were travelling through a flat grass steppe, but later on in the day the country became rolling downland, and finally quite hilly. Kuznetzk itself is in the foothills of the Altai mountains, and not more than 150 miles from the Mongolian frontier.

We subsisted on the food brought from Moscow. There was a midday halt at a place which was supposed to provide dinner, but the buffet was so crowded with workmen and peasants off the train that we only managed to get a plate of rather thin oatmeal soup. Most of our fellow travellers belonged to the various mining and metallurgical works along the line.

Towards evening troubles began again. Our tickets had been mistakenly taken to a place called Ussiaty, which, we now learned, was thirty miles from Kuznetzk. When we got there further tickets had to be bought. The booking-office clerk was in such a hurry, however, that he simply added our names to the voucher he issued to two women who were travelling "hard." We had no desire to travel like Siamese twins, nor had the women. The train nearly left during the resulting altercation, but the muddle was fortunately disentangled just in time.

When we reached Kuznetzk, four hours late, it was nearly midnight. There was, of course, no one to meet us. It was dark, cold, and muddy, and we learned that the town was four miles away. Fortunately the sporadic arrival of American engineers in the last few weeks had accustomed the Authorities to the sudden appearance of benighted foreigners. We knew from meeting one of them on the train from Moscow that there was some sort of hostel available, and thither we hoped to be eventually guided. A policeman cheered us up by saying that he had telephoned for a cab, but having deposited us on the steps of the station post office, he disappeared, and, though half an hour passed, no cab arrived. My companion then got hold of someone who rang up the hostel. Of course they had never heard of us, but they promised to send a car. Just as we were expecting it to turn up, a railway official appeared and informed us that he was going to send us up the branch line to the works by train. Humping our luggage, we followed him for a good half-mile across sidings to his office in a wooden hut, whereupon he apparently forgot us completely until a message arrived that the motor-car was waiting where we had been before. So back we trekked. This time the car was actually there, and tossing and swaying like a dinghy on the ocean over quite the most slippery and muddy earth track I have ever seen, we fetched up after 2 a.m. at our destination.

"Kutznetzkstroi," the most important of the works in the district, is a big iron and steel plant, which is to produce 1,000,000 tons of steel a year when completed. It covers a square mile or more of ground. Work was begun in the spring of 1929, and should be finished by the end of 1932. At the time of my visit there was not much to be seen except foundations and scaffolding. Twenty thousand people, a good many women among them, were employed, some housed in a town of wooden huts, others living under canvas or in wretched dug-outs in the hillside. A great deal of the labour is necessarily temporary and seasonal, but operations are not entirely suspended during the winter. Building goes on under huge wooden shelters, which keep out the worst of the frost.

The American engineers, who are to supervise the construction, were only beginning to arrive. Eight of them were in the hostel in which we stayed, a bare but by no means uncomfortable wooden house, where the food was quite good and drink abundant. Russians have an idea that Americans will never complain so long as they are kept well supplied with brandy and vodka. There will eventually be about fifty of them, and several are bringing wives and families. They seemed uncertain as to their exact position. The Russians said they were only engaged in an advisory capacity. The Americans said they could not take responsibility without some executive control. They were, however, on the whole optimistic about the success of the enterprise.

Here, as is commonly the case in Russia, the deficiency of modern appliances has to be made up by the employment of large numbers of people using primitive methods. Boards, for instance, are mostly sawn out of the trees by hand and planed with adzes, a process in which Russians are adepts, but which is wasteful and slow. The majority of the workmen seemed totally untrained to the use of mechanical devices, but the Americans said they were willing, and quickly picked up the right way of doing things. In the higher positions the Russian engineers were said to have good theoretical knowledge, but to be deficient in directive ability.

We were unable to see as much of the district as we had hoped owing to the weather. Although it was only the end of August, summer was over. Rain had made the rough tracks impassable for motors, and we had to abandon a visit to the "Telbes" iron mines fifty miles farther South. Even at Kuznetzk itself there were no metalled roads, with the result that it was almost impossible to walk in the clayey and glutinous mud. In these circumstances most of the transport work was being done by horse-carts.

The day we left Kuznetzk was particularly unpleasant, as we were given good reason to remember. The railway station was four or five miles from the hostel. We started in ample time, but our *izvoshchik* took it into his head to hurry. The track was an absolute quagmire and full of holes. It was just about as much as we could do to keep the luggage balanced on various outlying portions of ourselves and the carriage. We escaped mishap, however, until we were a quarter of a mile from the station. Then the driver apparently determined to arrive in style, and started whipping up the horses. They broke into a gallop which was altogether too much for our shandrydan. A big pothole brought us to a sudden stop with a shattering jolt, and then the carriage tipped slowly over, and we all subsided gently into the mud. We escaped without getting very dirty, because the hood was up, and we rolled into it. We also had no difficulty in putting the carriage upright again. The horses just stood and waited as if this was the most ordinary thing in the world. After the driver had tied up a broken spring with a bit of rope, we finished the course in good time for our train, which took us back without incident to Novo-Sibirsk, whence we returned to the comparative civilization of Sverdlovsk on our way to Kazan on the Volga.

CHAPTER IX

GLIMPSES OF THE PROVINCES

(ii) THE VOLGA AND THE CAUCASUS

Timber felled in the forests of North Russia floats 2,000 miles down the Volga and its tributaries to the Caspian Sea and the oil-fields of Baku. This avenue of communication has been important throughout Russian history. Along the Volga are scattered colonies of many alien peoples, the Votiaks, the Mordva, the Mari, the Chuvash, the Kazan Tatars, the Bashkirs, the Volga Germans, the Kalmucks. The Caucasian isthmus is even more of an ethnological museum. Besides the Georgians, Armenians, and Azerbaidjan Tatars, which are the principal peoples of Trans-Caucasia, there are mountain tribes of obscure origin, while North of the main range a variety of peoples, roughly classified as Circassians, inhabit the western districts, and another group of peoples, equally roughly classified as Lesghians, occupy the wild country along the Caspian coast. A journey along this route gives some idea of the heterogeneous population under Soviet rule, besides affording glimpses of important sections of the Five Year Plan.

A regular steamer service plies on the Volga between Nizhni-Novgorod and Astrakhan. The famous summer fair at Nizhni-Novgorod exists no more. It is significant of the times that the wonder of the town is now the motor-car factory being erected by the Ford Company for the Soviet Government to produce 140,000 cars a year by 1937. At present both the factory and the new town, which is to house 50,000 people, are only in the early stages of construction. On the other hand, Astrakhan preserves its squalid picturesqueness, untouched by the modernizing hand of the Five Year Plan, which is apparently not concerned about caviare. I saw neither of the places, however, as I only covered the middle stretch of the river from Kazan to Stalingrad.

Kazan is an interesting old town. It is the capital of the Tatar Autonomous Republic, part of which, an undulating region of down and forest, is crossed by the railway from Sverdlovsk. Mosques appear in the villages and a new type of face at the stations. The Volga Tatars are not so Mongolian in features as many of their kindred. They bear a closer resemblance to the Ottoman Turk than, for instance, to the Kirghiz. Kazan has always been the intellectual centre of Tatar culture, a legacy of the days when it was the capital of a kingdom which included a large part of Russia. It symbolizes Russia's contact with the Moslem East, just as Kiev symbolizes contact with the Catholic West.

Although Kazan is generally spoken of as being on the Volga, it is actually five miles from the river. On a hill above the little river Kazanka stands the Kremlin, a picturesque agglomeration of walls and towers and church domes, somewhat similar in character to the Moscow Kremlin, but altogether less impressive. Generally speaking, the town is dirty, the streets atrociously paved, and the houses squalid. It has atmosphere, however, but the atmosphere of drowsy maturity, in contrast to the uglier but more vital atmosphere of incipient industrialism which is noticeable in places like Novo-Sibirsk or Sverdlovsk. We were directed to visit the old University and the Muse m rather than new factories.

Three-quarters of the population of the town is Russian, so that the Tatar element is not so much in evidence as it is in the country districts. There are many mosques, but they are unobtrusive, and minarets are not a feature of the scenery. All names and inscriptions are, however, written up in Tatar as well as in Russian. A Latinized Tatar alphabet, similar to that adopted in Turkey, is coming into use in place of the Arabic script, but both are often placed side by side.

The Tatar Republic is a good example of the policy of encouraging the autonomous development of national groups. Since Ivan the Terrible put an end to the independent Tatar Khanate of Kazań in 1552, the Tatars have been gradually pushed away from the main centres of civilization by Russian settlers. Although the Tatars number 52 per cent. of the whole population of the Republic, the Russians are in a majority in the towns and river valleys. Before the Revolution all the big landowners were Russians. Now, the Tatars, who were formerly treated as inferiors, are taught to regard themselves as the dominating race within their own territory.

Economically the Tatar Republic is poor. Only one important railway line crosses its territory, though others are now under construction and projected. The main avenues of communication are still by river on the Volga, Kama, and Viatka. There is little mineral wealth, though hopes are entertained that oil may be got from near the Volga, where an English company had workings about thirty years ago. The principal effort now being made is to raise the standard of grain cultivation, and to substitute wheat for rye as the chief crop. Such industries as exist are secondary, such as tanning, timber mills, chemicals, and furs. An interesting example of the last of these was a factory which makes imitations of the better furs out of cat, dog, sheep, marmot, and other common skins. Formerly, the raw skins were exported to Germany. They claim to be producing 250,000,000 roubles' worth of goods a year,

TOP: THE KREMLIN AT KAZAN

BOTTOM: TIMBER RAFTS, FLOATED DOWN FROM THE UPPER VOLGA, BEING BROKEN UP AT THE STALINGRAD SAWMILLS

about 25 per cent. of which are exported. There were 700 people employed at the time of my visit, but the business is expanding rapidly, new buildings are going up, and this number is soon to be increased to 5,000.

The population of the Republic is about 3,000,000. Outside the towns the Russians and Tatars live in separate villages, and there are more or less definitely Tatar and Russian districts. Russian and Tatar are both official languages. Everyone learns both at school, but instruction is primarily in the language of the particular village. To raise the Tatar to the same cultural level as the Russian is the principal object for which Tatar autonomy exists, and it is in cultural respects that there is most independence. Prior to the Revolution, the tendency was to repress rather than encourage a Tatar national culture. There are now many more Tatar newspapers, and much larger provision is made for the education of Tatars. The Republic has been in existence since 1920. It was claimed with some pride that in ten years literacy among the Tatars had been increased from 18 per cent. to 33 per cent., and that compulsory education was being introduced. One of the chief problems is the social status of women among a predominantly Mohammedan population. Tatar women were never, apparently, veiled, but segregation of the sexes was maintained, and this also is being broken down. All schools, for instance, are mixed.

The journey down the Volga was, frankly, a disappointment, though I can imagine its being quite a pleasant and restful trip under favourable conditions. There was nothing to complain of about the boat itself, but there was hardly anything to eat on board, and, though it was only the first week in September, the weather was wretched. It may fairly be said that between leaving Sverdlovsk on September 3rd and arriving at Stalingrad on September 8th we did not have a single square meal, and would almost have starved had it not been for the food we carried with us. The steamer provided nothing but cabbage soup, eggs, and *kasha* (a sort of buckwheat porridge) for three days; nor was it possible to supplement this fare at any of the stopping-places. Yet the Volga districts are purely agricultural. The only explanation is that every scrap of surplus produce is drained away to the industrial districts.

The scenery along the Volga is not such as would, in any circumstances, awaken much enthusiasm. The stream was about half a mile wide at Kazan, but the water was very low, and judging by the sandbanks which emerged from it, the level must be somewhere about twenty feet higher in the spring floods. The river freezes in winter over its whole length. Below the junction of the Kama it gets deeper and wider. It looked about two miles wide at Stalingrad. Owing to floods and marshes, many of the towns and villages are some distance from the banks. There are always a great many people at the landing-stages, and at nearly every stopping-place quite a crowd entered and left the boat. Occasionally these provided diverting types and some queer costumes. The country on both sides was usually monotonous, rolling forest, pasture or tilth. Traffic on the river consisted either of steamers similar to our own or of timber rafts.

Ulianovsk, the former Simbirsk, was the first town of any importance at which we halted. Its chief claim to fame is as the birthplace of Lenin, after whose original family name of Ulianov it is now called. There was not time to visit the historic spot. At Samara we had an hour or so on shore, but a walk through its straggling, squalid streets hardly repaid the effort. Samara is the capital of the Central Volga Region.

Below Samara we passed through the Autonomous

Republic of the Volga Germans. These are descendants of colonists brought in by Catherine the Great in the eighteenth century, and number nearly half a million. They still speak German, and many villages have kept to the dialect of their places of origin. Their buildings are quite German in style. They remain Protestants, and the spires of their churches form a surprising contrast to the domes of the Orthodox churches in the Russian villages on the other bank. As far as I could gather, there is not much difference between the cultural level of the two peoples.

Opposite Pokrovsk, the capital of the Volga German Republic, is Saratov, the capital of the Lower Volga Region. This is a somewhat larger and less dingy edition of Samara and had one remarkable feature. The bells still hung in many of the church towers. I was unable to discover how this came to be, but so far as my observation goes no other place in Russia is so favoured.

Stalingrad (formerly Tzaritzin) is far enough South to feel the influence of a warmer climate. The country looked dusty and dried up. To the South-East is the arid Kalmuck Autonomous Region,[1] which links up with the Trans-Caspian steppes across the Volga delta. This is a breeding-ground for camels and oxen, which are extensively used on the Lower Volga and in the Northern Caucasus.

From a moderate-sized town with one or two important industrial undertakings, run by foreign companies, Stalingrad is rapidly developing into one of the principal cities in Russia. It is the effective terminus of Volga navigation, and is the distributing centre of a large area. If the Volga-Don canal is ever constructed, it will become more important still, but this project has apparently once more receded into the background. Although the two rivers are here only

[1] The Kalmucks are a pure Mongolian tribe which emigrated from the Altai region in the seventeenth century. They are Buddhists.

forty miles apart, it is said that the soil is so porous that nothing but cement would hold the water.

Factories stretch along the river bank for nearly ten miles, among them the great tractor factory which is one of the show places in Russia. The buildings, including new tenement dwellings for about 10,000 employees and their families, cover some 1,200 acres. Originally designed to produce 25,000 tractors a year, the planned capacity has now been doubled. Construction was begun in the spring of 1929, but owing to the shortage of steel and the delay in the delivery of certain machines from America, production, which should have started in the summer of 1930, was negligible until the last months of the year. The first tractor to be produced was exhibited at the Communist Party Congress in Moscow in June 1930. Rumour has it that several parts were of wood. Four hundred and fifty tractors should have been produced in September, the month of my visit, but I believe only sixty were actually finished. According to one of the principal engineers, the rate of production should have reached half-capacity, i.e. at the rate of 25,000 tractors annually, by the end of the year, so it is plain that they are some way behind the schedule. The normal life of these tractors should be six or seven years, but with the kind of treatment they are likely to get at the hands of inexperienced mechanics and peasants, and with the work they will be expected to do, four years seems about as long as they will survive in Russia. The type of tractor is a copy of the American International Harvester, and the factory itself is modelled on Ford's works at Detroit. The whole place has been erected under American supervision, but it was only in the summer of 1930 that the Americans obtained full directive control. There are now over 300 Americans at work in the factory, most of them foremen in charge of various departments.

Their relations with the Russians have been strained at times, but as it is vital that tractors should be forthcoming for the fulfilment of the agricultural programme, the Russians have had to put their pride in their pockets. Practically all the machinery and constructional steel has come from abroad, mostly from America. We saw some German machines, a few Swiss, and one or two English (Ransome and Rapier) cranes. Russian steel production cannot, apparently, begin to cope with the demand. There is a steel-works within a couple of miles of the "Traktorstroi," but we were told that it did not produce good enough material.

At the opposite end of the town there are important timber mills. The timber is rafted down the river from the North. After it is sawn up 60 per cent. goes to Novorossisk to be exported. The best wood goes to make boxes for Palestine oranges, and, according to my informant, the wood is so good that it is afterwards used for making musical instruments. The mills are being modernized and extended. Some of the machinery is Russian (from a Moscow factory) and some German, but the greater part is Swedish. The rafts are broken up in the river, and the logs carried up the bank by conveyor. About 4,000 people were employed. These particular mills are called *Electroles*, to distinguish them from *Gorles*, where the primitive hand methods are still used.

One day, passing a church which had been turned into a Trade Union Club, we asked permission to look round. The nave was the auditorium of a theatre, and the stage stood where the altar had been. The spaces between the pillars of the nave were walled up and hung with portraits of Lenin, Stalin, and others. The aisles formed reading-rooms and a library.

The biggest church in the town, an ugly red-brick

building in the middle of the central square, is going to be a theatre, but is at present used as a garage for motor-lorries. There is a wooden ramp covering the steps to the main entrance, and the lorries are parked under a dome and along walls, from which frescoes of the Apostles stare with a Byzantine rigidity, not unlike stupefaction. Outside this church there was a peep-show depicting the methods of the Spanish Inquisition. It seemed a crude affair, but no end of people were paying a small sum for admission.

A little South of Stalingrad begins the North Caucasus Region, country which, with the Daghestan Republic and the three Republics of Trans-Caucasia, differs very much from ordinarily accepted ideas of Russia. The climate is warm and dry in the northern steppes, which are given up to grain-growing and the raising of cattle, sheep, and horses. The centre and South are wild and mountainous. On the Black Sea coast there are sub-tropical districts. Not only are the Russian inhabitants immigrant colonists, as they are in Siberia, but they are in many parts outnumbered by the indigenous peoples. The Russian conquest is comparatively recent. It was only completed about fifty years ago, and there has been much more recent fighting with insurgent tribes. The rivers Don, Kuban, and Terek mark stages of the Russian advance with their powerful Cossack settlements, now broken up in so far as they were organized on a military basis with special privileges. Everywhere there are remnants of peoples whose historical associations, stretching back in many cases to remote antiquity, bear witness to the traffic which has ceaselessly moved across this bridge between continents. Part of Georgia is the traditional site of Colchis, the land of the Golden Fleece. In the Kuban countless mounds in the steppe attest the remains of bygone civilizations. Alexander the Great's name is still remembered in Armenia. It is hard to imagine more fascinating country, with more picturesque inhabitants, or more beautiful scenery.

The greater part of the North Caucasus Region has but a small share of these attractions. Rostov-on-Don, the capital, is a large commercial and industrial city. A new agricultural machinery factory, "Selmashstroi," is situated there, and is one of the first enterprises promoted by the Five Year Plan to have started production. Several thousands of ploughs, mowers, seeders, rakes, binders, and harrows have been turned out, but the output has not yet reached full capacity.

East of Rostov are some of the largest of the State farms, notably the one called "Gigant," which has an area of a thousand square miles. "Gigant" is entirely devoted to wheat, and has 400,000 acres under cultivation. It is the show agricultural undertaking in Russia, but is really nothing more than a "stunt." A friend of mine, who investigated the costs of production, says that conditions are so peculiar that no useful conclusion can be drawn. No depreciation is apparently charged on machinery. "Gigant" can get all the tractors it wants for the asking, so it indents for a new outfit every year, and sells off the old stock to collective farms at the same price it pays for the new ones.

On the River Kuban, near the small town of Kavkazkaya, about 250 miles South-East of Rostov, there is a German agricultural concession known as "Drusag," which is short for Deutsch-Russische Sahtbau Aktien Gesellschaft. Here we were the fortunate guests of the Director, Dr. Ditloff, and spent some very pleasant days exploring the neighbourhood. The concession covers 25,000 acres, and includes six former private properties, whose homesteads are now utilized by the concession staff. Most of the land is under plough, but there are also large herds of cattle and flocks of merino sheep. On the whole Dr. Ditloff seems to have been able to keep on good terms with the Soviet Authorities, but the position is not without its difficulties.

The Concession marches with a *sovhoz*, or State farm of some 7,000 acres, which appeared to be well equipped and quite efficiently run. The Authorities are naturally anxious that their own venture should not suffer by comparison with its foreign neighbour, but it seemed fairly clear that with all their efforts they could not emulate the standard of farming on the Concession. The *sovhoz* had, we were told, one tractor for every 250 acres of ploughland, which was double the proportion on the Concession; they also employed considerably more hands; yet their production was appreciably lower. The manager of the *sovhoz* was, as is commonly the case, qualified rather by his political than by his agricultural attainments. He was a former steel-worker. His predecessor had been a tailor. The technical work was done by a staff of agronomists, of whom there were at least half a dozen.

In the immediate neighbourhood of the Concession there were two or three small Russian villages and a larger village of German-speaking colonists, who came from the German settlements on the Volga some fifty years ago. The latter, Novo-Ivanovka, consists of whitewashed adobe houses, much smarter looking than the timber houses of the North, strung out on each side of a long wide street bordered with acacias. It is partially collectivized, but there were no very obvious signs that this fact had as yet raised the standard of farming. Grain, which should have been gathered in a month before, was still lying in the fields. There was little agricultural machinery, and there were no tractors. There was even a shortage of horses and oxen, and such as were available were overworked and undernourished. As happened everywhere during the winter of

TOP: PEASANTS IN THE KUBAN

BOTTOM: TROOPS BIVOUACKED OUTSIDE THE CATHEDRAL OF MTZKHET, NEAR TIFLIS. THE CHURCH ITSELF HAD NOT BEEN ENTERED

1929, many draught animals had been slaughtered. There seemed no system by which the neighbouring *sovhoz* came to the help of the collective farm in any way. The chairman of the farm committee knew very little about farming, and had been appointed from outside.

The country round "Drusag" is a slightly undulating and almost treeless steppe, but mountains are visible to the South on a clear day. There are two ways of reaching Tiflis on the far side of the Caucasus range. The first, the more comfortable but duller route, is direct by the railway, which, passing along the northern side of the main mountain range, finds its way round the eastern end by the shores of the Caspian, and then doubles back westwards through Baku. The second and more interesting route is over the mountains by the Georgian military road from Vladikavkaz. This is the one I took on my first visit in 1929.

The Moscow express decanted us on a glorious morning, late in October, at Mineralye Vodi, or "Mineral Waters," a junction which, as the name implies, serves a number of health resorts in the neighbouring hills. Here, while waiting for the train to Vladikavkaz, we made our first acquaintance, in the animated market-place, with the Caucasian mountain tribesmen. I am quite unable to say which was which, but some were tall and fair, others squat and dark, and with their various distinctions of costume, the knowing eye could doubtless have recognized Circassians, Kabards, Ossetes, and others.

The train, a local one, upon which we now embarked, rattled slowly along the valley of the River Terek, passing Cossack *stanitzi* and tumble-down native villages. For a space we ran parallel to the main range of the Caucasus, with nothing but a bare plain between. The mountains rose sheer into the air, a jagged line of peaks outlined against a deep blue sky. Elbruz stood out prominently with its rounded, volcanic-looking summit and snow-covered slopes sparkling in the sun. Evening came while we were still some way from our destination, and our carriage began to fill with a crowd of peasants. An amiable Persian offered my wife a bit of the corn cob he was gnawing, but the conversation he was attempting to open soon languished from lack of a common vocabulary. Then a smart young man in a Russian blouse and breeches, who had been eyeing us doubtfully for some time, addressed us in hesitant but excellent English. He explained that he was a member of the Communist Party, and held a good position for his years. He had evidently been pondering the propriety of having anything to do with two manifest bourgeois tourists, but courtesy and curiosity had triumphed. He wanted us to know that a Communist was a civilized human being, he wanted to do his day's good propaganda deed, he wanted to hear what strange ideas we might have about Russia and the outside world, and he wanted to practise his English. We were soon engaged in an animated conversation, which attracted the fixed but uncomprehending attention of the other fifty or so passengers. By the light of a flickery lantern, which made the bearded faces and sheepskin hats of the audience seem even wilder and more theatrical than ever, we argued ponderously about the merits of Leninism. The young Communist would now and then turn to the others and give them the gist of the proceedings. I particularly astonished him by saying that I had read some of the works of Lenin and other Bolsheviks in English translations. Nothing but the production of a volume from my bag would convince him that their publication was allowed by a capitalist British Government. I took the opportunity of comparing freedom of opinion in England with its absence in Russian, but he stoutly maintained that anyone could say what he liked, adding quite seriously that of course bourgeois sentiments were excluded. When I pressed him with rather more intimate political questions he responded well enough at first, but suddenly broke off the discussion by asking whether we played tennis; nor would he touch politics again. We parted quite cordially when we reached Vladikavkaz, but he would neither tell us his name nor be seen with us after we left the train.

We spent the night at Vladikavkaz, but sleep was not easy, because, until a very late hour, the greater part of the population promenaded in a double column up and down the boulevard outside our window. The next morning we had to be up by six o'clock to catch the motor-bus over the mountains. We piled ourselves into an open Fiat, holding ten people and some luggage, and bumped off after some delay in starting. The road would not rank high according to English standards, but the actual fact of being metalled throughout makes it almost unique for Russia. It climbs steeply, through wild country and a deep gorge overhung by granite rocks, to a height of 7,000 feet. On the top of the pass the view opens out and discloses the snowy peak of Kasbek, the second highest in the Caucasus. Up here there lives a small tribe, to which legend romantically, but probably erroneously, ascribes a crusading origin. They are called Khevsurs, which is said to be a corruption of *crève-cœur*, and are reputed to wear a red Maltese cross upon their sleeves. Up till very recently they retained the use of the chain mail which was universal a century ago in the Caucasus. I was able to obtain a suit of this armour, and am informed that none of it has any indication of a Western origin.

We have now left the North Caucasus Region of the R.S.F.S.R. and entered the Trans-Caucasian Republic of Georgia. The road begins a long winding descent through the more friendly country of the warmer southern slopes. Hitherto the gradient had prevented our chauffeur from speeding, but now he let himself go, and I hope never to experience another such hair-raising performance. We tore down the long zigzags, bumping and swaying, then stopping almost in our own length, skidding round the corners, and shooting off again. We charged carts and cattle at full speed, hooting furiously. A child and a dog had narrow escapes, but the rest somehow scattered to the sides, though why a dozen horses did not plunge over the precipice remains a mystery. An Armenian engineer, and a Russian Government clerk on holiday with his wife, sat beside us. The latter, who came from Leningrad, were in ecstasies over the mountain scenery. We picked up a young Georgian *en route*, who said he was employed in the museum at Tiflis, and proceeded to discourse to us excitedly about the history, geography, ethnology, and archæology of his country, shouting above the roar of the engine and waving his arms. He addressed himself, mostly in Georgian, to a soldier who sat dangerously perched on the luggage in the back seat, and who occasionally condescended to translate. We arrived in Tiflis nerve-shaken, hot, and dusty, after ten hours on the road. It is a journey worth doing once, but on my next visit I decided to circumnavigate the mountains sedately by train.

Tiflis is an agreeable city, but is likely to disappoint anyone who approaches it with romantic expectations. The core of it is Oriental, the super-structure Western. The old town is more squalid than picturesque, though not without interest. The newer quarters are spaciously planned and gaily laid out with gardens. Considering that since the Revolution the city has been successively occupied by German, British, and Bolshevik armies, that the Turks were at one time in the neighbourhood, and that the

Azerbaidjan Tatars have been at war with the Georgians, it is surprising to find the place so little affected.

The Georgians are an attractive, light-hearted, but somewhat feckless people, whose strong national sentiment does not find its best expression in politics, though they have produced some of the prominent personalities of the Revolution, including Stalin. More cultivated than the Azerbaidjan Tatars, but with less practical ability than the Armenians, the Georgians seem to show a preference for the more graceful qualities of civilization. The mountain clans are not devoid of dashing valour, which has endowed the country with a long line of epic heroes, and, greatest of all, a heroine, Queen Tamara, a contemporary of Charlemagne, round whom innumerable legends have collected, and with whom nearly all prominent features of the countryside have been associated.

The Georgians are specially noted for their cooking and their dancing. They also produce the best wine in Russia, though where it all goes to is a mystery. Like everything good in the Soviet Union, it is exported, but I have yet to find a restaurant in Europe which displays a "Napariouli" on its list. There are only one or two places left in Tiflis now where these delicacies may be sampled, and then only for fantastic charges. In this respect there was a notable change for the worse between my visits in 1929 and 1930.

The revival of national culture under the Soviet policy of national autonomy plays a great part in the intellectual life of Tiflis. It is rather annoying, after having learnt to decipher the Russian alphabet and to murder a few Russian phrases, to find a determined effort being made in Tiflis to promote the currency of Georgian, which has quite a different alphabet. The same perplexity obtains in Armenia and Azerbaidjan. The study of native lore is the natural refuge of an intelligentsia which has little sympathy with

Bolshevism. In the University we found people digging out old manuscripts from remote hiding-places, and an enthusiastic professor gave us a most enjoyable day by taking us out to Mtzkhet, the picturesque old capital of Georgia, where part of the cathedral dates back to the sixth century.

Tiflis is both the capital of Georgia and of the Trans-Caucasian Federation, an Union Republic of the U.S.S.R. Union, which also includes Armenia and Azerbaidjan. The three constituents have no racial or linguistic affinities, and are traditionally enemies. The Georgians and Armenians are among the oldest Christian nations. The Tatars are Moslems. The Armenians supply most of the driving-force and business capacity of the Federation, and occupy a high proportion of places in the Federal Government.

Among the acquaintances I made in Tiflis in 1929 was an American engineer who had just come out with his wife on a two years' contract to advise the Trans-Caucasian Government on irrigation works. They had never been out of America before, knew very little about Russia, and were full of amazement at everything they saw. The country round Tiflis, they said, reminded them very much of Arizona. We renewed our acquaintance a year later. They had just come back from a holiday in Constantinople, which the Authorities had somewhat reluctantly allowed them. They seemed rather depressed, and sighed for the gaiety and plenty of Istanboul. Life in Tiflis, they said, had been slowly getting harder all the year. There had been trouble in the mountains in the spring, presumably due to the collectivization campaign. Mrs. —— had an amusing account to give of the demolition of the Cathedral which stood almost opposite the hotel. This was a large modern building, not the old one which the European Press reported to have been destroyed. The site was wanted for some new Government buildings, and the first intention was to blow the place up. A message was sent to the hotel telling the inmates not to be alarmed by the explosion. In order that there should be less disturbance it was proposed to fire the charge at night! Different counsels, however, ultimately prevailed, and the building was eventually demolished in the ordinary way. Mrs. —— complained that they could get practically nothing sent out from home, as nearly all articles are either prohibited or subject to enormous Custom duties. Some mosquito netting which I sent out to them was returned to me. Some silk stockings never arrived at all. They had to pay 48 roubles on half a dozen handkerchiefs, and they refused to accept delivery of a tin of bath salts on which the charge was many times the value.

Mr. ——, who had travelled all over the country, particularly between the Kura and the Araxes and along the Persian and Turkish frontiers, was impressed by its potentialities, but seemed doubtful about its suitability for cotton, which is what they are trying hardest to grow. In many of the southern districts, where irrigation works are now planned, there are extensive remains of former canals, and the ground is strewn with the débris of ancient villages from which he has retrieved a number of curious bronze ornaments. At one spot there is a cuneiform stele, half of which is still standing, and which records the irrigation operations of an Assyrian monarch. Mr. —— spoke in sorrow rather than in anger of the Soviet Authorities with whom he has to deal. Waste and inefficiency are rampant. There was plenty of keenness, he said, but no one had any practical common sense. The amount of unnecessary investigation and discussion made him wild. The staff in his office worked night and day, but most of the time they were compiling quite unnecessary reports, tables of statistics, and returns for the State Planning Commission. In his judgment there were some sincere people at the top, then a layer of careerists, or what he described as "racketeers," and below these a layer of young fanatics. He did not pretend to have any views on the ultimate results, but was inclined to be pessimistic about the effects of present methods.

There is a British Military Cemetery in Tiflis, where about thirty people who died during the occupation of 1919–1920 are buried. It is a poor little patch of waste ground, some fifty yards square, on a hill in the suburbs, surrounded by a rickety barbed wire fence, and with nothing but rings of stone to mark the graves, except for one cross, put up by an officer's relatives. The Trans-Caucasian Government has apparently made difficulties about giving permanent possession of the land, and allowing the erection of a wall and proper headstones. But for the devoted attention of a few elderly ladies of British nationality in Tiflis, it would long ago have gone to ruin.

A night's journey West from Tiflis is Batoum, on the Black Sea, the southernmost port in the Soviet Union, only a few miles from the Turkish frontier. Here is a place, if ever there was one, "Where every prospect pleases and only man is vile." All along the hilly coast luxuriant sub-tropical vegetation flourishes in the warm damp climate, and on a fine day the peaks of the main Caucasus chain are visible to the north. The scenery is enchanting, but the town itself is miserable and dirty, with a mixed population, which may inaccurately, but aptly, be described as Levantine. In spite of having been under Russian sovereignty for over fifty years, Batoum still has a Turkish look. The local population are Moslem Georgians, known as Adjars. In spite of anti-religious propaganda, their women are still quite frequently veiled, but perhaps a more tolerant attitude

AN ADJAR (MOSLEM GEORGIAN) HAWKING QUAILS NEAR BATOUM

A GEORGIAN WOMAN IN NATIONAL DRESS

is adopted by the Authorities near a frontier where it might be injudicious to antagonize the people.

There is also a British Military Cemetery at Batoum, but as there are no resident British subjects, it has been much neglected. The only cross is lying broken on the ground, the fence has been removed, and the land, which contains the graves of about sixty British and Indian soldiers, has been planted with maize.

Other traces of the British occupation are still observable, among them several Ford cars, which were left behind, but are still plying the streets. I noticed on a wall near the harbour the words "NO SMOCKING" (*sic*) painted up in large letters. This was apparently part of the *mise en scène* of a Soviet film which featured the intervention of the British Imperialists.

Batoum is a busy place because it is the terminus of the pipe-line from Baku, which carries about 10 million tons of oil a year. About two-thirds of this is handled by the Soviet Oil Trust "Azneft," the rest by the Standard Oil Company. The most up-to-date oil port, however, is now Tuapse, with a pipe-line from the Grosny Fields, which allows ships to be loaded by gravitation.

Near Batoum are the Chakva tea gardens, which were started long ago, but are now being greatly developed in order that a large proportion of the huge Russian consumption of tea should be home-grown. At present only about 250 tons of tea are produced a year, but a new factory has just been erected with a capacity of 1,200 tons, and there are plans to plant eventually no less than 175,000 acres of tea. The Chakva tea has a taste unlike either China or Indian tea. It is perhaps most like Java tea. The aim is to reproduce as nearly as possible the qualities of Ceylon tea. This was the only factory I saw in Russia with any quantity of new British machinery.

CHAPTER X

GLIMPSES OF THE PROVINCES

(iii) THE BLACK SEA COAST AND THE UKRAINE

The Caucasus has the reputation of providing better living conditions than any other part of the Union, and it is consequently everyone's dream to be sent there. Any reference to it in other parts of Russia always provokes sighs of longing. To most Russians the Caucasus is very much what Scotland is to a great many Englishmen, primarily a holiday resort, and this aspect of it throws an interesting sidelight on existing social conditions.

The Eastern shore of the Black Sea, between Sukhum and Tuapse, is one of the great playgrounds of Russia. It consists of a series of small seaside towns, dotted along the forest-clad hills of the coast, in the neighbourhood of which wealthy Russians, under the old régime, possessed villas. From the sea the effect is not unlike a less highly developed Riviera.

Everything is now under Government control. Hotels and villas have been turned into sanatoriums and rest-houses, where representatives of every industry and profession are sent to recuperate from illness or exhaustion. A few such places are open to the general public, but most are only available for chosen members of particular organizations or for sufferers from particular diseases. Better food is provided than is normally available. Public 'buses run excursions to neighbouring points of beauty and interest. There are opportunities for sport and games, and particularly for sun and sea bathing.

I spent a few days at Sochi, the principal resort, in 1930.

All the important people, including Stalin, come here for the summer holidays. No one ever sees the great Communist leader, but I caught a glimpse of two celebrities, Kalinin, the President of the U.S.S.R., and Voroshilov, the Commissar for War.

The Kavkaskaya Riviera Hotel, reputed to be the best in the place, was filled to its utmost capacity, so much so that many of the rooms would be more accurately described as dormitories. The guests consisted chiefly of minor officials and professional people. Most of them were a good advertisement for the power of Sochi's sunshine, but fat men with shaven heads do not look their best in singlets and white duck trousers, while cheap cosmetics only drew attention to the natural defects of the feminine portion of the assembly. They were all supremely unconscious, however, of their æsthetic deficiencies, and obviously enjoying themselves. The neighbouring country was delightful and the bathing delicious, but life in the hotel was not so enticing. Meals were like a Feast of the Passover in a railway refreshment-room, served in relays, eaten in haste, and consisting mostly of rissoles, unleavened buns, and weak tea.

We had made tentative plans for a shooting expedition, which, owing to lack of time and our inability to make cut-and-dried arrangements beforehand, came to nothing, or rather degenerated into a farce. Bear, wild boar, and chamois had been talked of, and we had borrowed arms and ammunition. A friend was to have had a scheme ready for us, but he had been unable to make all the necessary preparations. He suggested, however, that we should see what we could do in one day, so we took a 'bus to a farm some miles away, the abode of a mighty hunter. We arrived heavily equipped with our "pieces"—I hardly know whether to call them guns or rifles, as one had two shot-barrels and one rifle-barrel, and the other one shot-barrel and two rifle-barrels. In any case they were a terrible weight, and it was very hot. We did no more, however, than walk perfunctorily through a large orchard and some small woods. I do not know how effective our weapons may have been against larger game, but all we saw was a single quail, and that escaped, as it was practically out of range. For anyone who cares to organize a serious expedition, there is, however, excellent shooting still to be had in the Caucasus, not only in this district but even more so farther south and inland. The authorities are well disposed towards foreigners, and all the necessary facilities are easily obtained.

I met an ardent Trotskyite on the beach at Sochi. He seemed overjoyed at the opportunity of unburdening himself with comparative safety to a foreigner. He had been quite a prominent Party man. Now he was driven to the indignity of picking up a living by private trading! As a convinced Communist this seemed to him the "most unkindest cut of all." There were thousands like him, he said, expelled from the Party for refusing to bow to the condemnation of Trotsky's views. He seemed very bitter about it, and gave me to understand that Communism was going to the dogs.

A regular service of steamers plies all round the Black Sea coast from Batoum to Odessa, a journey of about four days. I went the whole way from Batoum in 1929 and as far as Sochi in 1930, on both occasions by the same ship, the *Lenin.* The food and accommodation were, by Russian standards, good, and, on the two new German-built motor vessels on the route, they are reputed excellent. I could not describe the *Lenin* as luxurious, but, although the meals were perhaps a trifle less ample in 1930 than in 1929, they were on both occasions adequate and cheap.

There is no conspicuous display of Communism on the

Lenin, such as we experienced in travelling from London in the *Sibir*. The passengers, instead of being anxious to see how Communism works, were perhaps glad not to have lessons in Socialism too conspicuously thrust upon them. They were nearly all holiday-makers, a friendly company made up from every class of society. There were workmen, technicians, civil servants, an opera singer, a general, and a journalist. Although politics were taboo, they were more open in their conversation than any other assembly of Russians I have met. Incidentally I may say that this was the only occasion on which I ever heard a Russian sing the Volga Boat Song. One peculiar individual came from the Moldavian Republic on the Bessarabian frontier, and I found the best method of communication with him, though not a very effective one, was a mixture of schoolboy Latin and broken Italian.

One couple interested me particularly. They were of the generation that grew up during the war, and belonged to the class of small landowners. In the natural course of events the man would have inherited a country estate and a house in Moscow. The Revolution, of course, upset everything. Fortunately, he had studied engineering, and was therefore catalogued as a "specialist" rather than a "bourgeois." He had steady employment, and found it fascinating to work for the "Five Year Plan." "After all," he said, "the industrialization of Russia is worth working for, no matter what political régime is in power." He was no Communist, but no "counter-revolutionary" either. Life was grim, especially if one had been used to better things, but one managed to get along somehow. He and his wife lived in two rooms of the Moscow house which should have been his property. The rest of it was occupied by four or five other families, who, of course, used his furniture. It would be no good to him now, so he did not mind. Their chief regret was the scarcity of social refinement.

Starting from Batoum, the ship calls first at Poti, the port for the Chiatouri manganese mines, then at Sukhum, the centre of a tobacco-growing district, then at the string of holiday resorts, Gagri, Gadauti, Novi-Afon, and Sochi. Further North comes Tuapse, the oil port, followed by Novorossisk. This is the scene of *Ciment*, one of the best of the recent Russian novels dealing with the Revolution. The Ciment works where the story takes place can be seen at the extremity of the deep bay round which the town straggles.

The next stopping places are in the Crimea, another playground, with a string of holiday resorts along the coast. The most famous is Yalta, once a fashionable watering-place, and now, like Sochi, a conglomeration of sanatoriums and rest-houses.

The last port of call before reaching Odessa is Sevastopol. From the sea the country round looks comparatively flat, contrary to the engravings of the Crimean War with which one is familiar. It is certainly much flatter than the eastern part of the peninsula, but it is cut up by ravines, which are scarcely visible from a distance. The entrance to the bay of Balaclava is just discernible. An hour or two after passing it the steamer enters the magnificent harbour of Sevastopol itself, the headquarters of the Russian Black Sea Fleet, not a very formidable-looking array judging from the appearance of the units lying there. The town itself is an insignificant place, whose one dramatic moment seems to have been the memorable siege. There is a museum devoted to the Crimean War, and, where the citadel stood, a picture panorama illustrating the final assault by the allies. It is somehow a little unexpected to come across this corner of familiar history in a country where one of the principal impressions to-day is of its isolation from the rest of the world.

When I saw Odessa in November 1929 it seemed in a state of suspended animation. It is a fine town, better laid out and more European, or perhaps I should rather say more cosmopolitan, than other Russian towns. The devastations of the Civil War, which are said to have injured a third of the houses, are no longer apparent, but nothing is going on. Were it not for the brighter colouring of a southern climate, and the greater animation of its inhabitants, one might seek a comparison with Leningrad. There was little traffic in the streets. There were no ships in the harbour. The biggest hotel was almost empty. It may be that with the resumption of Russian grain exports Odessa is waking up a little, but it cannot yet be anything like the busy city it once was.

Odessa is in the Ukraine, which is the principal State of the Union next to Russia proper. The Ukrainians, or Little Russians, are about as different from the Great Russians as are the Lowland Scots from the English. Moscow is to Kiev as London is to Edinburgh. It is a difference which can be minimized or accentuated according to circumstances. It is now the fashion to encourage a Ukrainian national consciousness. Ukrainian is treated as a separate language. It is as if Scotland were given home rule and the authorities officially adopted the writings of Burns as the standard for vocabulary, orthography, and pronunciation. The Ukrainian is a gayer person than the Russian and his peculiarities are largely due to Polish influence in his speech and custom. It was because Kiev, the traditional centre, was suspected of being too Polish in sentiment that the capital was transferred to Kharkov. There is a secessionist movement in the Ukraine which has, so far, been successfully kept under. Besides those who support the present régime, there are a few who favour a Union with Poland and a larger number who would like to see an independent Ukraine including the Ukrainian districts now under Polish rule.

Kiev, the old capital of the Ukraine, is one of the few Russian provincial cities with an historical atmosphere. It has been an important place longer than Moscow. It has maintained for centuries a unique religious significance as a centre of pilgrimage. Standing in a commanding position on a terraced bluff above the River Dnieper, the roofs of its houses, and the domes of its churches and monasteries, rise in gilt-pointed tiers above the flat surrounding plain. Here, as in Moscow, a touch of fairyland expresses the underlying mysticism of Russia. Two peculiarities distinguish Kiev from other Russian towns. Its outlook is westwards, not eastwards, and nearly half the population are Jews. Psychologically Kiev belongs to Central Europe. In spite of its present decadence, the slatternly shabbiness of more northern cities is not so evident, people are better dressed, and the shops more attractive. When I commented on this to a casual acquaintance, his reply, though naïve, expressed the difference very well. "Ah, you see," he said, "Moscow and Leningrad take their fashions from London, *we* take them from Paris."

Kiev to-day is a sad town and seemed especially so to me in grey damp autumn weather with the last leaves hanging brown and sodden on the trees. In what was formerly the opulent residential district plaster was peeling off the houses, and the streets were uneven and slushy. The centre of the town is animated enough, but where formerly pilgrims streamed to do homage at the famous shrines, there is hardly a soul to be seen. The great "Lavra" has been turned into a home for disabled ex-service men of the Civil War. In the courtyard, untouched, is the granite

TOP: STATUE OF LENIN AT BATOUM

BOTTOM: THE TEA GARDENS AT CHAKVA

tomb of Stolypin, who inaugurated, too late, land reforms which might have changed Russian history, and who was shot in the Opera House at Kiev in 1911. A flagged pathway and stairs, worn by the tread of innumerable feet, and perhaps also by the knees of the more devout, leads down to the cave monastery. To-day a single footstep echoes in the silence. The entrance to the monastery is on a terrace, overgrown with weeds, and bordered by a rotting balustrade. An old, ragged, and filthy priest stands by the door and hands you a candle. You pass into a semicircular passage hewn in the cliff. This is where some of the most venerated saints lived and established their sanctity by unheard-of asceticisms. Some were walled up in tiny cells with only a small hole to admit air and food. Others existed for years wearing heavy chains, or forced into some intolerably cramped position. Such extremities of maceration were still being practised when the Revolution came and the Soviet Authorities turned the monks out. But the bodies of these holy men still lie in open coffins, covered with vestments, in niches along the wall, and as you pass along the priest still recites the exploits by which they acquired merit. He no longer pretends, however, that the bodies have not suffered decay. This superstition has been too thoroughly exploded by demonstration, and he will even go so far as to show how the illusion was created. Perhaps it is on these terms that he is allowed to fulfil his present miserable office.

And now let us turn away from the past, from stagnant ports, and mildewing sanctuaries, to the present centre of Ukrainian life, where the Soviet authorities are trying to drown the past in a crescendo of roaring machinery. This is Kharkov, formerly a "county town" of no particular significance, now a capital city of nearly three-quarters of a million inhabitants, the administrative and economic centre of a highly developed industrial region, of an area which is to be revolutionized by the vast new hydro-electric power station on the Dnieper, and of some of the richest agricultural districts in Russia.

Kharkov is in process of entire reconstruction. Already there is little outside the centre of the town to remind one of pre-revolutionary Kharkov. Apart from Moscow no city in Russia can compare with it for movement and activity. I was reminded of some South American cities like São Paulo, where everyone always seems to be moving into a new building. Acres of new houses have grown up in the suburbs, but the pride of the city is the fifteen-storied "Palace of State Industry," which houses the chief Government and business offices. The advantages of a skyscraper in the middle of the Russian plains is not very apparent, but the result is certainly impressive.

Away to the South-East are the coal-mines of the Donetz basin. Serious labour troubles were being experienced when I was there in 1930. Workmen were persistently leaving. The food had been too poor to make the heavy work tolerable. For these mines are old and wretched places to work in. They are from two to three thousand feet deep, and access is by low narrow tunnels. A good deal of cutting machinery has been installed, and the coal is brought to the surface by electric hoists, but the men have to crawl for an hour at least to reach the face. This in itself is exhausting. Yet conditions are better than they were before the Revolution. Hours are shorter and the living quarters are being rapidly improved. Presumably the workman will no longer stand what he put up with in the bad old days. Things are still so unsatisfactory, however, that of nearly two thousand German miners, who were engaged during 1930 to give the workers a stiffening, all refused to stay after a few weeks.

Two hundred miles South-West of Kharkov is "Dnieperstroi," the colossal hydro-electric power station which is to revolutionize industrial conditions over a large part of the eastern Ukraine. It will ultimately develop a total of 850,000 horse-power with an output of two and a half thousand million kilowatt hours. Construction has been proceeding, under American direction, since 1927. The dam across the Dnieper, 1¼ miles long and 200 feet high, is nearly finished. A new city for a population of 500,000 is being built. It is said that the population of the area affected by the station will eventually rise from one to eight millions. New factories are planned in the immediate neighbourhood and around the city of Dniepropetrovsk, 50 miles away. Power will be transmitted as far as the banks of the Don, 180 miles to the East. In typical Russian fashion the most striking feature of the scheme, the power station itself, has been undertaken first. It will be a good many years before there are industries to absorb all the electricity. Nevertheless, this is an impressive example of the scale on which industrialization is proceeding.

I shall not have conveyed the impression I intended unless the reader has grasped that a visit to Soviet Russia is a mixed experience. It is fascinating, but by no means wholly enjoyable; with all the advantages vouchsafed to the foreigner, life is still a strain. One scarcely cares to contemplate what it would be like to be a Russian. As the train nears the frontier one's heart lightens. One needs to curb one's impatience while the tedious formalities are taking place. Then the refreshment-room on the Polish side claims one's whole attention. What comfort! What abundance! And then Warsaw! It is not a particularly attractive place really as European capitals go, but to eyes accustomed to Russian scenes, how gay! How spick and span! What a number of motor-cars! How bright with illuminated signs at night!

And yet I found myself missing something. I had come back to an adipose world, where rich food and bulging waistcoats seemed to play a disproportionate rôle. Looked at from this angle the Russian caricatures of capitalists are not so grotesque. The newspapers appeared to be overflowing with inconsequent babbling. The superficial and the garish seemed to claim a surprising amount of attention. It might be true that untold energy was going to waste in commercial competition and individual self-seeking. I missed the bracing feeling of life being carried on without any margin, of a necessary concentration on essentials. I missed the feeling that the main object of life was not money. I missed these things but I did not regret them. I was only astounded that the atmosphere of Soviet Russia could produce such a psychological impression in a few weeks.

Things appeared to me thus after leaving Soviet territory. For a moment I stood upon a frontier of the mind and seemed to view the two dispensations clearly and separately. Then I plunged once again into what is, for me, normal life, and Soviet Russia became a memory.

PART III

BOLSHEVISM IN ACTION

CHAPTER XI

THE COMMUNIST DICTATORSHIP

Were the Soviet System worked as a free system, were freedom of speech and opinion and organization permitted, were elections allowed to express the feelings of the voters, were the congresses of Soviets places of frank discussion, did the "Tsik"[1] exert its powers as a legislature, and did the "Sovnarkom"[1] act unhindered as the reflection of the prevailing mood of the country, it is possible that these institutions might constitute the form of democratic government most suited to Russian conditions. But the Soviet Union, in appearance a federal democracy, is in fact and admittedly a Communist dictatorship.

The "October" Revolution gave power to the Bolshevik section of the Russian Social-Democratic party.[2] Henceforward the supreme object of the Bolsheviks has been to retain power so as to make effective a communist dictatorship in Russia and to make themselves the spear-head of the World Revolution. Compared with these, all other aims are subsidiary. The Bolsheviks, therefore, devoted themselves from the start to putting their party in a position of absolute authority. Steps were taken to ensure that the Communist Party, and the Communist Party only, should lay down the policy of the country.

It goes without saying that since the "October" Revolution the principal political posts have been held by Com-

[1] See Appendix for the meaning of these and other abbreviated names for the organs of Government.

[2] The name was later changed to Russian Communist Party in order to dissociate it from the Social-Democratic parties, which were said to have betrayed Socialism by supporting their national Governments during the war and by not responding to the call to world revolution.

munists; a more remarkable development has been the organization of the Party so that it duplicates the ordinary machinery of government at almost every stage. From the "fraction" in the village or factory, through the hierarchy of local Congresses of Soviets, up to the "Tsik" and its inner conclaves, the Party keeps its watch and ward, faithful to the traditions of discipline and training instilled by Lenin when he insisted on the organization of a fighting force at the decisive Social-Democratic Conference in 1903.

Quality rather than quantity is aimed at just as much to-day. No one can become a member of the Party without sponsorship, without a period of probation, and without passing a course of "political grammar." Applicants are divided into three categories. In the first are workers and Red Army soldiers of proletarian or peasant origin. These require two recommendations from party members, who must be of one year's standing in the case of workers, and of two years' standing in the case of soldiers. In the second category are peasants and private craftsmen "who do not exploit another's labour." These require three recommendations from party members of three years' standing. In the third category are all other applicants, and these require five recommendations from party members of five years' standing. The period of probation is six months, one year, and two years respectively for each category. Anyone who makes an "unworthy" recommendation is liable to exclusion from the Party. Specially stringent conditions apply to any applicant who has ever been a member of any other party, whatever his social origin.

The Russian Communist Party is a close corporation. Discipline is very strict. Orders must be obeyed without question. Differences of opinion within the Party are settled by the simple means of excluding all those who refuse to accept the decisions of the central authority. On several occasions there have been purges which substantially reduced the number of members. The adoption of the New Economic Policy for instance, which aroused considerable opposition among the purists, resulted in the expulsion of some 200,000 members. After Lenin's death the struggle between Stalin and Trotsky ended in the latter's banishment, and the expulsion of many thousands of his adherents.

Party controversies are commonly expressed in terms of Communist doctrine. The conflict of rival policies and personalities is thus inclined to turn, in form at least, on points of political orthodoxy. All sides support their cases with quotations from Lenin, and, to the uninitiated, it is often very difficult to discover the point at issue. There is something in the published discussions strangely reminiscent of the proceedings of the Councils of the early Christian Church. Once a point of dogma has been settled, a member must either conform or he will be expelled as a heretic.

It is difficult for English people to realize what government by a party dictatorship means. Whatever party is in power in England takes on a national complexion. While it is in office a British Government is relatively independent of the caucus of the party to which it belongs. In Russia, the Party organization is the only real power. Stalin,[1] who

[1] Joseph Vissarionovich Djugashvili, generally known by his revolutionary pseudonym of Stalin, was born in December 1879, at Gori, not far from Tiflis. He is a Georgian. His father was a cobbler, and destined him for the same trade. His mother, who is still alive, and lives in the former Vice-Regal Palace in Tiflis, which is now the Headquarters of the Trans-Caucasian Government, wanted him to be a priest. He studied at the theological seminary in Tiflis, but left before his time, whether because of ill health, as his mother has stated, or because of his revolutionary views, is a little uncertain. He was, at any rate, a member of the Social-Democratic organization in Tiflis in 1898. Between 1900 and 1917 his political activities brought him into constant conflict with the police. He was six times sentenced to various periods of detention in North Russia or Siberia, but escaped on each occasion. At the outbreak of the revolution he was in exile near Turukhansk

is virtually dictator, derives his power from being General Secretary of the Central Committee of the Party. He is not a member of the Government, though he is a member of the Presidium of the "Tsik."

The direction of the Party is vested in the Central Committee, about seventy in number, which is elected by the Party Congress; but, as in the case of the Soviets, power actually devolves on a small inner group. The Central Committee has three sub-committees, a Political Bureau of nine, an Organization Bureau of thirteen, and a Secretariat of five members. Several people belong to more than one of these sub-committees. Stalin sits on all three, so does Molotov. The Secretariat does the day-to-day business, the Organization Bureau or "Org-Bureau" deals with purely party questions, the Political Bureau or "Polit-Bureau," the most important of the three, concerns itself with all aspects of general policy.

In accordance with the practice adopted all through the machinery of government a check is kept on one body by another. The Party Congress also elects a Central Control Commission, on which no member of the Central Committee may serve. Representatives of this body attend the meetings of the Polit-Bureau, Org-Bureau, and Secretariat of the Central Committee. Its chief duty is "to cultivate a party tendency in all Soviet organs." Local Party organizations have local Control Commissions.

The dictatorship of the Communist Party, itself dominated by the Polit-Bureau, is exercised through various channels.

In the first place the Party controls the elections to

where the River Yenisei crosses the Arctic Circle. He was released, with other political prisoners, by the Provisional Government, and took part in the activities of the Petrograd Soviet. He was Commissar for Nationalities in the original Bolshevik Government. He has three children, a son aged twenty-four by his first wife, and a son aged eight and a daughter aged five by a second marriage.

Soviets and Congresses of Soviets. Since 1920 no political organization except that of the Communist Party has been allowed to exist. Candidates are described as "party" or "non-party." The election of a proportion of non-party men is tolerated, partly because the Party cannot man every post, partly because it is a means of bringing selected people of a neutral turn of mind under Communist influence, and partly because it gives the impression of tolerance of other points of view. The procedure is for someone to propose a list of candidates as having received the approval of the Party "fraction," that is the Party organization, which corresponds to the organ of government concerned. This list has never been known to be rejected.

In the second place the Party controls administration. The Central Control Commission dominates the Collegia of the various Commissariats, and, moreover, particularly identifies itself with the work of the Commissariat of Workers' and Peasants' Inspection. This department has general supervisory functions over all Government activities, and naturally looks to the appropriate Communist organ to indicate the lines on which to work. One of its particular duties is to watch the effect of Government policy on the relations between town and country, so as to guide the assimilation of the peasants to the workers' point of view. It is the authority on the progress of socialization, and is specially charged with checking bureaucratic tendencies and corruption. The Commissar is customarily a member of the Presidium of the Central Control Commission.

In the third place, the Party controls political opinion through the G.P.U., and, while the army continues to be a Red army, it possesses the means of suppressing any revolt.

The policy of the Party automatically becomes the policy of the Government. The position of a Minister, even if he is a Communist, is always precarious. He is subjected to what must be almost intolerable supervision. The outside world sees no difference between the activities of the Government, the Party, and the Third International (which is also dominated by the Russian Communist Party). Nevertheless, Party control is not exercised without some friction. The two chief official newspapers, *Izvestia*, the organ of the Government, and *Pravda*, the organ of the Party, do not by any means always sing the same tune. The Government has to deal with actual situations. It has to administer a country, the vast majority of which is non-Communist, and to maintain relations with other countries, all hostile to Communism. It works with a staff of officials and technicians, very few of whom are Communists. It has a natural inclination to compromise. The Foreign Commissariat, anxious to maintain friendly relations with Foreign Powers, may genuinely deplore the activities of Communist propagandists abroad. The Trade Commissariat may think economic reconstruction would get on faster if things were made easier for foreign capital. But it is the Polit-Bureau which takes the ultimate decisions.

The Communist Party, including candidates, numbers less than a million and a half members. Including the Communist League of Youth or *Komsomol*, the total is under 3,000,000. This minority completely dominates a population of 150,000,000. Starting as an obscure revolutionary group, which even in April 1917, a month after the outbreak of the revolution, only claimed to represent 76,000 workers, the Bolshevik Party was able, through the skill and determination of its leader, to seize its opportunity. Having possessed itself of the centre of government, and, what was just as important, of a substantial part of the country's armed forces, it proceeded to consolidate its position, stamping out opposition by terrorism, if necessary. Gradually it extended and perfected the machinery for imposing its will, always so contriving matters, however, that what it willed should not be beyond its power to enforce. In spite of mistakes and reverses, it regained control over the greater part of the Tzar's dominions. In spite of hazardous experiments and some startling reversals of policy, it has clung to its general principles of social philosophy. The history of the Communist Party in Russia is but another example of what may be achieved by people who hold tenaciously to a central idea, and are ready to adopt any means for its realization. That its dictatorship is firmly entrenched is certain; whether its course is progressing so surely towards the realization of Communism as it alleges is not so certain. Even a dictatorship, however absolute, is neither infallible nor completely impervious to outside influences.

CHAPTER XII

GOVERNMENT BY PROPAGANDA

The Communist objective is twofold. Ultimately, it is nothing less than a fundamental alteration of social standards, first in Russia, then all over the world. More immediately it is the economic reorganization of Russia on a Socialist basis, and the forcible conversion of the population to the Socialist point of view, by intimidation if necessary, but mainly by propaganda. The Soviet System has been made the instrument of class war.

The stranger soon notices something peculiarly abnormal and yet vaguely familiar about the atmosphere of Soviet Russia. It is vital that this atmosphere should be apprehended, because it is the clue to much that appears incomprehensible to those who draw their information mostly from the newspapers. Soviet Russia is a world apart, cut off by the political, economic, and cultural restrictions imposed by the present régime from normal intercourse with the rest of civilization. It is a country living under the conditions of a self-imposed blockade, a country struggling to evolve a new technique of life, a country fighting for its spiritual as well as for its material life. The outstanding quality of the Soviet environment is the predominance of a war mentality.

Analogies to war-time conditions are obvious. There is the concentration of everything in Government hands, the restriction of private trading, the occupation of private houses and hotels for Government offices, the shortage of commodities, the inferior and *ersatz* quality of others, the ration-card system, the queues outside food-shops and eating-houses. There is the scarcity of all but official news, the prevalence of rumours, the pervasion of propaganda. There is the sensation of constant strain.

The Bolshevik ruling class is deeply infected by the war mind. Every problem is discussed in military phraseology. Such words as "front," "shock troops," "front line" are constantly being used. The battle is against all the traditional loyalties, and some of the most inveterate prejudices in human nature. Religion, patriotism, personal liberty, and the incentive of private gain, everything, in fact, that is implied by the term "bourgeois ideology" are condemned and fought.

The Communists are surrounded by hostile forces, both at home and abroad, and, in proportion as they are energetic in the pursuance of their revolutionary doctrines, they credit their opponents with scheming counter-revolution. They are quite serious in their fear of an attack by the combined forces of the Western capitalist countries. The "bogey" of foreign intervention is no doubt also a useful instrument of propaganda. Patriotism has its uses even among Communists. Alleged foreign aggression is a good rallying call, and justifies the maintenance of a large and expensive Army. The possibility of war is, nevertheless, a real and constant preoccupation. Such an outlook is responsible for an undercurrent of nervousness, which breaks out from time to time in attacks of spy-mania and in political prosecutions on a large scale. The Bolsheviks have no more compunction about sending their political opponents to the scaffold than troops have about shooting their enemies in war-time. There have been cases of blood-lust, no doubt, but, generally speaking, the killing of the "bourgeois" is simply regarded as a regrettable necessity. The loss of life involved in the carrying out of a political and economic plan is thought of in much the same way as might be the casualties in a battle. There is no desire to waste life, but loss of life is a minor consideration in view of the objective to be reached.

To inoculate a hundred and fifty million people with a new philosophy of life is an ambitious task. Russia was probably the only country in the world where this particular experiment could be attempted. The former Russian Empire, an agglomeration of overwhelmingly agricultural and largely uncultured people, was made the scene for the application of theories developed from observation of quite different conditions. Communism had always been thought of as the logical outcome of industrialism. As a matter of fact, its only chance of success was in a region where industry hardly existed, for, as in an industrialized country, the economic system is such a delicate and complex organism, and so bound up with the lives and interests of the people, that few could contemplate its destruction with equanimity. In Russia, however, once the superstructure of Tzarism was overturned, there remained only a primitive social organism, on the one hand almost insensitive to rough treatment, and on the other a virgin field for propaganda.

There is scarcely a branch of social life where propaganda does not penetrate. Even in his entertainments the Russian is not left to follow his preferences. Fully half the programmes provided at theatres and cinemas have some element of propaganda. Plays glorifying the Revolution are naturally much in favour with the Authorities. It is somewhat incongruous, however, to find that the lesson to be conveyed is sometimes the dire consequence of rebellion against the present régime. The villain of the piece is a dissatisfied worker, an insubordinate commander, or a Trotskyite, just as often as he is a *kulak*, a bourgeois, a White counter-revolutionary or a foreign "interventionist." Anti-Imperialism, illustrated by capitalist oppression of coloured races, and especially of the Chinese, is a common theme; so is anti-religious propaganda, and the portrayal of Russian history in terms of oppression by Tzar and Church. The positive side of Bolshevism is the subject of innumerable films covering industrialization, collective and mechanized farming, the advantages of various Soviet institutions, the need for education, hygiene and so on. When the lesson is in the form of a story the hero is always a Communist who, by superior qualities and attainments, overcomes the inertia of the older generation.

The Radio, the Press, the Poster, and the Platform all contribute their quota of the propaganda which pours forth in torrents from official sources. Public squares, restaurants, and station waiting-rooms are equipped with loud speakers, which blare out the official version of whatever may be considered of public interest, or deliver homilies on the avoidance of measles and the importance of cleaning the teeth daily. Every place of work is hung with charts, diagrams, and pictures. Marxian texts, pictures of Lenin, red flags, and Soviet emblems, adorn factories, public buildings, trams, in fact every prominent position. All the space usually devoted to Pears' Soap, Bovril, and other commercial advertisers is utilized for the advertisement of a single political party. On appropriate occasions demonstrations are organized with processions, bands, and banners, culminating in fiery oratory from a red-draped rostrum. Naturally in a country with so many illiterates as Russia the mass appeal has to be to the eye and ear. The Press has principally to consider the educated minority. It supplies material for the party worker. It answers awkward questions. It indicates the limits within which controversy should keep.

The general public gets rather tired of being treated like school children to these perpetual object lessons in good Communism, but it has to put up with what it can get. There is always a rush to see an American film. Translations of H. G. Wells and Edgar Wallace are very popular. But any encouragement of bourgeois emotions, such as romance or personal success, is officially frowned on.

On the other hand, there is no doubt that, one-sided though it is, all this propaganda has led to a far more widespread interest in what is going on than can ever have been the case before. The Russian enjoys discussion, but he has never been trained in discrimination. It is nothing new for him to have to accept an official version of events, and he does not think it odd that he should only hear one side of a case. Public opinion and free speech are almost meaningless expressions to the mass of the population. Nevertheless, discussion flourishes in the village, in the club, and wherever people congregate. Every workman and peasant is surprisingly well informed on current topics, but the effect of propaganda is an extraordinary similarity in the questions put to a stranger, and in the facts that are commonly accepted. The only opposition to the official version of contemporary history comes from personal experience, and this is usually too limited to have much effect.

It is very difficult to get anyone to understand conditions in a democratic country like Great Britain. The assumption always is that things go on in capitalist countries very much as they did in Tzarist Russia. Although everyone knows that there are Communist parties abroad, and indeed thinks them more important than they are, no one realizes that the very fact of allowing Communist candidates to stand at elections argues liberty of statement for Communist views. The assumption always seems to be that the party must be working underground. I often tried to explain that the only thing forbidden in England was the attempt to alter the Constitution by revolutionary instead of Parliamentary means, but this distinction was not easily grasped. Parliamentary Government in the English sense is quite outside the experience of the ordinary Russian.

Freedom of speech and of the Press is not understood because it has never been experienced. I had great difficulty in persuading a certain member of the Party that English translations of Lenin's works, and of the writings of other prominent Bolsheviks, could be had at any English bookshop. Many people were surprised that I had been able to buy, in England, two or three translations of recent novels about the revolution. One man was even sceptical when I told him that I got my guide book to Soviet Russia from Cook's in Berkeley Street. Yet freedom of discussion in conversation or in print is not entirely suppressed, and in one direction is actually encouraged. Communists are instructed to undertake "self-criticism," by which is meant comparison between actual performance and what is theoretically desirable, as a disciplinary exercise. This is intended to help stimulate effort. It is rash, however, to put forward views inconsistent with Communism. Workers and peasants often express themselves extremely frankly about the Government, and seldom come to any harm by doing so. The bourgeois and "specialist," classes on the other hand, prefer not to talk politics.

Of all propagandist activity in Russia that directed against religion strikes the stranger as the most remarkable. Countries with no official religion are common enough, but an officially Atheist Government is something new.

The Bolshevik attitude towards religion is comparable to our own attitude towards Communism, making allowance, of course, for the fact that the similarity of Russian conditions to war conditions are responsible for very much stricter repressive measures in that country. There is no general prohibition of worship in Russia, any more than the expression of Communist views is prohibited in democratic countries, but every member of a religious body in Russia is a potential enemy of the Communist State, just as every Communist is a potential enemy of what, for want of a better word, I must call the Capitalist State. The line between legitimate activity and action calculated to be dangerous to the existing order is hard to draw, but in both cases there is a point at which the authorities feel bound to interfere.

Religious organizations are on much the same footing as any private society or corporation, that is to say a body of people can legally form themselves into an association for carrying on the rites of any creed, so long as they keep clear of politics. Once registered they can acquire the use of a church, whose upkeep must be defrayed by voluntary contribution, and the services of a priest, who, although automatically disfranchised by his calling, is free to carry out purely religious duties. Of course, the stigma attached to religion of any kind, and the association of the Church with counter-revolution, amount in themselves to serious disabilities. The weight of the constituted authority is biased in favour of the Communist position. Anti-religious propaganda has official support. The prohibition of political activities extends to the imparting of religious instruction to anyone under eighteen. Any demonstrative assertion of religious convictions, such as the ringing of church bells, and processions, is forbidden. A religious devotee is *ipso facto* suspect of hostility to Communism, and must consequently expect differential treatment when it comes to admission to schools, or the allocation of work and rations.

Some courage and a readiness to bear opprobrium, extra privations, and persecution are required of open adherents to a religious faith. It is not surprising therefore that many prefer to keep their religious convictions to themselves, and that many more, especially among the younger generation, are content to follow the orthodox attitude laid down by the Communist Party.

Communism has often been itself described as a religion. It lays claim to universal validity, and purports to supply a self-sufficient explanation of the universe. It deduces a code of morals and æsthetics from its principles. In its own way it might even be said to have a touch of Puritanism. It is a hard creed, and has the same disregard for everything irrelevant to the main goal, the same contempt of anything that savours of relaxation. Its insistence on physical fitness is almost ethical. It demands a devotion, and aims at exciting a missionary zeal, which can only be described as religious. If it has no God, it has recognized in Lenin something very like a prophet. With these characteristics Communism inevitably comes into conflict with every existing form of religious organization. Communism brooks no rivals.

The Lenin cult is not so much anti-religious as pro-Communist. Lenin's writings have taken the place of Scripture, and his effigy the place of ikons. The politicians quote Lenin against each other as if invoking a supreme authority. His sayings, inscribed on lengths of red bunting, adorn the inside and outside walls of every building. His bust is on every writing-table, his statue on every market square. There is a Museum in Moscow, devoted to his life, where his personal belongings are exhibited like relics. His tomb, where his embalmed body lies open to the public gaze, has been an object of pilgrimage for thousands.

All religions, Jewish, Moslem, and Buddhist, as well as Christian, fall equally under the condemnation of Communism, as a glance at the numerous anti-religious posters shows. But it is the Russian Church that has suffered most heavily at the hands of the present régime. The number of churches still used for services must be a small fraction of the total number, though probably enough for existing church-goers. Those of the greatest historical and architectural interest have been turned into museums, others, and particularly the monasteries, are used as institutions and dwellings.

In order to emphasize materialistic views, and to counteract belief in a literal resurrection of the body, Communism shows a decided preference for cremation. The new Moscow Crematorium occupies quite a prominent place in the list of sights. Funerals, however, remain occasions for pomp and ceremony. I witnessed the funeral of a prominent Trade Union leader, who was also an important Party man. He had been accorded interment in the Pantheon of Communism, the strip of ground behind Lenin's Mausoleum, under the Kremlin walls, in the Red Square. Thousands followed the hearse bearing the ashes, but, except that there was no priest, the superficial resemblance to the traditional ceremony was strong. Wreaths tied with red and black ribbons were carried by the chief mourners, and the four pall-bearers actually wore top hats and frock coats. To invent new forms of ceremonial respect is evidently harder than to change the meaning of the ceremony itself.

There is an Anti-Religious Museum in every big town, frequently situated in a church. The one described here is in Moscow, but the arrangement always follows similar lines. Crude blasphemy is generally avoided, but the effect of what is shown is well calculated to make an uneducated person, with revolutionary sympathies, feel that religion is a Capitalist fraud. There is really very little that an educated person would dispute, so far as facts are concerned, but they would be a shock to the average working-class Russian, and would make him receptive to conclusions which do not necessarily follow from these facts.

The first section of the Museum shows the process of evolution so as to suggest that man is only a superior animal. Then the likeness of Christianity to other religions is illustrated. This section is rather like a summary of the *Golden Bough*. The Virgin Mary is compared to the Earth Mother. Examples are shown of the likeness between her images and those of Demeter and other goddesses. There are examples of the Trinitarian idea in other mythologies, and several old ikons are displayed on which the Christian Trinity is represented by a figure with three heads. The idea of the dying and the resurrecting God is shown to be analogous to the myth of Osiris. A great deal is made of the existence of the Cross as a symbol in other cults. The lesson to be conveyed is that man made God, not God man.

The majority of the exhibits concern the Russian Church. Several famous saints have been dug up and put in glass cases to destroy the idea that their bodies did not decay. There is a section demonstrating how false miracles could be worked. The subterfuges by which a certain family attempted, some twenty-five years ago, to obtain the canonization of their father, who had not died so very long before, are set out in elaborate detail. The Church is represented as obtaining money by exploiting the piety of the poor. A great deal is made of unhygienic practices, such as the kissing and touching of objects of veneration. Ascetic extravagances are denounced. The ideas of Hell and Penance are so presented as to suggest that the Church's power is based on fear. It is explained that the Church and the autocracy united to keep down the masses by Inquisitional methods, and by the betrayal of the secrets of the confessional to the Tzar's agents. The close union between Tzarism and the Church is illustrated by pictures of coronations, by the use of religious symbols in military decorations, by presents given by Tzars to monasteries, and by photographs of the ceremonies which accompanied the "ennoblement" of St. Nicholas by the late Tzar. Finally, a collection of vestments is meant to teach that the Church made itself impressive by theatrical methods. The case against the Russian Church is cleverly marshalled, and it is easier to understand the anti-religious movement in the light of this attack on the superstitions with which Church and State, from Patriarch and Tzar to "pope" and moujik, must have been grievously infected.

The success of anti-religious propaganda is hard to estimate. The old traditions are still strong in the pre-revolution generation, from whom most of the surviving congregations are drawn. The younger generation is, apparently, at best indifferent. It is hard to believe that the religious impulse can be stamped out, or Communism made to take its place, but it is permissible to doubt whether a religious revival would be on Orthodox lines. The Church has not played the part in the revolution which its enormous social and political influence would have led one to expect. It seems to have sunk into silent impotence from the moment the Tzar disappeared. Even during the time of the Provisional Government few references can be found to it as an active force. A new religious movement might come from one of those waves of mystical excitement which have swept the country before now. It might coincide with an intellectual revival, and arise through science and mathematics. Russia might produce a prophet of quite an original character.

What is the general effect of all this propaganda on the rising generation? The Bolsheviks themselves recognize that the best they can hope for from the majority of the pre-revolution generation is acquiescence. Their hopes are centred on the generation over whose education they have had control, and no effort is spared to saturate children with Communist ideas.

The system by which working mothers leave their children, during their hours of work, at the crèches and kindergartens attached to the factories has undoubtedly some excellent features from the point of view of social welfare, but it also accustoms children from infancy to look elsewhere than to their parents for the answer to the first questions of awakening consciousness. The answers given in these institutions are necessarily Communist answers. Upon the walls a portrait of Lenin as a small child impresses on them the source of the social organization of which they are part. The family and religion are cut out from the very beginning and replaced by the State and Leninism.

When the child goes to school at seven or eight years old, he has already been made receptive to ideas, which he must now be taught to grasp intellectually, and to make the mainsprings of his life. There is, again, much that is excellent in the educational system as it is planned to be applied eventually to the whole country. So far it is only fully running in a few model schools in the large towns. The only unfortunate thing is, that the more efficient and widespread the educational system becomes the deeper will Communism go.

This is a dilemma which has constantly to be faced. There is not the slightest doubt that the efforts of the present régime in the social and intellectual fields are paving the way for an immeasurable advance on anything the people have known before. But every reform is used as a means of propagating Communism. It cannot, however, be seriously contended that the people ought to be left in ignorance and filth, for fear of their becoming Communists. It can only be hoped that the fallacies of

Communism will become apparent to an educated and healthy people.

Nearly every child in an efficient school becomes a "Pioneer," the equivalent of Boy Scouts and Girl Guides. Here, along with many useful things, they begin to learn their duty as good Communists. When, at the age of about fourteen, they are too old any longer to be Pioneers, their legitimate ambition is to join the Young Communists' League (*Komsomol*). But this is a select body, admission to which requires evidence of serious intention to work for the Party, into whose ranks a *komsomoletz* may expect to graduate after his novitiate in the junior organization. The *komsomoltsi* in a school are its acknowledged leaders. They are the Prefects, the eleven, the eight, the fifteen, all rolled into one, but the standard that puts them there is not one of lessons or games, but of political faith. On leaving school or the University, it is the *komsomoltsi* who get first choice of jobs. No one who is not of proletarian origin stands a chance of becoming a *komsomoletz*, and not much of getting a job. A child of bourgeois stock is made to feel his social inferiority as acutely as the child of a parvenu might have been made to feel his in the most aristocratic establishment in England half a century ago.

Everything is done to inculcate Communism and to glorify it, and in an efficient school it is "the thing" to be a Communist. It is religion, patriotism, and sport in one. Young people are being imbued with an attitude not unlike that which was common in Germany before the War. They have a similar self-confidence in the present moral and ultimate material superiority of their system, and the same belief that, one day, those who cannot see the light will be made to bow down before its strength.

CHAPTER XIII

THE FIVE YEAR PLAN AND PRODUCTION

The Communist ideal is the organization of human endeavour so that the life of each individual is completely and inseparably absorbed into the life of society as a whole: and society is conceived as working with the same co-ordinated precision as the machinery which it is considered the highest result of human endeavour to construct and operate. It follows that industrialization, or the mechanization of production, must be a primary objective for a Communist Government in a predominantly agricultural country like the former Russian Empire. The Bolsheviks rely on industrialization both to increase the existing proletarian element on whose support their power rests, and ultimately to proletarianize the mass of naturally individualist peasantry which forms the vast bulk of the population. To these considerations of principle are added urgent considerations of expediency, for it is essential that a régime which proclaims its opposition to the existing social system of the civilized world should be as far as possible economically independent.

The Five Year Plan is an attempt to lay the foundations of a modern industrial State entirely through State enterprise. So far as it is consistent with Communist theory to adopt a Capitalist model, that model is the United States. Methods of large scale mass production conform to Communist ideology, and there are obvious analogies between the size and geographical features of the two countries. The Soviet slogan is "We must catch up and pass America."

The Five Year Plan began to operate on October 1,

1928. It is claimed that the Plan is being fulfilled a good deal faster than was originally expected, and the slogan now is "The Five Year Plan in Four." An outside observer obviously cannot get any accurate check on the progress of so vast a scheme, but it seems quite possible that the Soviet Authorities will have statistical justification for claiming a substantial measure of success before the scheduled time. It must always be remembered, however, that Soviet statistics have a political import. It is necessary to stimulate the ardour of the population and to maintain the momentum required for the achievement of what is nothing less than a consciously directed economic revolution. While, therefore, there do not seem to be any grounds for believing that figures are deliberately falsified, Soviet statistics, like those, be it said, of most partisan organizations, often do not tell the whole truth. When, for instance, it is said that the production of boots exceeds that of pre-war years by so much, it is not stated that there was only one big boot factory in Russia in those days and that the bulk of home production came from the village cobbler, a source for which no figures exist. Again, when it is said that production in a certain industry has been so much in such and such a time, it is not always clear that allowance has been made for defective articles.

Soviet industry cannot be correctly judged unless it is realized that the ordinary standards of measurement can only be applied with important modifications. An American engineer once told me that his advice was asked about some plans for an irrigation dam, and that he gave an adverse opinion on the grounds that the water to be obtained was not worth the expenditure. A tremendous hue and cry was thereupon raised, and a local committee decided that someone must be sent to jail for having put up an unsound scheme. The American was, however, first approached with an appeal to modify his opinion. He eventually agreed to add a paragraph to the effect that whereas such a scheme would not be considered economic in America, the same might not be the case in Russia where conditions were so different.

Costs of production, to take one example, neither have the same meaning nor importance as they have in a capitalist country. It is true that the Soviet Authorities emphasize the necessity of reducing costs of production, and are not satisfied with what has been achieved, but when these costs are reckoned in roubles they are simply a measure of the relative efficiency of various industries in Russia. They have no relation to any absolute, or even world standard. Every reproductive undertaking is counted as so much gain to the national wealth, and the cost of it is not to be measured in roubles, but only in the materials and commodities which have gone to its erection and to the payment of labour. When it is said that oil is exported at a loss, it may only mean a loss taking the rouble at its par value. It does not necessarily mean that there is actually a loss to the State. It is even a matter of comparative indifference whether particular industries show a profit or not, so long as the whole economic turnover of the country shows a gain. Tractors, for instance, are marketed below cost price, because the loss will be more than counter-balanced by the gain in agricultural production. Sometimes, when factories show a deficit, the workers are told that they have not worked efficiently or hard enough and that as they are the owners, they must stand the loss in lowered wages until the deficit is made up. But when the industry makes a loss because of national policy the deficit is made up by a subsidy.

The Five Year Plan is not proceeding smoothly. A scheme worked out in such detail and requiring such exact synchronization was bound to get out of gear. According to the Plan, new blast furnaces and power stations should be ready to supply steel and electricity just when new factories are completed, and new railways should be waiting to carry the increased flow of goods. What is actually happening is that the whole economic fabric of the country is creaking and groaning under an almost unbearable strain. Materials of all kinds are lacking. There are not enough bricks, there is not enough steel, there are not enough locomotives and rolling stock. But the work must go on just the same, because, at all costs, every organization must show that it is keeping up to schedule. Makeshifts, as was shown at Novo-Sibirsk, for instance, are resorted to in order to avoid delay, while preliminary undertakings such as road making, which would save time in the end, are neglected because there is nothing immediately to show for them.

There is a very noticeable difference when the works are under the direction of foreign experts. This dependence on foreign technical assistance is an indication of where the Russians are weakest. There are something like 5,000 Americans and Germans scattered about the country (very few members of any other nationality have been engaged). Wherever one goes, be it to the new coal and iron fields of Siberia, or to the Ural mines, or to the older industrial area of the Donetz Basin, or to the semi-desert regions of Trans-Caucasia and Turkestan, Americans will be found directing new works. The Germans usually occupy subordinate positions in the already established industries. The tale they tell is always the same. The conception of the Plan is excellent, the workman, when shown how to set about a job, is keen and quick to learn, but there are not the men with practical executive ability and knowledge. The older generation of engineers and technicians, who were mostly trained abroad before the Revolution, are out of date, the younger generation is keen, but has only learned from books, and has often only been through an abbreviated intensive course of instruction. Moreover, the younger generation no longer brings an adequate background of home and general education to their technical studies, while capable instructors are rarer than before the Revolution. The lack of intercourse with foreign countries is prejudicing the standard of all the learned professions. It is said that much excellent research work is being done, but the training of doctors, teachers, and others suffers from lack of contact with foreign practice.

The situation is aggravated by political exigencies. It is not only necessary that the work should be done, but that it should be done in the way indicated by the Communist Party. The nominal head of an undertaking is often a member of the Party who has no technical qualifications. An industrial worker may become director of a state farm, an agitator the manager of a factory. The technical subordinates, who have to do the real work, usually belong to the amphibious class of "specialists," which is neither proletarian nor bourgeois. It is indispensable, but it is not above suspicion. Party men are constantly being shifted to prevent them losing the purity of their political faith in concentration in technical efficiency, a process which is often assisted by political intrigue.

In these circumstances the question of foreign technical assistance assumes additional importance. Even before the war Russian industry was largely run under foreign technical direction, and it may well be asked whether the Russians are not even less likely now than formerly to be able to undertake this work. One can hardly be surprised that Russian technical experts are not inclined to take responsibility, and seek shelter behind the opinions of their foreign advisers. There is little doubt that if foreign technical assistance were withdrawn the result would be a substantial decline in efficiency. At present, however, the tendency is to engage more and more foreign experts. It is of course intended that as soon as Russians can be properly trained they should be left to carry on, but it is open to argument whether this day will ever come. There have certainly been cases where the necessity for getting on with the job has resulted in foreign technical experts, originally engaged in an advisory capacity, being given more direct executive control. This is apparently what happened at the Stalingrad "Traktorstroi," and is likely to happen at the Kuzetzk and Magnetogorsk steel works.

The Soviet Authorities are not blind to the dangers that beset them. It remains to be seen whether they will be justified in relying on their ability to train up the rising generation of proletarians to fill the positions of the decimated and repressed bourgeois classes. Of more immediate significance are the attempts to counteract the tendency to careless workmanship which the insistence on production at such high pressure has produced. This is the first step towards inculcating those habits of accuracy and of getting the best results by the shortest route, which are so alien to the Russian character, but so much the essence of efficiency. Without them Russian industry will find it hard to stand on its own feet. A great deal of attention is being given to industrial psychology, and such institutions as the Central Institute of Labour in Moscow are both a training ground and a laboratory from which interesting results may be expected. Meanwhile, in the factories themselves, an intensive propaganda is being constantly waged against slackness. Workers are encouraged to organize themselves in "brigades," which compete against each other. The factory newspapers give weekly results, illustrating the status of the group concerned by representations of various modes of locomotion, from the aeroplane to the tortoise. Films on the same theme are frequently included in the cinema programmes. Money prizes are given for the best producers in a factory. There was a box at a cinema in Kharkov, over which was displayed an inscription in red lights, "For Shock Workers," these being people who had earned a free show.

It may be mentioned that piece-work has been introduced wherever possible, and that the three-shift system is commonly employed. In several factories, which I visited, the work ran in three shifts of seven hours, the night shift receiving an extra hour's pay.

One of the most striking alterations in working conditions is the introduction of the five-day week. This began to be put into force when I was in Russia in 1929. It had not yet become general when I was there in 1930. The idea is that a fifth of the workers in any office, factory, etc., shall be off duty every day, so that everybody gets one day's rest in five, while no office or factory is ever closed. The advantages of the system are supposed to be the additional employment it will give, and the possibilities of increased production. An incidental effect, and a highly desirable one, from the point of view of the Government's anti-religious policy, is the abolishing of Sunday and the old Christian holidays. The only general holidays are now the two days for May Day and the Anniversary of the Bolshevik Revolution (November 7th), and the "World Peace Day" on August 1st. The disadvantages of the scheme are obvious. For instance, everyone's job has to be done by somebody else on one day in five. It may be a good collectivism to say that it ought not to matter what particular individual does a job, but the individuals who do the jobs may take another view, especially when A mislays B's tools, or a customer has to wait while C tries to find out what D did with some relevant correspondence. At present people often forget which is their day off. I have several times made appointments only to find that the person I wanted to see was away. Then the system cuts into social and family relations. Facilities are supposed to be given to members of the same household to arrange for the same day off, but it is not very easy to do this in practice. An abstruse calculation is required before two friends can meet, and it must require good staff work to get the whole of a football team on the field the same afternoon. The difficulty of working such a system is evident and may prove insuperable as a universal rule. Stalin's speech in June 1931 indicated that modifications would be necessary.

Most of what has been said hitherto applies primarily to industry, but agriculture plays just as important a part in the Five Year Plan. The attempt is being made to introduce modern methods of large-scale mechanized farming in a country where the most primitive methods have hitherto existed, in itself a gigantic task, and complicated, even more than in the case of industry, by the peculiar notions of social organization with which it has to be reconciled.

In order to understand what is happening, something must be said about the agrarian system as it existed before the Revolution, at least in as far as peasant holdings are concerned. The Russian village formed a community called the *mir*, which, amongst other things, administered the village common land. When the serfs were freed in the sixties, land was distributed to the villages on the basis of 2½ acres for each adult. This land was held communally, and redistributed among the villagers every six years. It was laid out in strips, and each holding might consist of several strips at a considerable distance from one another, for each person had to share in the good and bad land alike. Not only was this system wasteful of time, but no one was interested in improving the land beyond a certain point, and, the total amount of land remaining the same, the individual's share became smaller as the population grew. Peasants, however, could, and did, buy and lease other land of their own. It was the object of Stolypin's land reforms to facilitate this process, and to turn the peasantry into a class of real individual small-holders. Had this reform been started a generation sooner there might not have been the land hunger which fed the flames of the Revolution. As it was, the process had scarcely begun when the war broke out, but it is interesting to notice that in the Smolensk district, where there are said to have been most small-holdings, there has been an exceptionally large portion of *kulaki*, or wealthier peasants. The same is probably true of Siberia also, where there were few big landlords, but many large farms held by colonists.

At the beginning of the Revolution the peasants seized as much land as was within their reach, though many of the large properties fell directly into the hands of the State. The number of individual peasant holdings increased very much between 1917 and 1924, but production decreased greatly during the period of Civil War and War Communism. It was always the intention of the Soviet Authorities to introduce some form of collectivization, and to carry the class war into the villages, but within the last year or two the campaign against the comparatively well-to-do peasant has been waged with as much fierceness as that which characterized the earlier struggle against the big landlord. Up till recently it has been necessary to be lenient with the individualist peasant so as not to risk a breakdown of the food supply. It is thought that now the State farms are organized on a larger scale, collectivization can be pushed on with less risk. The risk, however, is still there, hence the alternating policies of terrorism and cajolement, which are from time to time adopted.

It is claimed that the time is in sight when what is known as the "socialized sector" of agriculture will produce enough to make the country independent of the "private sector." State farms, namely farms run directly by a State trading organization such as the grain or milk trusts, have been widely developed, and appear, generally speaking, to be reasonably well run. The collective farms do not seem to be doing so well. The best elements in the village have probably been ousted as *kulaki*. There is a great deal too much talk and too little work done. Nevertheless, as the introduction of tractors and other agricultural machinery progresses, much greater production is possible than with the primitive methods hitherto almost universally employed.

Considering the permanent state of unsettlement in which the collectivization and anti-*kulak* campaigns keep the countryside, it is surprising that results are as good as they are. During the great campaign in the winter of 1929 something like half the live-stock in the country is said to have been slaughtered rather than that it should be yielded up to the "collective." Even if this be an exaggeration no one denies that the subsequent shortage of meat was the result. Apart from material losses, the ruthlessness of the campaign involved immense hardship, and it must be remembered that the drain on some of the sturdiest elements in the country has been continuous. The social structure of whole districts has been violently altered. Undesirable elements are transported to other parts of the country, and strangers come in to take their places. The Cossacks, for instance, have been entirely broken up as an organized class. Thousands of people have been packed off, with what they can carry, to live or die in the frozen North. The word *kulak* covers a multitude of sins. It may mean someone whose property it is desirable to seize in order to make up the quota of grain demanded by the Government. It may mean an influential person who made himself unpopular with the local authorities.

The picture conveyed by a description of the facts which any careful observer must record is at first sight a gloomy one. It is necessary, however, to guard against attributing the same consequences to incompetence, disorganization, privation, and oppression in Russia as would be justified in a Western country. Notwithstanding evidence to the contrary, it is rare to find any foreigner, who has been in close touch with the situation for any length of time, so pessimistic as to forecast a breakdown. Most assert both that the position of the present régime is unshakeable, and that the final result of the present economic effort will be to leave the country as a whole substantially richer than it was. Whatever may be said about the methods by which the Five Year Plan is being carried through, the fact remains that a large proportion of the national income is yearly being capitalized, and that the productive capacity of the country is being steadily increased. Several competent observers put the efficiency of the Soviet economic system at about 60 per cent. of what it might be in English, American, or German hands, but, even so, there is a substantial margin of achievement left. Whether it will be possible for the Bolsheviks to advance, as they expect to do, from State Capitalism to something nearer pure Communism seems improbable. It is always when the Party insists on putting some purely Communist idea into operation that crises occur.

The critical point remains where it has always been, in the land and the peasantry. There is one absolutely essential requirement for the continued development of the country without a breakdown and that is its ability to feed itself. The failure to contrive an effective system of agricultural production by insisting on a policy of centralized collectivization might have disastrous effects, but it would be rash to count on such a failure.

The fulfilment of the Five Year Plan is a tactical objective. The fate of the present régime is not necessarily involved in its complete attainment. Naturally a failure so marked as to lead to a breakdown of the apparatus of government would imply much more than a tactical defeat. On the other hand a partial failure, leaving the Government able to consolidate a new line after claiming substantial successes, might rather increase than diminish its strength. This is what happened when the New Economic Policy was introduced, and, though the present situation seems to approximate more and more to the conditions of the War Communism period, it is not yet so bad as it was in 1920 and 1921. "War Communism" was a confused attempt to impose Communism by a *coup de main*. "Nep" had strategic significance because it involved the re-casting of the whole plan of campaign. The Five Year Plan is in a different category of operations. It is an offensive in a war of attrition. Its object is to gain certain economic positions. It means the acquisition of material resources, without which the morale of the population in the rear cannot be sustained, and an aggressive foreign policy cannot be attempted.

It does not look as if the Five Year Plan was going to produce all the results claimed for it, but, unless the Bolsheviks are so foolish as to ignore facts, they will not force the pace to the breaking-point. There is still a large balance of probability in favour of their being able to create conditions under which the Soviet Union could supply the bulk of its requirements for a standard of living much below that of Western countries, but which would mark an advance on what the Russian masses have hitherto known. The attempt to whip up effort by appeals to get the Five Year Plan finished in four years may partly be due to a realization of the difficulty of inducing the population to stay the full course. It would be easy to camouflage shortcomings by blaming Capitalism for the world economic depression, which is throwing out their foreign trade calculations, and at the same time to make a favourable comparison between actual achievement and the original estimates, which have been progressively raised as the Plan proceeded. If it is true that a Fifteen Year Plan is being prepared to follow the Five Year Plan, it is clear that it is not intended to maintain the present hectic *tempo* indefinitely. No one could contemplate fifteen years of the present exhausting efforts with equanimity, and it must be that a more normal and steady course of development is foreshadowed.

CHAPTER XIV

THE FIVE YEAR PLAN AND THE STANDARDS OF LIFE AND LABOUR

The Five Year Plan was considered in the last chapter from the point of view of the Government. Its effect on the people must now be examined, and an answer found to the riddle of how a country so impoverished by revolution and so largely dependent on its own resources could embark on such a gigantic undertaking.

The cost of the Five Year Plan falls entirely on the people. There is no longer a wealthy minority to be mulcted in taxation. The whole burden falls on the masses. The wretched conditions of life now prevailing are the result of the sacrifices they have been called upon to make.

In the first place, capital equipment and technical assistance are required from abroad, and must be paid for by exports. The population is deliberately kept on short commons so that as much oil, wheat, timber, butter, eggs, and every other commodity as can be collected without causing a famine may be sent abroad. The chief reason for the recent epidemic of Soviet "dumping" is the fall in world prices, which has forced the Soviet Government to sell a much larger quantity of goods in order to realize the sums needed to meet its foreign obligations.

In the second place, the State only supplies a bare minimum of goods for consumption, because its energies are concentrated on building up the basic productive industries. Capital expenditure is being met out of income. Owing to the State's monopoly of foreign trade, and its control of foreign trade, the Government can direct the use of a large proportion of the national income. The Five

A POSTER IN WHICH LENIN IS SHOWN DISPLAYING THE NEW COMMUNIST ERA TO THE ASIATIC PEOPLES. KRUPSKAYA, HIS WIDOW, IS SEEN WRITING MESSAGES IN THEIR VARIOUS LANGUAGES

Year Plan is financed out of the compulsory savings of the people.

The peculiarity of the financial position is that the Government's control of trade enables the country to be virtually independent of the rest of the world. There is no free market in currency. Rates of exchange are officially fixed at about par, and, although much lower unofficial rates can be obtained abroad, the business done is not large and must chiefly be for illegal purposes, since the import and export of roubles into and out of Russia is prohibited. Inside Russia one is told that foreign currency can be sold for a handsome premium. I have heard dollars, nominally worth two roubles, quoted at ten and even as much as forty roubles. Such transactions are, however, strictly illegal, and expose the participants to very severe penalities. The official rate of exchange is purely arbitrary, and, even were it possible to make allowances for the different conditions under which commercial transactions are conducted, no satisfactory standard of comparison with prices and wages in other countries exists. The internal value of the rouble cannot be translated into terms of foreign currencies.

It is perhaps misleading to speak of inflation in the ordinary sense in connection with Russia, but many of the symptoms are there. The currency issue has been rapidly expanded, and no corresponding supply of commodities has been put on the market. This is partly due to the fact that more and more money is required to pay the increasing number of persons employed on new works which do not yet produce anything. Money is useless to a person beyond the comparatively small sum required to meet his immediate needs.

Efforts are made to induce people to utilize the only forms of investment which exist, namely savings banks and internal loans. The success of this expedient is limited, even though moral pressure is applied. The result, combined with the effects of political uncertainty, is a certain shyness of paper roubles. There is a tendency to hoard silver, and to convert money into goods at every opportunity.[1] Better value can be obtained on the open market by barter than for cash. These factors only operate, however, in a small section of the economic field, since the vast bulk of financial transactions are Government transactions. Moreover, there can be no question of a flight from the rouble because there is no alternative currency.

Private trade is insignificant in relation to the business of the whole country, but it is still a substantial factor so far as individuals are concerned. Sixteen per cent. of the retail trade remains in private hands, but the real importance of the open market lies in the fact that it supplies a large proportion of essential foodstuffs. During the eight months, October 1929 to May 1930, only 5·3 per cent. of manufactured articles were sold on the open market, but 26 per cent. of agricultural produce, and this included 65 per cent. of the butter, 60 per cent. of the milk and eggs, and 14 per cent. of the meat sold in the country. Articles of prime necessity are either rationed in such small quantities, or the supply is so irregular, that few people outside Moscow and some other big towns depend entirely on the controlled market for food supplies. The *Moskauer Rundschau* (a German weekly newspaper published with official sanction) stated in August 1930 that the proportion of a worker's purchases made in the open market was 28 per cent. in the

[1] While I was in Moscow in 1930 supplies of sugar, on one occasion, and of feathers for stuffing pillows, on another occasion, were released in the controlled market at fixed prices without restriction on the amount any individual might buy. Both times the stocks were sold out in a day, people buying up to the limit of their spare cash and of their ability to carry the stuff away.

Ural Region, 21 per cent. in White Russia, and 17 per cent. in the North Caucasus Region.

Prices in the controlled and open market differ widely. The open market prices are much the higher. Butter may cost as much as 25 roubles a kilo, and is never likely to be less than 10 roubles a kilo. Eggs in Siberia in August 1930 were from 20 to 25 kopeks each, and bread 2 roubles a kilo. On the Volga, a few weeks later, a roll of white bread, not more than a pound in weight, cost 1 rouble. Boots cost from 100 to 150 roubles a pair. These prices were from five to ten times the controlled prices. People can afford goods at such prices because they cannot satisfy their requirements in the controlled market, and there is always a margin of unexpended wages and salaries waiting for an outlet. The difference between controlled and open prices is partly accounted for by competition, and partly by the disabilities under which private traders suffer and for which they have to recoup themselves.

There is, naturally, a temptation to buy in the controlled market for reselling in the open market at a huge profit. This is a serious offence, generally known as "speculation," and may be punishable by death.

It is difficult to gauge the standard of living under such conditions. The value of wages and salaries depends to some extent on what proportion is spent in the controlled and what proportion in the open market, as well as on the special rates and free services to which people are entitled according to their social status. The official rations are a bare subsistence minimum. Bread, which is a much more important article of food in Russia than in Western Europe, is seldom lacking. A regular factory worker gets a good meal in the canteen for a very small charge, say, 30 or 40 kopeks. There are many public dining-rooms in the larger towns where meals of varying cost and quality can be obtained without restriction.

Clothes are harder to get than food, and have to be made to last longer than the quality justifies. It is common to hear people grumbling because a new pair of shoes or goloshes have split after having been worn a week or two. The stores at the new works arising out of the Five Year Plan seem to be comparatively well stocked in order to attract workers, and as an inducement to permanence of employment.

The regular industrial worker has the advantage of important free social services. His children are well cared for without charge whenever there are crèches and kindergartens attached to factories. He may be housed rent free, and as a member of a Trade Union he obtains admission to museums, theatres, and cinemas at reduced rates. He is entitled to a yearly holiday on full pay, and, if he is lucky, he may get a free trip to the Caucasus or the Crimea. This type of worker is, however, a favoured minority. The casual labourer, the peasant, and the office worker is not so fortunately situated.

Is anyone materially better off because of the Revolution? The short answer is that until the final results of the Five Year Plan are known nothing can be said for certain. It is important, however, that this question should not be confused by any comparison between the standard of living in Russia and Western countries. The worker and peasant lived before the Revolution, and still live, in conditions which no Englishman would tolerate. How far anyone is actually better off than he was is hard to ascertain, but no one seems to suggest that there is, as yet, any very marked difference. Supporters of the present régime point out the improvement since the worst years of revolutionary disorganization, and emphasize the leeway that has had to be made up. It is absurd, however, to say, as I have heard it said quite seriously, that the rise in the standard of living in Russia has been greater than in England during the last ten years. The obvious truth that the higher the standard from which one starts, the more difficult, and the slower, must the rate of progress be, is conveniently forgotten.

Speaking generally, it may be said that in some ways a few people are better off, but that in most ways practically everybody is worse off. The bourgeoisie and the intelligentsia are much worse off in every way. They are meant to be. The peasant, who forms nine-tenths of the population, has got more land, but not so much as he hoped, and, until the Government comes to terms with him, and modern agricultural methods begin to be generally adopted, he will gain nothing materially by the substitution of officials for the local squire. The industrial worker is the best off, but complaints are not wanting that the "good time" he hoped for is a long time coming. His hours are shorter. He has opportunities of taking a more active part in organizing his working and social life. He gets a good deal done for him. On the other hand, the practice of supplying so much in services and kind, that would elsewhere be paid in money, curtails his freedom to please himself. Nor is he given enough for his needs. Then there are deductions from wages for political and other purposes to be considered. Some of these, such as subscriptions to Government Loans and Funds, are supposed to be voluntary, but this is something of a euphemism. Moreover, he cannot save, and he cannot become his own master.[1]

[1] The function of "organized labour" is, of course, fundamentally altered in theory under the Soviet régime. Now that the proletariat has become the ruling class there should be no need to fight for better conditions. The "capitalist exploiter" has vanished. Trade Unions simply become the instruments for applying Government policy in its vocational aspects. That the

This brings me to the general question of labour conditions, one with which the future of the Soviet régime is intimately connected.

Labour in Russia is by nature much more migratory than in the more industrialized countries of the West. It was usual for factory workers before the Revolution to remain officially domiciled in their native villages. Workers went to and fro between town and country, and might be employed for part of the year in a factory and for the rest on the land. The Donetz coal-mines, for instance, had a different personnel in summer than in winter. Even now the interchange has not ceased. A large proportion of the labour engaged in the various construction works under the Five Year Plan is peasant labour. Contrariwise, the fact that special brigades of industrial workers are sent into the country to stimulate and direct collectivization is not so absurd as it seems. Many industrial workers have still close ties with the land.

One of the problems of the Soviet Authorities is to make labour more stable. There are constant complaints that workers will not stay any length of time in the same employment. One reason is that living conditions are not good enough. The permanent staff at a works may be well enough fed, but it seems that the rations provided for the lower grades of workers is insufficient in view of the heavy manual labour they are required to do. The case of the Donetz miners referred to in Chapter X is an example. Labour is scarce and fitful in the port of Leningrad for the same reason. Workmen will not do the heavy labour of loading timber ships under the prevailing conditions. Workers recruited from distant villages for new construc-

need for defence against the State as the only employer is just as great as it is against multitudinous capitalist employers seems to be occasionally realized, but such a heretical doctrine is naturally discouraged.

tion works often come only because they see a chance of moving at public expense. When they reach their destination many of them go off after a week or a fortnight's work. Efforts are made to provide decent housing accommodation at these new works, but building cannot keep pace with requirements. In the neighbourhood of big cities—Baku and Kharhov are outstanding examples—whole towns of new houses have sprung up in connection with new enterprises, but in remoter parts it is common to find workmen living under canvas or in turf dugouts on a hillside.

The number of industrial workers is increasing rapidly with the progress of the Five Year Plan, and energetic steps are needed to anchor the new proletariat to their jobs. Special propaganda brigades go about preaching the doctrine of collective ownership. The workman is told that he owns the place where he works and that he has a social duty to stay there and see things through. Another device is to induce workmen to sign long-term contracts. The tendency for neighbouring works to compete for labour by offering higher wages is also being eliminated.

While the Authorities are only gradually getting a hold on this large floating mass of low-grade labour, the situation is quite otherwise with the old proletariat and the "specialists." These classes have very little freedom of movement. If a man leaves a job with a note on his papers that he has gone at his own request he will find it extremely difficult to find other employment unless there is a great shortage in his particular trade. "Specialists" find it very difficult even to get a transfer.

It is obviously necessary, with growing industrial development, that permanency of occupation should be encouraged among the new industrial population, but the action of the Authorities tends to go far beyond what is strictly necessary. The justification put forward is the progress of socialization. It seems that the socialization of industry involves the robotization of the proletariat.

That socialization means the loss of all individual freedom is made even clearer by the position in the country districts. Here the aim of collectivization is not only the excellent one of improving the methods of farming, but also the much more debatable one of proletarianizing the peasantry. So far as the *sovhozi* (State farms) are concerned the labourer is already in the position of a wage-earner. What is more interesting is the process by which in the *kolhozi* (Collective farms) also the peasant is losing his independence. The nucleus of the *kolhozi* are the *bedniki* (poor peasants), who never had any property. The anti-*kulak* campaign has made it practically impossible for anyone to hold more private property in the shape of live-stock or agricultural implements than just serves to produce the needs of a family. The members of a *kolhoz* are swelled by people who, having nothing left of their own, have no alternative but to join a collective organization, or it may be that *kolhozi* are formed to save what little is left. The result is that the *kolhozi* are often poorly equipped, and run by the least thrifty and enterprising members of the community. The problem is how to raise the standard of administration and farming in the *kolhoz*. It is difficult to see how this can be done without importing managers and agronomists, and thus assimilating the *kolhoz* to the position of the *sovhoz*, on which they are likely to become increasingly dependent for advice and the loan of machinery. It may well be that in many *kolhozi* the necessity of organizing better production will, in fact, do away with its theoretically co-operative basis, and turn the member of a *kolhoz* into something very like a wage-earner.

Although the individual has not the same freedom to dispose of his labour as in this country, it is going too far to describe labour generally as forced. The Soviet Authorities cannot, however, deny that forced labour exists, although they would perhaps prefer to call it by another name. There is no concealment of the fact that *kulaki*, who have been "liquidated," have been deported to the number of well over a million and set to work, chiefly in the lumber districts of the North. As a *kulak*, the unfortunate man has no civic rights. Like a heretic condemned to the galleys by the Spanish Inquisition, it is considered that he ought to think himself lucky to be given a chance of salvation by doing something useful.

The bulk of the labour in the timber camps probably consists either of *kulaki*, and similar political offenders, or of nominally "free" labour recruited under pressure. It is generally stated that the villages in the lumber districts have to provide a certain quota of men and horses for work during the winter when farming is at a standstill. If sufficient volunteers are not forthcoming, the quota is made up by ballot or men are told off by the village Soviet. As a man is expected to keep his horse as well as himself on a wage of not more than 2½ roubles a day, it is clear that volunteers will be few. There are, of course, a large number of professional lumbermen, who have no other means of livelihood, and there may be a few "shock brigades" of enthusiastic Communists, who are probably quite unfitted for the work and whose job is really to provide moral stimulus. It is not surprising if women are employed, as they habitually perform heavy labour in Russia, and are encouraged to do so under the Soviet system.

Conditions in the timber camps undoubtedly differ greatly. Some are said to possess bath-houses, reading-rooms, heated quarters, and canteens where more or less adequate meals can be obtained at low charges. Others are extremely primitive, and this is where one would expect to find most of the deportees. Given a brutal overseer, starvation and ill-treatment involving numerous deaths are more than possible. No one would get into serious trouble for the death of a few *kulaki*.

In any case, workers in the timber districts are likely to be worse off for food than elsewhere. There would be fewer opportunities in these sparsely inhabited regions of supplementing official rations by purchases in the private market, on which, as has already been stated, workers in the provinces rely for between 15 per cent. and 25 per cent. of their food supplies. As regards clothing, official figures declare that Centrosoyuz provided the timber districts during January and February, 1931, with 893,000 pairs of boots, 344,000 pairs of shoes, 109,000 pairs of *valenki* (felt knee-boots), 368,000 fur jackets and nearly 5,000,000 pairs of gloves or mits. Even if these supplies cover several million people, it seems that in these respects, at any rate, the timber workers are as well provided for as any other section of the population. After all, it is not in the interest of the Soviet Government that it should allow the physical efficiency of workers in one of its most remunerative export businesses to fall too low. Still, quite clearly, this is not the employment one would choose if one could help it.

Although it is not always easy to draw the line between forced and convict labour, the latter, in the sense of the unpaid labour of persons sentenced on definite criminal charges, can hardly be an appreciable economic factor. Prisoners are, however, usually given work of some kind. An interesting example is that of a camp of some thirty convicts which a party of foreigners came across accidentally while on a shooting expedition. Their task was to distil turpentine. They were given a pound and a half of bread a day each, and nothing more. They had to build their own shelter. A militiaman visited them once a day to call the roll. There was no permanent guard. Escape was apparently considered impossible. This happened in summer. Whether they were moved to better quarters in winter is uncertain, but it is hardly possible that they could survive in the open in such a rigorous climate.[1]

It has been said that the collectivization of the peasantry virtually amounts to the reintroduction of serfdom. Strictly speaking, this is not a proposition which could be sustained, but as a rhetorical expression it contains some truth. On the other hand, it is also true that for the first time in history the Russian peasant is being taught to organize himself, and, when the process has developed further, the effect may be very important. Already it is said that the Authorities find it harder to squeeze an excessive quota of grain out of a *kolhoz* than out of individual peasants. It may be that some day the peasants will develop an organized political consciousness of their own, which will differ fundamentally from the essentially urban outlook of Communism.

[1] The *Report on Russian Timber Camps* (Benn, 1931), made on behalf of the Anti-Slavery Society and the Howard League for Penal Reform, seems to be the most complete and impartial investigation of the whole question yet made.

CHAPTER XV

WILL BOLSHEVISM LAST?

If conditions of life in town and country are such as have been described, why do people stand them? Do any large number of people really think that the Five Year Plan, with its social as well as its economic implications, is worth all this bullying and all these privations? There are two answers.

The first answer is that the Five Year Plan represents something more than the policy of a Communist Government. It also stands for reconstruction, for better times to come, and for the economic progress of Russia. Few really understand and care about the fulfilment of the Five Year Plan as a policy, but many are mesmerized by the hopes held out to them. The example of the ardent Communists, the effect of propaganda, unhindered by counter-propaganda, suffice to secure the benevolent neutrality of large numbers among a habitually docile and long-suffering population. Moreover, there are not wanting those who conform because it pays, and those for whom the fulfilment of the Plan provides an interest in their work.

The second answer is that public opinion matters comparatively little. There is a point, of course, beyond which even the Communist Party dare not go, but foreigners, imbued with democratic traditions, can easily miscalculate the effects of popular unrest. To hear the continuous grumbling among all classes, it might reasonably be concluded that the country was seething with discontent. Perhaps it is, but no one seems to think there is anything to be done. There are neither the means nor the will. A million people might revolt without upsetting the country as a whole. A fatalistic helplessness seems endemic in the people.

Half a century of dogged and persistent labour, crowned by the efforts of a great leader, assisted by the circumstances of an exhausting foreign war, were needed to overthrow a tottering monarchy and place the Bolsheviks in power. A decade has not seen them weaken.

Will Bolshevism last, then? There can be no direct answer to such a question, but it is worth asking in order to consider a variety of possibilities and arrange them according to their probability. I hope, however, that no one will think I am posing as a prophet.

If by "Will Bolshevism last?" is meant, "Will Communism eventually triumph?" the answer is almost certainly "No." The concessions which Communism must make to human nature and to the logic of events, if it is to be at all workable, seem to be such as would fundamentally alter its principles. Its materialistic and mechanistic philosophy, with the consequent rejection of spiritual religion and of personal liberty, is too narrow and too intellectual to be the permanent basis of a social system. Man is not purely an economic animal, nor can his spiritual instincts be extinguished. Even were Communism to be successfully imposed on Russia it would inevitably come to grief in the conflict which the pursuit of World Revolution would precipitate.

On the other hand, if the question means, "Will the present régime collapse?" the answer is almost equally certainly "No." A repetition of 1917 is most unlikely, except as a result of widespread famine or unsuccessful war. This generation has had enough of revolution.

If, therefore, by "Will Bolshevism last?" is meant, "Will the Communist Party remain in power for another decade?" the answer is that it probably will, for lack of an alternative, if for no other reason. It does not follow, however, that the situation is static.

The political changes that are likely to occur in the near future must be looked for within the Communist Party. At present the dictatorship of official Communism does not seem in jeopardy, but disintegrating forces are at work. Ruling out complete triumph or collapse, the Communist Party is faced with two alternatives, either to follow the tradition of judicious realism inherited from Lenin, or to stand by its doctrinal guns whatever the consequences. The dictatorship of the Party is the principle at stake. Will the dictators, in case of need, rely on popular support at the expense of strict Communist theory, or will they rely solely on the strength of a well-drilled party machine?

The first alternative means an eventual compromise with bourgeois ideas, but it is the surest way of preserving the dictatorship. A strong Central Government is required in Russia, at least until the economic position is assured. Concessions that would satisfy the majority of the population would put off the realization of Communism indefinitely, but it would reconcile the country to its present rulers. Peace would have been declared in the class war.

The second alternative means fighting the class war to a finish, with the risk of having to make the party machine so rigid that a bad defeat would break it up. The practice of expelling "heretics" from the Party has not so far had serious political consequences because the retention of power by the Communist Party is still regarded as essential even by those who are expelled. But should the official Communists ever show signs of losing their grip on the situation and of heading for a collapse, an organized Communist opposition might come into existence. With two regular Communist parties in the field the dictatorship comes to an end. Although at first the conflict would be between different brands of Communism, opposition to Communism itself could no longer be suppressed. Political fluidity would be restored.

There can hardly be any doubt as to which alternative sound statesmanship should choose. Lenin himself showed that while it was necessary to be absolutely uncompromising in order to gain power, compromise was justified in order to keep it. Stalin is a worthy disciple of Lenin, but he lacks many of his qualities. He may not find the right policy an easy one.

Stalin's problem is to know just how far he can go towards putting Communism into practice. Unless he goes far enough, his followers will be dissatisfied. If he goes too far there will be a smash. On the whole the tendency is to avoid a smash at the risk of political trouble. A party will yield to argument, but facts will not. The most sensational recent example was the sudden alteration of the collectivization policy at the beginning of 1930. After having given the Party its head to annihilate the *kulak* and force the peasants into collective farms, Stalin, impressed by the effects on the food supply, and disturbed by murmurs in the army, suddenly applied the brake. The Party obeyed.

At the same time, what some call realism others call opportunism. Every time Communism is checked it is weakened, and some think that the danger to Communism is greater when the check takes the form of restraining enthusiasm than when it is brought about by compromise with unpleasant facts. This fear lest the momentum of Communism should slacken because the apostles and disciples of the movement are becoming politicians and bureaucrats has been voiced by Trotsky and others. The danger is a real one. A revolutionary faith like Communism cannot live in an atmosphere of settled order. The more settled conditions in Russia become the more difficult will it be to keep up enthusiasm. There are those who, believing as all good Communists should that the ultimate success of Communism is inevitable, would rather see Communism crash in Russia than have the purity of its doctrine contaminated by compromise. They are probably right in believing that Communism cannot evolve without ceasing to be Communism, that it must fight or perish.

This type of opinion is held both by older purists and by a section of the younger generation. Part of its significance lies in its tendency to encourage a premature attempt to force the issue with the rest of the world. There is every indication that though the Bolshevik leaders have not given up the idea of world revolution supported by Soviet arms, they have no intention of adopting an aggressive foreign policy until the internal situation is secure enough to support an open struggle.[1] At present they are doing no more than fish in troubled waters. There is always a chance, of course,

[1] It is difficult to form any opinion of the real extent and effectiveness of Soviet military preparations. Such matters are obviously not discussed with foreigners by anyone possessing inside knowledge, and there is little for the ordinary traveller to observe. The loyalty of the Red Army to the present régime does not seem to be questioned. The soldiers are well looked after and they can, of course, be more easily propaganded than any other section of the people. The Army is, in fact, a very effective school of Communism, and a particularly important one because it is mostly recruited from the villages, where time-expired men may be expected to have considerable influence. For this reason also, the Army provides a useful indication of peasant opinion. It was partly owing to information obtained through letters received by soldiers, and to the dissatisfaction revealed in them, that the collectivization campaign was abruptly modified at the beginning of 1930.

So far as casual observation goes, the Red Army does not make a very good impression. Soldiers usually look slovenly and dirty, march badly, and handle their rifles carelessly. This is particularly noticeable in the provinces. The G.P.U. troops are in quite a different class, but there are only a few thousand of them. The general opinion, however, seems to be that the Army as a whole is as good as the pre-war Russian Army. It would be formidable in defence, but of no more than moderate value for an offensive campaign.

that events may be too strong for them, but a more serious danger is the impetuosity of the fanatics. Many of these people have been brought up on such mendacious presentations of the facts and tendencies of the modern world that they may both overestimate their own powers and be hopelessly at fault in their appreciation of the situation in other countries. Although, as the older generation of Bolsheviks, with their background of foreign exile, dies out, Communism in Russia is likely to become less rather than more international, there is always the chance of a situation arising which would bring the international tradition into the foreground again. Even if the World Revolution were to fade from the active Communist consciousness as the apprehension of the Day of Judgment faded from that of early Christianity, the Third International might yet remain to bear witness to the ideal of Universality in the same way as the Catholic Church has done. And events may yet occur in China, in India, or even in Germany, which might encourage the young hotheads to put all they have been taught to the test of arms. Even if ultimate defeat were certain no one could estimate the effects of such a conflict on civilization.

The question of leadership is evidently vital. Everything depends on the character of the actual head of affairs. Stalin is an able man and has so far coped successfully with the problems that have arisen. But Stalin's strength seems to lie rather in his gifts as a political organizer than as a constructive statesman. When he is gone there is no saying what may happen, for one of the consequences of his somewhat narrow outlook has been to alienate many of the other most experienced leaders. Trotsky, Kamenev, Zinoviev, Rykov, and many more have either been expelled from the Party or reduced to the ranks. Their places have been taken by men whose primary qualification is that they are safe. Readiness to obey orders rather than administrative ability seems more and more to be the test of preferment. The older generation of Bolsheviks, who were single-minded and had a wide experience of the world, have not infrequently made way for careerists and pedants.

If the strength of the Communist Party depended entirely on its own resources, the outlook would indicate its gradual decline, but the Communist Party is really only the narrow form into which the energy released by the Revolution has been forced.

Many people have wondered at the comparative ease with which the tiny Communist minority has established and maintained its domination over a population more than ten times its number. The innate apathy of the Russian people does not, I am convinced, supply the whole answer. The fact that resistance to the Bolsheviks has mostly been passive accounts largely, it is true, for their having been able to set up Communism as the official social order, but even terrorism, acting on a traditional subservience to despotism, would not have sufficed to maintain them in power had they not received the support of those to whom the desire for a new order of some sort was a potent influence. None of the counter-revolutionary movements supplied that need. A vast reservoir of human energy was released by the Revolution. It was almost unconscious and entirely without form. The Bolshevik régime survived, not because it was Communist, but because it was able to catch up and give expression to a great deal of this underlying spiritual ferment. What gives Bolshevism life is not its Marxian doctrines, but its correspondence to a current of thought which is noticeable outside as well as inside Russia, the kind of thought which is much in favour among our young intellectuals, irreverent, irreligious, amoral, mechanistic, and materialistic in its expression, but vital, because it is founded on a realization of the failure of an old dispensation, and goes forward to conquer a new heaven. This is something more than what Communism has hitherto implied, but it may be what Communism will come to mean, and if so there are far more Communists among us than we suspect. Bolshevism makes its appeal to this side of the younger generation's mind, and what they will make of it no man can tell. But the tendency of most intellectual movements is to dissipate themselves, and it seems more than likely that the narrower aims of old-fashioned Bolshevism will gradually fade.

CHAPTER XVI

BOLSHEVISM CONTRA MUNDUM

The conclusion that Bolshevism will neither succeed nor fail is too vague to be left without further explanation. What it means is that while Bolshevism is strong enough to have a profound effect on the development of Russia and some influence on the world at large, it is strong enough neither to remain unaffected by the material on which it works nor to sweep over the human race like a new Islam.

Russia remains Russia, even if it is an altered Russia. *Plus ça change, plus c'est la même chose.* A tremendous social upheaval has taken place in Russia, but Russian methods and Russian habits of mind are too deeply planted to be eradicated by orders from above, especially when the rulers themselves are children of the same environment.

Many are the observations made by foreigners in the past which might refer to the present day.

Sir Bernard Pares, describing a journey made in 1907, writes in his recent book:[1] "We passed through Perm, where we saw a number of convicts in chains marching up to the town from the river. They looked full of bitter protest; they were probably on their way to Siberia. At this time the Government sent into exile whole masses of men and women, and vengeance was taken for everything that had been done in all the troubled years." The same might be said about the forced labour gangs of to-day. Laurence Oliphant, who travelled through Russia in 1852, made the following comments on the economic conditions of that time. "The whole system seems most elaborately devised to destroy all enterprise, and to depress as much

[1] *Russian Memories*, p. 157.

as possible the spirit of trade, in a country which naturally possesses it in but a very limited degree; and it must be long ere the resources of the country can be properly developed while the Government seeks its own aggrandisement regardless of the prosperity of the community."[1] These words could appropriately be used of the Five Year Plan from the point of view of subordination of the needs of the people to the realization of Communist theories. Oliphant further wrote: "It is evident that an extensive intercourse with European nations would open the eyes of this enslaved population, and introduce those principles of freedom which would soon prove utterly subversive to the imperial power as it at present exists."[2] Substituting the word "Bolshevik" for "Imperial" this is a view which can reasonably be held at the present time.

The Russian character has not changed in essentials but only in its mode of expression. Many mistakes are made in appreciating the Russian situation because people in England insist on applying the same critical standards to Russians as they would to themselves. We are accustomed to think of Russia as a European Power, and to assume we know all about Russians. We really need to approach the study of Russia with the same diffidence as we should feel in studying China.

The Russian is a blend of European and Asiatic. Along with the fertile imagination of the Slav he has inherited the sterile fatalism of the Tatar. Behind a few generations of association with the West he has centuries of subjugation to a series of Oriental despotisms. He is at the same time impulsive and apathetic, unstable and stolid, lacking in perseverance yet endlessly patient, full of a sense of the dramatic yet slow to act. He is temperamentally a person

[1] *The Russian Shores of the Black Sea, etc.* (Blackwood, 1853).
[2] Ibid.

of extreme moods, and he lives in a world of dreams which he has not the ability to realize. He will aim at the moon and neglect the most elementary necessities of his immediate surroundings. The gap between conception and performance is one which he has the utmost difficulty in bridging. *Niechevo*[1] and *seichass*[2] are the words which constant reiteration make the foundation of the foreigner's Russian vocabulary. There is a certain characteristically peasant concreteness about the Russian mind where personal interests are concerned, but the predominant impression is one of indefiniteness. A conversation begun on some specific subject will nearly always swell insensibly to a discussion of general principles. Particular points run together like notes played on the piano with the loud pedal held down. Perhaps it is this irresistible attraction of universals which makes Russians so easily affected by mass suggestion.

Compared to an Englishman, what the Russian particularly lacks is that personal independence which is conveyed by the German word *Selbstständichkeit*. How much of this is inborn and how much due to environment is hard to say, but the fact remains that no Russian has anything but the vaguest conception of the meaning of liberty. The intelligentsia knew of it as a liberal ideal, but had the crudest notions of its application. The masses have still to learn that it is not merely a release from social restrictions. Russians are accustomed to the reign of authority rather than the reign of law. They accept subjection to arbitrary power, which we regard as something akin to slavery, as a normal condition. Liberty, and particularly its manifestation in democratic political institutions, grows out of organization from the bottom. Though the Russian has

[1] "Never mind."

[2] Literally "in an hour," but used as the equivalent of "immediately."

a strong collective sense, he has not yet learnt to discipline it, and thus create a framework within which the individual may freely express himself. England passed through this stage five hundred years ago. For an apt analogy with the political mentality of the Russian peasant during the Revolution we should have to go back to Wat Tyler and the Wars of the Roses. To say that a Russian is incapable of understanding democracy is only as true as it would be to say that a child cannot understand John Stuart Mill. He may come to do so, but in the process he must pass through the fire of a hard school. Russia is absorbing modern ideas in its own way, which is a different way from ours.

The old and the new are so bewilderingly mixed, in spite of the obvious contrast between them, that the balance between them is not easily kept. On the one hand everything can be seen in the light of a struggle towards a new and better world. Russia, it may be said, had to die in order to be reborn. The débris of the past seems of small account beside the signs of fresh life, and of long-suppressed energy released. On the other hand, everything can be seen as evidence of an orgy of destruction. The discrepancy between the standards of living in and out of Russia is glaring. The lack of comfort, refinement, beauty, gaiety, and all the decorations of life saddens and repels. The attacks on all that Western civilization reverences and admires strike home with a shock of horror. Sometimes one, sometimes the other point of view gets the upper hand on the observer who is trying to be unprejudiced. Neither represents the whole truth, and it is immensely difficult to focus the two at once. When it comes to practical politics the trouble is that the development of Communism and of the new Russia are so interwoven that to hinder the one is to retard the other. This can easily be shown by examples in the departments of social welfare, education, industrial reconstruction, and the modernization of agriculture. It is almost impossible to attack the present régime without attacking the new Russia, and the gradual recuperation of Russia is the one thing longed for by all Russians regardless of political opinions.

Bolshevism is certainly a challenge to Western Civilization, but it is not merely destructive. It is a positive theory of life, which is trying to draw to itself the energy released by the Russian Revolution in a large and compact section of mankind. Western Civilization cannot meet the challenge of Bolshevism simply by negative criticism. It must advance with its own conceptions of life, and penetrate the defences which the Bolsheviks have thrown up round the Soviet State. The proper answer to Communism is a better social system.

What then should be our attitude towards the problem?

There is really no tenable position between a policy of outright hostility and a policy of accommodation. Both of these involve a risk of strengthening Bolshevism, the former by rallying support to any Government against external pressure, the latter by helping the present régime to be the instrument of the rehabilitation of the country. The choice depends on the chances of the situation evolving peacefully from within, and for my own part I should be prepared, for the present at least, to take the second risk.

The dangers and difficulties of a policy of active hostility to the Soviet régime make me extremely reluctant to see this course adopted. There is nothing to be gained by pin-pricks. An effective hostile policy can only have for its object the downfall of the Communist Party. To achieve this the co-operation of the principal capitalist countries, the United States and Germany especially, would have to be sought. This is exactly what the Soviet Government expects. It is the eventuality which its military preparations, its economic plans, and its manipulation of public opinion are designed to meet.

A distinction must, of course, be made between protection and aggression. It is one thing to take defensive measures against a foreign competitor on economic grounds; it is quite another thing to adopt measures whose primary object is to harm another country. We should be perfectly justified in restricting Soviet imports if we thought it economically advantageous, but as soon as political considerations involving the character of the Soviet régime are brought in, we embark on a line of action which involves much more serious consequences. It may be said that, whatever the motive, the result would be the same, but whereas a defensive policy would defer the crisis as long as possible, in the hope that the danger may pass with the adaptation of Bolshevism to the facts of life, an offensive policy assumes the inflexity of Bolshevism and the inevitability of a conflict.

The steps by which a conflict might be precipitated are clear. An embargo on Soviet products would be the first step. The next would be an attempt to form an anti-Soviet combination of several countries. Such a combination could not be formed on economic grounds alone, although economic action would be its first object. In order to induce countries with important Russian trade interests to sacrifice these interests, and in order to get the support of public opinion, a moral appeal would have to be made. It would be essential, for instance, to persuade the United States to stop assisting Russian economic development, and this could only be done by an appeal to religious and humanitarian sentiments.

A combination of Great Britain, Germany, and the United States would find it comparatively easy to obtain the support of other countries through which the Soviet

Government might make good its needs. The way would be open for the re-establishment of what was called the *cordon sanitaire* just after the war. We should be in sight of the imposition of an economic blockade, and from an economic blockade to war the transition is easy.

Apart from the wisdom or otherwise of such a policy, it is open to practical objections. The formation of an anti-Soviet coalition would be an exceedingly difficult task, but without international agreement anti-Soviet action could not be effective. The futility of half measures cannot be too strongly emphasized. What people who use moral arguments to support an anti-dumping campaign forget is that Russia is too large and powerful a country to be overawed by gestures and demonstrations. It was comparatively easy to force reforms on the Turkey of Abdul Hamid, though it was not so easy to make them effective. The inhuman exploitation of native labour in Putumayo and the Congo, slavery in Abyssinia and Liberia, are matters which can be dealt with by the overwhelming pressure of world opinion. But the Soviet Government is not exposed to pressure from a limited display of force, and is completely indifferent to foreign public opinion, except when it has something definite to gain by deferring to it. Unless the advocates of an anti-Soviet policy are prepared to face a war, their efforts will be ineffective, and unless they can be sure that public opinion will back them in the event of war, they may only succeed in bringing war nearer, without being able to make adequate preparations for it. Is public opinion so impressed by the menace of Communism that it would stand even for an economic blockade? Would people accept the necessary restriction of the rights of commerce? Would those who refused to let the Russians starve in 1921 agree to starving them out in 1931? It is often suggested that an anti-Soviet policy is justified by consideration for the welfare of non-Communist Russians, but if the only way of making protests effective is through blockade, or by force of arms, Russians can scarcely be expected to be enthusiastic. Foreign intervention is no more popular in Russia to-day than it was during the Civil War. Russia would rather be left to work out her own salvation.

Another possibility must also be discussed. Supposing that an anti-Soviet policy were so successful that it brought about the collapse of the Soviet system by economic pressure alone, what would be the result? People often talk about the collapse of Bolshevism as if there was some alternative ready to take its place and to establish a Government on orthodox lines. There are no grounds for such an assumption. The economic collapse of Russia would almost certainly be followed by political collapse. The same centrifugal forces which manifested themselves in 1917 would operate once more. The Ukraine, the Caucasus, Central Asia and the Far East would fly off into space, and it would be impossible to prevent foreign Powers from taking a hand in the game. What would be the relations of Poland to the Ukraine, of Turkey, to say nothing of other Powers, to the Georgians, Armenians and Tatars of the Caucasus, of Great Britain to the peoples on the Indian and Afghan frontier, of Japan and China to the country East of Lake Baikal? No one can foresee, but it may be confidently predicted that such a situation would lead to trouble. This time, perhaps, the army, not being in the demoralized state to which the war of 1917 reduced it, might take charge. A Russian Napoleon is not yet an impossibility.

The alternative to a policy of hostility is to encourage relations between the Soviet Union and the outside world. It means counting on contact with the outside world to modify the present régime by the force of events. It means giving common sense and practical necessities the best possible chance. Diplomatic relations should not be severed unless it is intended to adopt a policy of active hostility to the Soviet Union. So large and powerful a State cannot be ignored just because it is ruled by Communists. To treat Bolshevism as if it were a temporary attack of lunacy is entirely to misread the situation. A Bolshevik Government exists, and the British Empire is so circumstanced that the two cannot help coming into contact with each other. It is better that this contact, even when inharmonious, should be to some extent regulated through recognized formal channels than that the situation should simply be allowed to drift.

It may be that, in spite of every effort, time may not bridge the gulf which separates Bolshevism from Western Civilization. If both remain unchanged in their outlook, a conflict seems inevitable. They cannot exist permanently side by side as they are at present. A case has, it is hoped, been made out to support a reasonable expectation that Communism may become so modified as to make a common basis of understanding possible. But it is no use pretending that this will happen unless Communism abandons some of its fundamental claims. The West cannot yield on essentials, though Western countries are also changing, and we may live to experience profound alterations of our social system. The crucial point is the restoration of the sovereignty of human personality in Russia, and such liberty can only come with peace in the class war. Then the war mentality will pass and the way be opened for the harmonization of such lessons as the Russian Revolution has to teach with the vital changes already in evident progress throughout the rest of the world.

APPENDIX

APPENDIX

THE POLITICAL ORGANIZATION OF THE U.S.S.R.

I. Organization on a National Basis

The political map of Russia has very considerably altered since the Revolution, and many people are still unfamiliar with the reorganization which has taken place.

Since the Revolution Russia has lost, with Finland, the Baltic States, Poland and Bessarabia, an area of rather more than 170,000 square miles and a population of about 40,000,000.[1] The formation of the Soviet Union fundamentally altered the organization of the State, giving it a federal instead of a unitary basis. New territorial units have come into existence, partly to suit the Soviet system, and partly in accordance with the alteration of policy towards the non-Russian peoples.

The Soviet Union came into existence at the end of 1922 in consequence of a treaty of federation between the Russian, Ukrainian, White Russian and Trans-Caucasian Republics. To these have been added the Turkmen (1924), Uzbek (1924) and Tadjik (1929) Republics. These seven Republics are known as Union Republics. Two of them, the Russian and Trans-Caucasian, are themselves federations, and most of them contain subordinate autonomous units.

Except in so far as their independence is limited by the Treaty of Federation the seven major Republics are

[1] The population of the present territory of the Soviet Union in 1914 was 140,000,000; in 1922 it had fallen to 132,000,000 owing to emigration, civil war, famine, and disease consequent on the Revolution; in 1930 it was estimated at 158,000,000. The rate of increase is now greater than in any European country, namely, 2·4 per cent. compared with 1 per cent. in Italy, 0·8 per cent. in Germany, and 0·6 per cent. in Great Britain.

sovereign States. The right of secession is explicitly reserved to them, though it cannot be exercised without the consent of all the other States in the Union. The Union Government has exclusive control over Foreign Affairs, War, Foreign Trade, Transport and Communications. Internal economic questions are federally directed but locally administered. It is only in such matters as Justice, Education, Public Health and Social Welfare that the local Governments have any wide discretion. Thus, in practice, the power of the Central Government is supreme, and here the dominating influence is the R.S.F.S.R. There can be no serious departure from the general line of policy enunciated in Moscow and controlled by the headquarters of the Communist Party. The federal system does, however, allow of this policy being administered with adaptations to local requirements, and it would be misleading to underestimate the importance of the changes implied. However slight autonomy may be in essentials, the fact remains that every self-conscious national group has at least been able to get a place on the map as an administrative and cultural unit.

Besides the major Union Republics there is a subordinate category of Autonomous Republics, complete with Council of Peoples' Commissars and the whole machinery of a Government. One distinction between them is that, while the language of the Union Republic is the only official language, the language of an Autonomous Republic has to share this position with the language of the Union Republic of which it forms part. Perhaps the closest familiar analogy to be found would be the status of the Irish Free State and Northern Ireland Governments in relation to the British Empire.

The position of the three constituent Republics of the Trans-Caucasian Federation, namely Georgia, Armenia and Azerbaidjan, is peculiar. Each was for a time a separate independent State. The Federation was formed, as preparation for a wider Union, in March 1922. Each is mentioned by name in the preamble of the Treaty of Federation, and they include subordinate Autonomous Republics and Regions of their own. They have thus an exceptional intermediate status.

There is a further category of Autonomous Regions, which represent yet another stage in the political hierarchy. In this case autonomy is mainly linguistic. These Regions are administered as an integral part of the Union Republic of which they form part.

A Soviet of Nationalities sits in Moscow to which these various national groups send representatives. The Union and Autonomous Republics send five delegates each,[1] the Autonomous Regions one each. The Soviet of Nationalities together with the Soviet of the Union (a body elected by the Union Congress of Soviets) form the Central Executive Committee of the Union, about which more will be said later.

Not unnaturally the territories of many national groups lie on the frontier; indeed, they form an almost continuous string. This is a fact of some importance because there is usually a kindred people on the Capitalist side of the boundary, among whom, no doubt, it is hoped to make Communist propaganda particularly effective. Next to the Ruthenian and Galician provinces of Poland lie White Russia and the Ukraine, each closely related ethnologically and politically to each other. On the Rumanian frontier the Moldavian Republic maintains, on Soviet soil, its affinity with the disputed province of Bessarabia. In the Caucasus the Republics of Adjaristan, Georgia, Armenia, Nakhichevan and Azerbaidjan represent peoples closely connected with those just across the Turkish and Persian borders. In Central

[1] The Autonomous Republics of Adjaristan and Abkhazia send only one each.

Asia the Turkmen, Uzbek, Tadjik, Kirghiz and Kazak Republics join hands across the frontiers of Persia, Afghanistan and Chinese Turkestan with very similar peoples in the deserts of Khorassan and the mountains of the Hindu Kush, the Tian Shan and the Altai. Finally, the Buryat Republic on the shores of Lake Baikal is nearly related to Mongolia. These are so many jumping-off grounds for the day, if ever it comes, when Communism makes its bid for world domination.

The Russian Socialist Federal Soviet Republic, or R.S.F.S.R., is the overwhelmingly predominant partner in the Union, comprising 92 per cent. of its area and 69 per cent. of its population. It includes the whole of Asiatic Russia, with the exception of the comparatively small area in Southern Turkestan occupied by the Turkmen, Uzbek and Tadjik Republics, and all European Russia except the south-western corner and Trans-Caucasia. It contains a large proportion of the non-Russian peoples of the Union, which are apportioned among eleven of the Autonomous Republics[1] and thirteen of the Autonomous Regions.[2]

The Central Asian part of the R.S.F.S.R. is mainly occupied by the Kazak Autonomous Republic. Formerly the inhabitants would have been called Kirghiz, but for some reason this is now considered inaccurate and derogatory. There is a separate Kirghiz Republic in the foothills of the Tian Shan. The Kazaks are Turco-Mongols, whose ancestors were the rank and file of Genghiz Khan's Golden Horde. They are nomads and Moslems. The Kara-Kalpaks, who form an Autonomous Region within Kazakstan, are

[1] The Bashkir, Buryat-Mongolian, Chuvash, Crimean, Daghestan, Karelian, Kazak, Kirghiz, Tatar, Volga German, and Yakut Republics.

[2] Komi-Zyrian, Oyrat, Votiak, Mari, Kalmuck, Kabardin-Balkarsk, Adigey, Ingush, Karachay, North Ossete, Cherkess and Chechen. The seven last are all in North Caucasia.

a kindred people. The Oyrats and Buryats, who live farther East along the Chinese frontier, are Mongols by race and Buddhists by religion.

Many of the most important Autonomous Republics and Autonomous Regions of the R.S.F.S.R. have considerable Russian minorities, and their large towns often have Russian majorities.[1] The result is that Russian influence remains very strong in such cases. Although applicants for official positions have to know the local language, Russians often predominate in the Government offices, and Russian continues to be the normal vehicle of communication.

The two next most important Union Republics, the Ukraine and Trans-Caucasia, are described in Chapters X and IX respectively. The Ukraine comprises 2¾ per cent. of the area and contains 20 per cent. of the population of the

[1] The following are outstanding examples:—

Territory	Proportion of Russians	Chief Town	Proportion of Russians
	Per Cent.		Per Cent.
Bashkir Aut. Rep.	44	Ufa	70
Mari Aut. Reg.	42		
Votiak Aut. Reg.	45		
Tatar Aut. Rep.	40	Kazan	70
Volga German Aut. Rep.	35	Pokrovsk	44
Crimean Aut. Rep.	51*	Simperopol	52
Adigey Aut. Reg.	40	Krasnodar, Vladikavkaz, Batalpashinsk, and Grosny, the administrative centres of six out of the seven N. Caucasian Aut. Regions have Russian majorities	
Karachay Aut. Reg.	37		
Daghestan Aut. Rep.	under 3	Makhach-Kala	56
Kazak Aut. Rep.	34*		

* Including Ukrainians.

Union; Trans-Caucasia 1 per cent. of the area and 4 per cent. of the population. The only autonomous constituent of the Ukraine is the Moldavian Republic on the Bessarabian border. Trans-Caucasia includes the Nakhichevan Autonomous Republic and the Karabagh Autonomous Region in Azerbaidjan, and the Abkhasian and Adjar Autonomous Republics and the South Ossetian Autonomous Region in Georgia.

White Russia comprises only $\frac{5}{8}$ per cent. of the area and 3 per cent. of the population of the Union. The people differ less than the Ukrainians from the Great Russians. Perhaps the difference is not greater than between Yorkshire and Somerset. The real distinction is historical, and mainly accounted for by Lithuanian and Polish domination between the thirteenth and eighteenth centuries.

The three Union Republics of Central Asia are the least developed, culturally, economically and politically. Turkmenistan is a large and sparsely populated semi-desert region. Its people are wild tribesmen of Turkish stock. Uzbekistan comprises most of the territory of the former Khanates of Khiva and Bokhara. It is a country rich in historical associations and its capital is Samarkand. The Uzbeks are of Iranian stock, but speak a Turkish language. Tadjikistan is the smallest in area and population of all the Union Republics. It is a mountainous land, and the people, who are akin to the Uzbeks, have retained their Iranian language. Their principal peculiarity is that they belong to the Ismaili sect of Moslems, whose head is the Aga Khan. It includes the Autonomous Region of Badakshansk. Few foreigners have as yet been able to give any detailed account of what has been going on in these territories. The Soviet Government is as chary as the old régime of allowing access to travellers, and a special visa is required to visit them.

II. Administrative Organization

The "Soviet System" is a term commonly used as the equivalent of Bolshevism, but it has a more exact meaning. There is nothing specially significant about the word *soviet* itself. It is the ordinary Russian word for "council." For instance, the Council of State in Tzarist times was the *gosudarstvenny soviet.* The name has, however, come to be particularly applied to the revolutionary Councils of Workmen's, Soldiers' and Peasants' Deputies which first emerged in 1905, and through which the Bolsheviks climbed into power in 1917. Round this type of organization, which, with the collapse of the former machinery of government, was both the only one available and one eminently suitable to their needs, the Bolsheviks built up their system of administration. It is, therefore, convenient to restrict the use of the word *soviet* to those bodies which derive from the original revolutionary councils, and now form a continuous chain between the smallest administrative unit and the Soviet of People's Commissars for the Union, which corresponds to our Cabinet. There is the more reason for doing this because the peculiarity of the Soviet System, in an administrative sense, is that it starts from an economic unit, and that the tendency has been to make economic considerations the guiding principle in the formation of the administrative divisions of the country.

The local units of the old Russian Empire have now practically ceased to exist, and it is only a matter of time before new divisions are in force everywhere. The former province (*gubernia*) with its subdivisions, the *uyezd* and *volost*, has been discarded. The village, however, remains to-day, as it has always been, the basis of rural administration. In the R.S.F.S.R., on account of its size, a major division, the Economic-Administrative Area (usually called *oblast*, but in the case of Siberia and the Far East entitled *krai*), which is not to be found in the other Union Republics, has been introduced. There are thirteen of these, three[1] in Asia and ten[2] in Europe. They are separate from the Autonomous Republics, but they include Autonomous Regions. The next division, which applies throughout the Union, is the *okrug*, and below this is the *raion*. All of these divisions combine rural and urban units. A clear-cut distinction is, however, maintained between the representation of agricultural and industrial interests, with a heavy weighting in favour of industry, which, although of much less actual importance than agriculture, is both the field whose development is most earnestly sought and that from which the present régime gets most support. Town soviets have much the same functions as municipalities.

The soviet *par excellence* is the original Council of Workmen's, Soldiers' and Peasants' Deputies. In the country districts it is the village soviet, which is both a territorial and an economic unit. Elsewhere it is the factory, the regiment, the "workers' settlement,"[3] and so on, a more decisively economic unit. An isolated mine or power station, for instance, would have its own soviet, and not be included in the village area. These different soviets form congresses of soviets and city soviets, each body electing a proportion of its members to a higher body. The basis of representation is, however, different for rural and non-rural bodies. Rural bodies elect a number of representatives proportionate to their population, non-rural bodies elect a number of representatives proportionate

[1] The Far East, Siberia and the Urals.

[2] Northern, Leningrad, Western, Moscow, Ivanov, Central Black Soil, Nizhni-Novgorod, Central Volga, Lower Volga and North Caucasus.

[3] Where it is inconvenient for urban electors to be grouped according to where they work they are grouped according to where they live.

to the number of electors. It is in this way that the urban and industrial elements are given a larger representation than their numbers would justify.

Each administrative division has its congress of soviets, as does also each Autonomous Region, Autonomous Republic and, of course, each Union Republic. The Union Congress of Soviets preserves a uniform ratio of representation of 1 in 25,000 electors for urban areas and 1 in 125,000 inhabitants for rural areas. The electorate in all cases consists only of those who are constitutionally entitled to civic rights, namely, to quote the Constitution of the R.S.F.S.R.:—

"(*a*) All citizens gaining their livelihood by productive work useful to society, as well as persons engaged in domestic pursuits which enable the former to follow their callings.

"(*b*) Red soldiers and Red sailors of the workers'-peasants' Red Army and Navy.

"(*c*) All citizens included in the categories indicated in paragraphs (*a*) and (*b*) of the present article who are incapacitated for work."

Certain categories of persons, in addition to the usual discrimination against lunatics and convicts, are specifically excluded from the franchise. According to the same source these are:—

"(*a*) Persons employing hired labour for the sake of profit.

"(*b*) Persons living on an income not derived from their own labour, such as: interest on capital, income from industrial enterprises, landed property, etc.

"(*c*) Private business men, trade and commercial agents.

"(*d*) Monks and clergymen of all religious denominations.

"(*e*) Employees and agents of the former police, of the

special gendarme-corps and secret police, and members of the former ruling dynasty of Russia."

The voting age is eighteen. There is no secret ballot. All elections are "open," e.g. by show of hands. The formalities are managed by electoral commissions in each administrative area, responsible to a central electoral commission in the capital. The members are nominated by important local organizations. Thus the electoral commissions in Autonomous Republics should consist of a President and two members from the Central Executive Committee, two members from peasants' organizations and one each from the *Komsomol*, women's Communist organization, City Soviets, national minorities and the Red Army.

Every soviet and Congress of Soviets elects an Executive Committee, which, as the main body meets but seldom (in the case of the Union Congress only biennially), is much the more powerful body. Concentration of authority goes even farther. Except in the case of the ordinary soviet, the Executive Committee elects a Presidium which remains in more or less permanent session and upon which all real authority devolves. The power of all local organs is, however, considerably curtailed by the ability of every superior organ to overrule the decisions of the one below it. Control is thus in fact highly centralized. Even the ordinary soviet has a secretary whose appointment must be ratified by the presidium of the *raion*.

The Union Congress of Soviets is constitutionally the highest authority in the land, but as it meets only biennially for about ten days, and consists of something like two thousand members, it can obviously have no control over affairs. Its principal task is to elect the Union Soviet of about four hundred members, which, with the Soviet of Nationalities,[1] whose appointment it formally approves, together form the Central Executive Committee[2] of the Union, the nearest equivalent there is to a national legislature. As this body only meets about three times a year for a few days at a time, it does little more than ratify proposals set before it. One of its main functions is the election of a yet smaller body, its Presidium, composed of between twenty and thirty members elected as to one-third by the Union Soviet, one-third by the Soviet of Nationalities, and one-third by the Central Executive Committee as a whole. As all the powers of the larger body devolve upon the smaller when it is not in session, the Presidium of the Central Executive Committee is the only one that really counts. The Central Executive Committee also has the duty of electing the Soviet of People's Commissars,[3] which comprises the heads of Government Departments, and corresponds to a Cabinet.

The same procedure governs the formation of the Central Executive Committees, with their Presidiums, and of the Soviets of People's Commissars in the Union and Autonomous Republics.

The relation between a Soviet of People's Commissars and the Presidium of a Central Executive Committee is important, because while the former is the executive nominee of the whole soviet structure, the latter is a projection of the nominating authority. In the early years of the Revolution, and even after the formation of the Union, the "Sovnarkom" of the R.S.F.S.R. and then of the U.S.S.R. was the dominating body. This was partly because Lenin was its president and partly because the exigencies of a constantly fluctuating situation necessitated much being

[1] Elected by the Central Executive Committees of national areas (see p. 233).
[2] Commonly referred to, from its initials, as the "Tsik." The Central Executive Committees of the various republics are usually indicated by an appropriate prefix, e.g. "Uktsik" for the Ukraine, "Zaktsik" for Trans-Caucasia, etc.
[3] Commonly known, from the first syllable of each word, as "Sovnarkom."

done by executive decree. Latterly the Presidium of the "Tsik" has tended to increase its influence by becoming more and more the official initiator of measures, which the "Sovnarkom" simply has to put into force and administer through its various departments. As a further check on individual People's Commissars, each Commissariat has attached to it a committee called the Collegium, which must be informed of all decisions and can question them by referring the matter either to the "Sovnarkom" or the Presidium of the "Tsik." The Collegia, though appointed by the "Sovnarkom," are really part of the machinery by which the Communist Party keeps its hold over the administration.

There are three kinds of Commissariats, known as "Union," "Unified," and "Non-Unified." Union Commissariats are those which are exclusively federal. They comprise the five Commissariats of Foreign Affairs, War and Marine, Posts and Telegraphs, Ways and Communications, Foreign and Internal Trade.[1] Unified Commissariats are those which exist both federally and locally in Union and Autonomous Republics. They comprise the three Commissariats of Workmen's and Peasants' Inspection,[2] Labour, and Finance, together with the Department of the Supreme Economic Council, which is, in effect, the Commissariat of Industry,[3] the Central Statistical Department, and the Department of the State Planning Com-

[1] This Commissariat has relations with certain subordinate republics as a Unified Commissariat for internal trade only.

[2] The duties of this Commissariat, in the words of Ordzhonikidze, its head, at the Fifteenth Congress of the Communist Party in 1927, are to "see that the decisions of the Government and the Party are always carried out." For further mention of its functions see p. 195.

[3] The Supreme Economic Council was originally intended to direct the whole economic organization of the country, but was gradually restricted to the control of industry only. It has charge of the supervision of the Syndicates and Trusts and of their relations with Labour, the Banks and Trading Organizations.

mission. General instructions are issued from the federal centre and only minor adaptations are allowed locally. "Plenipotentiaries" of all the federal or Union Commissariats may attend meetings of a local "Sovnarkom" and may, sometimes, vote. Finally, Non-Unified Commissariats are those which are exclusively local and have no federal equivalent. They are the six Commissariats of Agriculture, Education, Interior, Justice, Health and Social Welfare. Responsibility for the co-ordination of policy in these instances lies ultimately in the powers of the Presidium of the "Tsik" of the Union to overrule the legislation of subordinate bodies. In the case of Autonomous Republics control is more directly exercised through the "Sovnarkom" of the Union Republic in which they are included.

Two departments remain to be mentioned through which central control is more directly exercised over subsidiary organs of government than by any of those already mentioned. These departments are the Union State Political Administration, which is the official title of the G.P.U. ("gay-pay-oo," or "ogpu"), and the Council of Labour and Defence.

The G.P.U. was the successor of the "Cheka,"[1] the difference between them being simply that the powers of the new organization were defined somewhat more closely and given stricter legal form. It has branches all over the country, and, besides controlling the secret police, and being responsible for the suppression of counter-revolutionary activities, it is also entrusted with the policing of the frontiers and the railways. There is a specially recruited military force of all arms at the department's disposal. The G.P.U. is attached to the "Sovnarkom" of the Union and its Chief is an advisory member of that body.

[1] The "Extraordinary Commission to Combat Counter-Revolution, Speculation and Sabotage."

The Council of Labour and Defence, known as S.T.O., or "Sto," is a Committee of the Union "Sovnarkom." It is the successor of the Council of Workmen and Peasants' Defence which had much to do with the enforcement of War Communism. Its scope and powers are very wide since it can promote any measures to mobilize the forces and resources of the country. It is, in fact, a sort of war cabinet, which has acquired permanent functions. The State Planning Commission ("Gosplan"), which is responsible for the organization of the Five Year Plan and the casting of schemes of national development generally, arose from it, and is in some sort its departmental organ. Its orders naturally have an extensive and unifying influence throughout the Union in all politico-economic questions.

There are many obscurities in the detailed working of the system of government which has here been roughly sketched, and it has been impossible to go into the many interesting points that arise. But reference is so often made to some or other of the bodies mentioned that it seemed worth while trying to give some idea of how they hang together. Enough has been said, moreover, to bring out once more the perpetual conflict between the centrifugal and centripedal forces at work in the country. It is generally true to say that whereas the forms of local autonomy are conceded, centralization is in fact the practice. The attempt to combine the two principles has, however, never been abandoned. The result is an exceedingly complicated system of compensations, checks and balances, many of which would be unnecessary under an ordinary democratic régime, and which would surely clog the administration of the present régime were it not that real power is concentrated in a few hands, and that a few direct channels have been kept clear for its effective exercise.

BIBLIOGRAPHY

Note.—The literature on the Russian Revolution is so large that only a small selection can be mentioned. I have merely picked out from the works known to me those which seemed of greatest general interest and most representative of various points of view.

I. GENERAL

Anonymous.—An Impression of Soviet Russia. (Reprinted from the *Economist* of November 1, 1930.)

A short and able consideration of the Five Year Plan.

Baerlein, Henry.—The March of the Seventy-Thousand. (Parsons, 1926.)

An account of the Czecho-Slovak Legion's exploits from the Czech point of view.

Batsell, W. R.—Soviet Rule in Russia. (New York, 1929.)

A study of the constitutional development and political machinery of the Soviet State.

Buchanan, Sir George.—My Mission to Russia. (Cassell, 1923.)

The British Ambassador's Memoirs.

Buchanan, Merial.—Petrograd, 1914–1918. (Collins, 1918.)

Eye-witness notes by the British Ambassador's daughter.

Bukharin, N.—Historical Materialism. (Allen & Unwin, 1926.)

A good example of Bolshevik philosophy.

Burns, Émile.—Russia's Productive System. (Gollancz, 1930.)

A description of the economic machinery of the Soviet State.

CHAMBERLAIN, W. H.—Soviet Russia. (Duckworth, 1930.)

A well-balanced account of the Soviet régime by a journalist after seven years in the country.

DENIKIN, A. I.—The Russian Turmoil. (Hutchinson, 1922.)

Covers the period March to November, 1917, from the point of view of a senior officer primarily concerned with the condition of the army.

—— The White Army. (Cape, 1930.)

An account, by its commander, of the Volunteer Army's activities in relation to the Civil War generally.

DOBB, MAURICE.—Russia's Economic Development. (Routledge, 1928.)

A study of War Communism and "Nep."

—— Russia To-day and To-morrow. (Hogarth Press, 1930.)

A pamphlet addendum to the above.

DUKES, SIR PAUL.—Red Dusk and the Morrow. (Williams & Norgate, 1922.)

Personal experiences of an Intelligence Officer during the Revolution.

FARBMAN, MICHAEL.—Bolshevism in Retreat. (Collins, 1923.)

For the earlier development of the Revolution and the introduction of "Nep" this account is still worth reading.

FISCHER, LOUIS.—The Soviets in World Affairs. (Cape, 1930.)

Contains much useful information. The point of view is that of the British Labour Party.

FÜLLOP-MILLER, RENÉ.—The Mind and Face of Bolshevism. (Putnam, 1927.)

A colourful account of many aspects of Bolshevism. A useful introduction to the subject, but not a primary authority.

GRONDIJS, L. H.—La Guerre en Russie et en Sibérie. (Paris, 1922.)

The experiences of a Dutch journalist, a shrewd and honest observer, on the Galician front in 1917, with the Volunteer Army and the Bolsheviks in 1918, and in Siberia in 1919.

HAENSEL, PAUL.—The Economic Policy of Soviet Russia. (King, 1931.)

The author held important official positions both before and after the Revolution.

HARPER, SAMUEL N.—Civic Training in Soviet Russia. (Chicago, 1929.)

A study of Soviet institutions from the point of view of their effect on the propagation of Communism.

HINDUS, MAURICE.—Humanity Uprooted. (Cape, 1929).

—— Red Bread. (Cape, 1931.)

The author is a Russian-born American. His sketches reveal, with intimate vividness, the attitude of the ordinary Russian, and especially of the peasant, to the Revolution.

HOOVER, CALVIN.—The Economic Life of Soviet Russia. (Macmillan, 1931.)

The most up-to-date, and in many ways the best, account of the subject.

HOUGHTELING, JAMES L.—A Diary of the Russian Revolution. (New York, 1918.)

An eye-witness account of the "February" Revolution.

KARLGREN, A. F.—Bolshevist Russia. (Allen & Unwin, 1927.)

KERENSKY, A. F.—The Catastrophy. (New York, 1927.)

An "apologia" for the Provisional Government.

KNICKERBOCKER, H. R.—The Soviet Five Year Plan and its Effect on World Trade. (Lane, 1931.)

A very readable but somewhat superficial appreciation of the present situation by an American journalist.

LASKI, H. J.—Communism. (Thornton Butterworth, 1927.)

A good introductory study, tolerant of Bolshevik aims but antagonistic to Bolshevik methods.

LAWTON, LAUNCELOT.—The Russian Revolution. (Macmillan, 1927.)

A collection of essay-articles which conveys a fair picture.

LENIN, V. I.

The general reader will not want to tackle the collected edition of Lenin's works in twenty-five volumes prepared by the Lenin Institute, which exists for research into everything to do with Lenin's life. An English translation is in course of publication by Messrs. Martin Lawrence (London) and International Publishers (New York). His most important writings, such as What is to be Done? Materialism and Empirio-criticism; The State and Revolution; "Left Wing" Communism, an Infantile Disorder; Will the Bolsheviks Retain Power? can be found in *Selections from Lenin*, issued by the same publishers (cheap edition in 4 volumes).

There is no really adequate biography of Lenin. Nearly every work on the Russian Revolution attempts an appreciation. Among books specifically devoted to Lenin, *La Vie de Lénine*, by Pierre Chasles (Paris, 1929), and *Lenin*, by D. S. Mirsky (Holme Press, 1931), are among the best for general information. The former inclines to an anti-Bolshevik, the latter to a pro-Bolshevik point of view. The recollections of his intimate friends and colleagues are naturally biased but give more vivid impressions of his personality. The most important of these are the *Mémoires* by his wife, N. C. Krupskaya (Lawrence, 1930); *Lenin*, by L. Trotsky (Harrap, 1925); *Lénine*, by Maxime Gorky (Paris, 1924). Several collections of personal reminiscences of Lenin have been published in Russian.

LUDENDORFF, GEN. VON.—My War Memories. (Hutchinson, 1919.)

Contains important passages concerning German policy towards Russia in 1917 and 1918.

MAVOR, J.—The Russian Revolution (Allen & Unwin, 1928.)
A collection of notes rather than a comprehensive history.

MCCULLAGH, FRANCIS.—A Prisoner of the Reds. (Murray, 1921.)
A British officer's experiences during Kolchak's retreat, and during a subsequent peregrination in Bolshevik territory.

MIRSKY, D. S.—Russia, A Social History. (Cresset Press, 1931.)
Russian history viewed particularly as the background of the Revolution.

PALÉOLOGUE, MAURICE.—La Russie des Tsars. (Paris, 1922.)

—— An Ambassador's Memoirs (English Translation). (Hutchinson, 1923.)
The diary of the French Ambassador in St. Petersburg from 1914 to 1917.

PARES, SIR BERNARD.—A History of Russia. (Cape, 1928.)

—— Russian Memories. (Cape, 1931.)
Particularly valuable as describing an Englishman's effort to understand Russia during thirty years.

REED, JOHN.—Ten Days that Shook the World. (New York, 1922.)
An eye-witness account of the "October" Revolution by an American Communist who had access to the Bolshevik leaders in the Smolny Institute.

RODZIANKO, M. V.—The Reign of Rasputin. (Philpot, 1927.)
An account by the President of the Fourth Duma of the events that led up to the "February" Revolution.

SCHUMANN, F. L.—American Policy toward Russia since 1917. (Martin Lawrence, 1928.)
Contains useful material for the study of allied intervention during the Civil War.

SHERIDAN, CLARE.—Russian Portraits. (Cape, 1921.)

The author executed busts of many Bolshevik leaders, and was consequently in close touch with them during some weeks in Moscow.

STALIN, JOSEPH.—Leninism. (New York, 1928.)

A selection of Stalin's speeches, etc., mostly about the Trotsky controversy. An illuminating commentary on Bolshevik orthodoxy.

TROTSKY, LÉON.—My Life. (Thornton Butterworth, 1930.)

A vividly written "apologia," particularly interesting for its trenchant though prejudiced comments on other prominent Bolsheviks.

VILLIAMY, C. F., and HYNES, A. L.—From the Red Archives. (Bles, 1929.)

The most important of this collection of documents are the diaries of two officers describing the progress of the Revolution in the Baltic Fleet, on the Northern front in 1917, and a report to the Provisional Government on the state of the provinces in May, 1917.

II. NOVELS DESCRIBING REVOLUTIONARY CONDITIONS

(Many of these are personal experiences disguised as fiction.)

BABEL, I.—Red Cavalry. (Kopf, 1929.)

GLADKOV, F.—Cement. (Lawrence, 1929.)

KATAEV, V.—The Embezzlers. (Benn, 1929.)

KRASNOV, P.—From Double Eagle to Red Flag. (Allen & Unwin, 1928.)

Nevierov, A.—Tashkent. (Gollancz, 1930.)

Ognyov, N.—Diary of a Communist Schoolboy. (Gollancz, 1928.)

—— Diary of a Communist Undergraduate. (Gollancz, 1929.)

Romanov, P.—Three Pairs of Silk Stockings. (Benn, 1931.)

INDEX

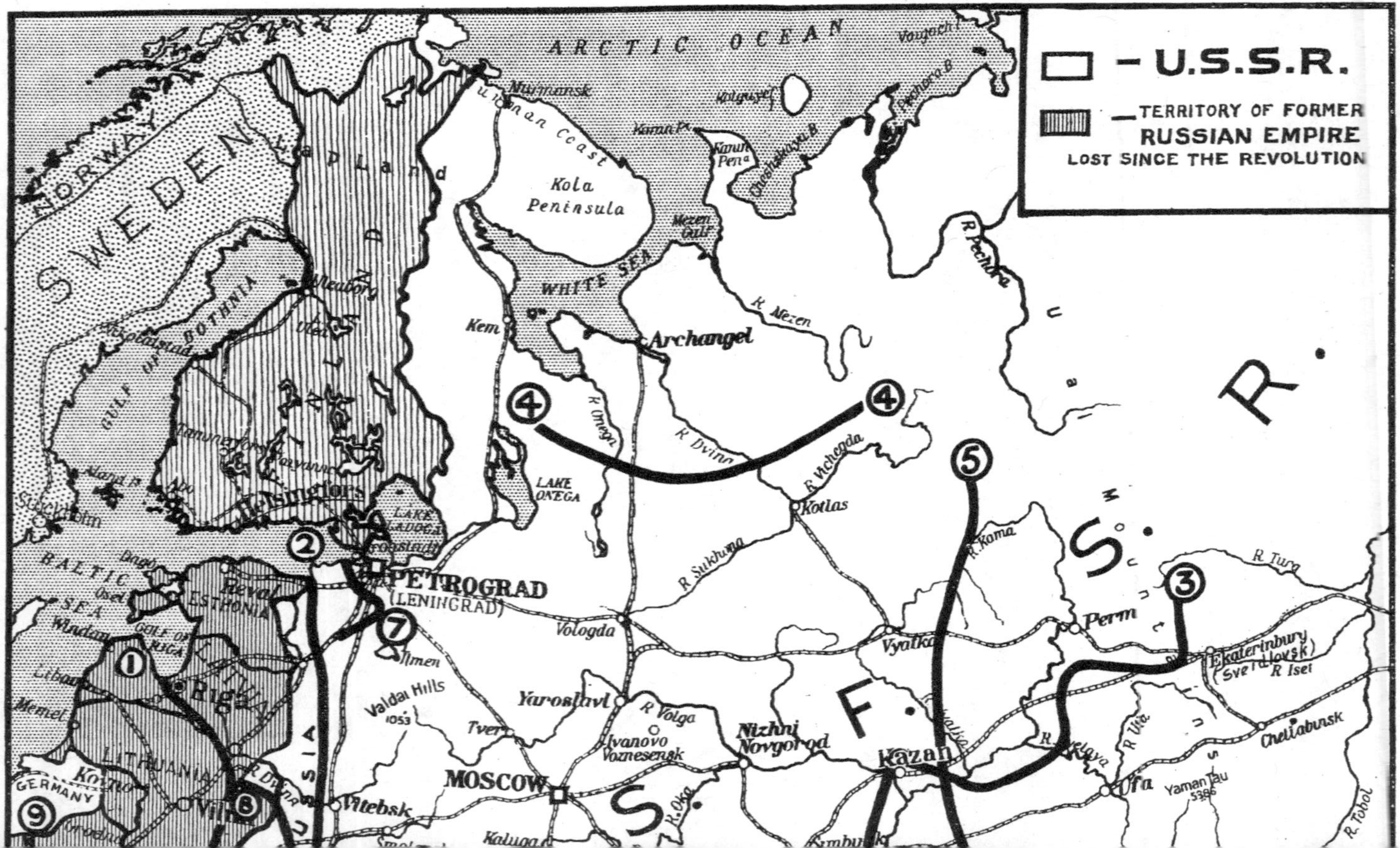
– U.S.S.R.
– TERRITORY OF FORMER RUSSIAN EMPIRE LOST SINCE THE REVOLUTION
ARCTIC OCEAN
Murmansk
Murman Coast
Kola Peninsula
WHITE SEA
Mezen Gulf
Archangel
Kem
LAKE ONEGA
LAKE LADOGA
R. Omega
R. Dvina
R. Vichegda
R. Mezen
R. Pechora
Kotlas
R. Sukhona
PETROGRAD
(LENINGRAD)
Vologda
Yaroslavl
R. Volga
Ivanovo Voznesensk
Nizhni Novgorod
Kazan
Vyatka
Perm
R. Koma
R. Tura
Ekaterinburg
(Sverdlovsk)
R. Isel
Cheliabinsk
Ufa
R. Ufa
Yaman Tau
3386
R. Tobol
MOSCOW
Tver
Valdai Hills
1053
Ilmen
Vitebsk
Kaluga
R. Oka
R. Dvina
SWEDEN
NORWAY
Lapland
GULF OF BOTHNIA
Helsingfors
Reval
ESTHONIA
GULF OF RIGA
Riga
Libau
Memel
LITHUANIA
Kovno
GERMANY
BALTIC SEA
Dago
Osel
Windau
R.
S.
F.
S.
R.
U S S I A

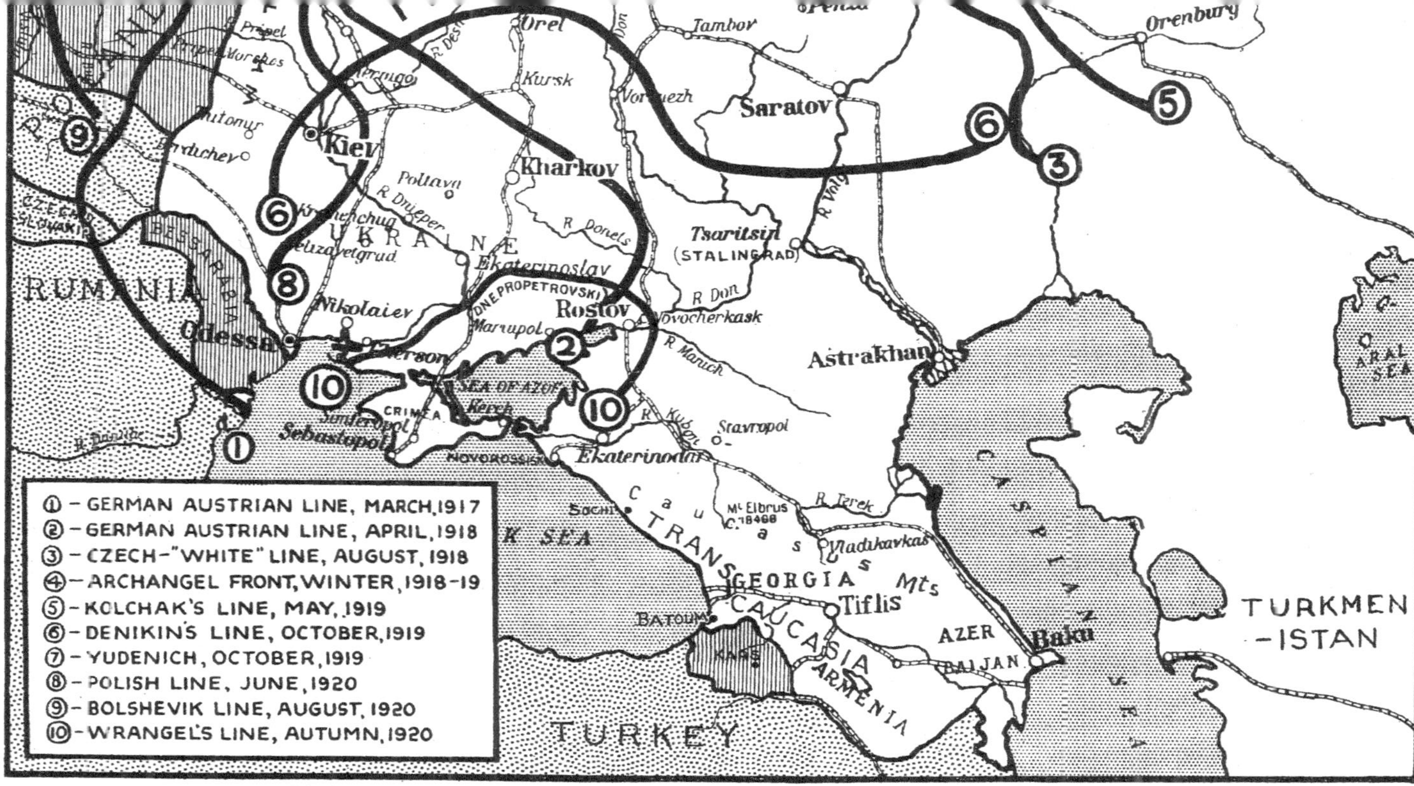

RUSSIA: TO ILLUSTRATE THE CIVIL WAR AND POLITICAL CHANGES

Common Core Lessons & Activities: Environmental Issues Around the World

By Carole Marsh

I by Gallopade International, Inc.

Printed in the U.S.A. (Peachtree City, Georgia)

I0895171

TABLE OF CONTENTS

G: Includes Graphic Organizer

GO: Graphic Organizer is also available 8½" x 11" online download at www.gallopade.com/client/go (numbers above correspond to the graphic organizer numbers online)

Losing the Amazon Rainforest

Read the text. Use the text to answer the questions.

The Amazon rainforest is the world's largest tropical rainforest. The rainforest is important to the environment of Brazil as well as the entire world. It is known as "the lungs of the earth" because the plants there convert carbon dioxide into valuable oxygen. The Amazon rainforest also plays an important role in weather patterns and is home to thousands of different species of plants and animals.

Today, the Amazon rainforest is threatened by deforestation. People have cleared large parts of the rainforest to create farmland, ranches, and new settlements. Others have cleared land for mining and logging operations, as well as to build roads.

The deforestation of the Amazon rainforest affects the entire planet. Without the rainforest, more harmful carbon dioxide remains in the air. The loss of the rainforest means less precipitation, leading to droughts and dry land where nothing can grow. In addition, thousands of valuable plant and animal species may be destroyed. That could affect the health of many people, since many medicines come from rainforest plants! Simply put, the rainforest ecosystem is critical to the health of our planet.

1. A. Use a dictionary to define threatened, as it is used in the text.
   B. Use a dictionary to find the meaning of deforestation. Write the definition in your own words.
   C. Define drought, as it is used in the text.
2. Use classroom resources and the text to write a well-developed paragraph explaining why the Amazon rainforest is important.
3. What benefits do some people gain from deforestation of the Amazon region? Use logical reasoning to support your answer.
4. Divide into groups. Research medicines that have come from rainforest plants. Create computer presentations and discuss in class.

CAUSE & EFFECT

Egypt's Aswan High Dam

Read the text and answer the questions.

Everyone depends on water. But sometimes there can be too much of it. When that happens, flooding can occur. In Egypt in 1970, workers built the Aswan High Dam on the Nile River to prevent flooding. The dam did its job to protect the surrounding areas from flooding, but it also had unintended consequences.

Farming has been successful along the Nile River for thousands of years because the soil is so fertile. This healthy soil is no accident. The river deposits silt into the land. Silt is mud, sand, or soil that sinks to the bottom of a body of water. It is filled with nutrients, which help crops grow. So, when the water flows, the silt is pushed downstream to enrich the farmland.

Unfortunately, the Nile overflowed its banks every year. Crops, buildings, and roads were destroyed. The Aswan High Dam let the Egyptians control the flow of water. It also used the water to make electricity. Thanks to the dam, some villages were able to have electric lights for the first time.

However, an unintended consequence occurred once the dam was built. The dam prevented the silt from being deposited into Egypt's soil. The land along the Nile River became less fertile than it used to be. Now, farmers use chemicals to help their crops grow. The chemicals cost a lot of money and can harm plant and animal habitats. Although the Aswan High Dam has helped people stay safe from floods, it has had some negative effects on Egypt's environment.

1. A. What are unintended consequences, as the term is used in the text?
   B. Give a synonym and an antonym for fertile.

2. Why is silt so important to the farmland along the Nile River?

3. In your opinion, should the Egyptians have built the Aswan High Dam? Use logical reasoning to support your answer.

4. Write two journal entries: one from the point of view of someone who was helped by the Aswan High Dam, and one from the point of view of a person who was harmed by it. Explain how the dam has affected your life.

Too Many People?

Read the text. Use the chart and the text to answer the questions

In the year 600 A.D., experts say about 200 million people lived on the Earth. Today, the world population is closer to 7 billion. Every year, millions of people are born all over the world. Each day, more and more people must share the same amount of space. We must also share the same amount of resources. What will happen when the number of people exceeds the space and resources of the planet?

Overpopulation is already occurring in many countries today. For example, more than 1.2 billion people live in India, compared to about 320 million in the U.S. Many Indians live in the capital city of New Delhi. Residents often live very close together in dirty conditions. In addition, it is very difficult to get items that are considered basic in the United States, such as water. If people do not have plumbing in their homes, they have to get water from a truck that provides a small amount just a few times per week. All of these factors can lead to the spread of disease.

China is another country with a huge population of about 1.4 billion people. Because there are so many people, more resources are consumed and more pollution is produced. In some Chinese cities, the air is choked with smog. Smog can make it hard to breathe. In other areas, polluted water has killed fish. Much of China's farmland has been turned into cities where people can live and work. Now, there are fewer areas to grow crops for the large population.

Overpopulation causes many problems for people and the planet. Areas that are overpopulated can have problems getting clean water to drink. Some farmers do not have enough water for their crops. Other people find it hard to get jobs because there are too many people and not enough jobs. Animal and plant habitats disappear when homes are built. Some areas do not have enough food to feed the people there.

You might think that overpopulation only causes problems in the countries where it occurs. However, it can harm countries around the world. For example, smokestacks in China create acid rain In Japan and South Korea. Diseases from one country can spread to others when people travel. Having enough food, housing, and oil and gas are concerns for a growing world population. The Earth's population is growing, but its resources are limited. Overpopulation is a serious problem facing the world today.

International Data Base World Population: 1950-2050

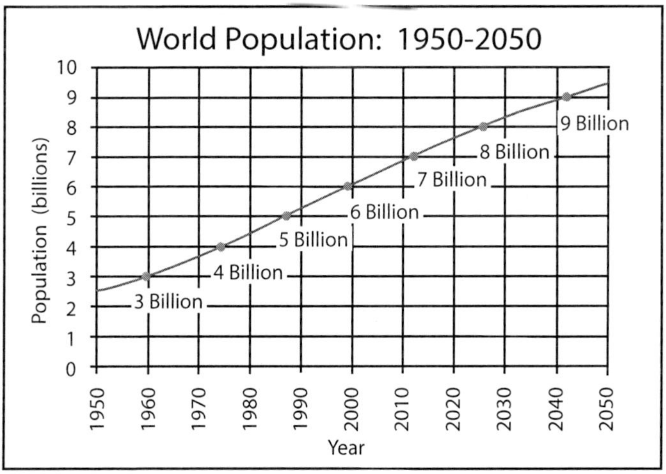

1. A. What is the meaning of the word resources? Give examples of three resources on Earth.
   B. Use a dictionary to define exceeds, as it is used in the text.
   C. Define overpopulation in your own words.
2. What is the main idea of this text?
3. A. List ways that overpopulation is affecting life in India.
   B. List ways that overpopulation is affecting life in China.
4. Review the chart. Imagine you are living in the year 2050 in an overpopulated country. Write a narrative about your life and describe how you are affected by overpopulation. Proofread and edit your work.
5. Divide into groups. Use the Internet to learn about an overpopulated country. Find out what problems are occurring there and what people are doing to solve these problems. Present your findings to the class and discuss.

Energy Sources

Use the Internet or another source to learn how renewable and non-renewable energy sources are similar and different. Then complete the graphic organizer below.

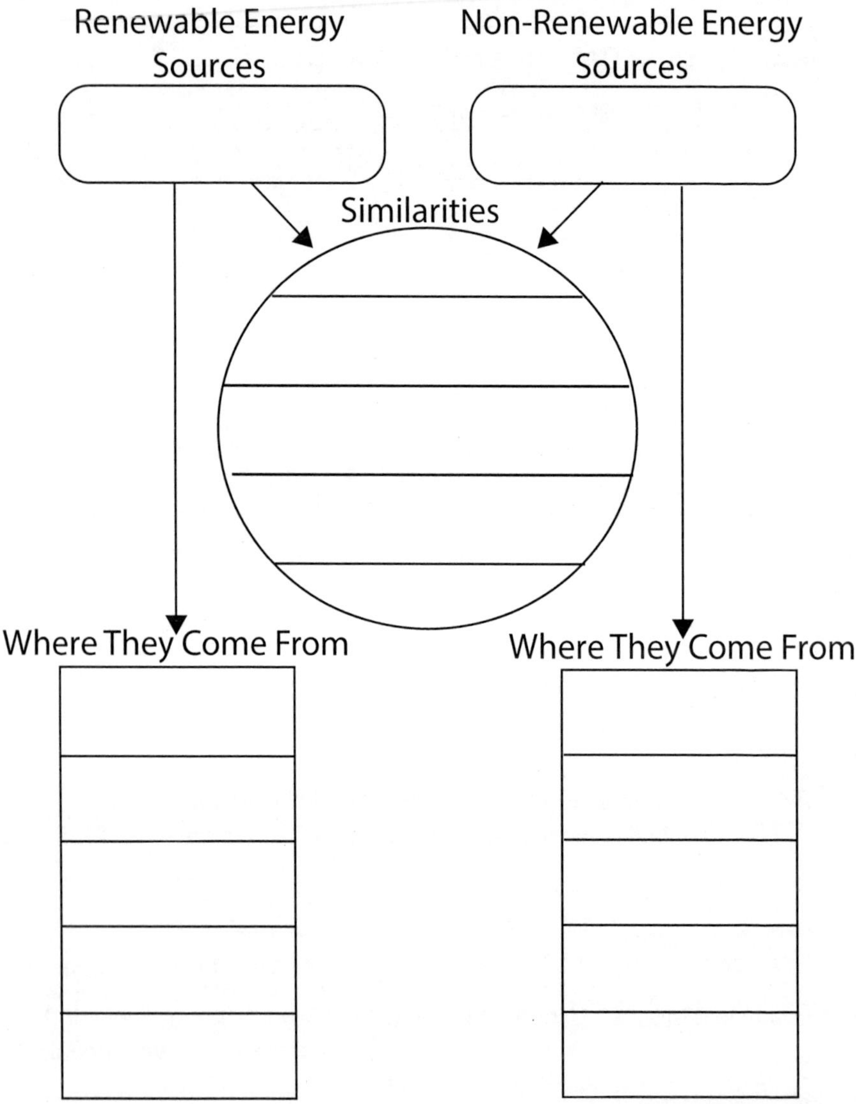

PRIMARY SOURCE ANALYSIS

Water Pollution in India

Experts say the world's biggest health risk is dirty water. In India, half the rivers are polluted. An estimated 2 million people bathe daily in the Ganges River, which is considered to be holy by the Hindu religion. However, it is dangerously polluted with chemicals, sewage, and human and animal remains.

Look at the photograph and answer the questions.

1. A. Use a dictionary to define the word sewage.
   B. Use a dictionary to define remains, as it is used in the text.
2. What health problems could be caused by cows bathing in the same river as people bathe in?
3. What do you see washed up along the riverbank? What health problems could be caused by what you see?
4. Infer why so many Indian people choose to bathe in a polluted river.
5. Write a journal entry from the point of a view of a tourist visiting India and seeing this scene. Describe the sights and smells you encounter, and your reaction to them. Compare this method of bathing to your life in the U.S.

Desertification in Africa

Read the text and answer the questions.

"Desertification" is a big word that means something very simple: land turning into desert. Desertification is a serious problem on the continent of Africa.

Deserts are among the hardest areas for life to survive. It can be difficult or impossible for vegetation to grow. When desertification occurs, land that was once able to support crops becomes dry. Healthy crops wither and die.

In Africa, people are the main cause of desertification. Farmers cut down or burn forests and bushland so they can plant crops. After harvesting the crops, they sometimes burn the stalks left behind. When strong winds blow, the wind carries away seeds and the top layer of soil. Little by little, the soil wears away and cannot support crops.

Farming can cause desertification in another way. Farmers in Africa sometimes use so much water for their crops that they drain an area's natural water supply. One of the reasons Lake Chad in West Africa has decreased in size is because people have used too much of the lake's water. Other reasons for African desertification include overpopulation, animals overgrazing (eating too much vegetation in one area), and decreased rainfall.

Desertification forces many Africans to abandon their homes because they cannot grow enough food, find enough water, or earn enough money. They settle in other areas away from the desert, hoping to start a better life.

1. A. Define vegetation as it is used in the text.
   B. What is a synonym for wither, as it is used in the text?
2. Summarize the main idea of the text.
3. A. Infer how desertification affects Africa's economy.
   B. Infer how desertification affects the health of Africans living in the damaged areas.
4. What factors causing desertification are out of people's control? What factors can people control?

Disappearing Lake Chad

Lake Chad provides water to millions of people in several West African countries, but it is shrinking dramatically. Look at the maps and answer the questions.

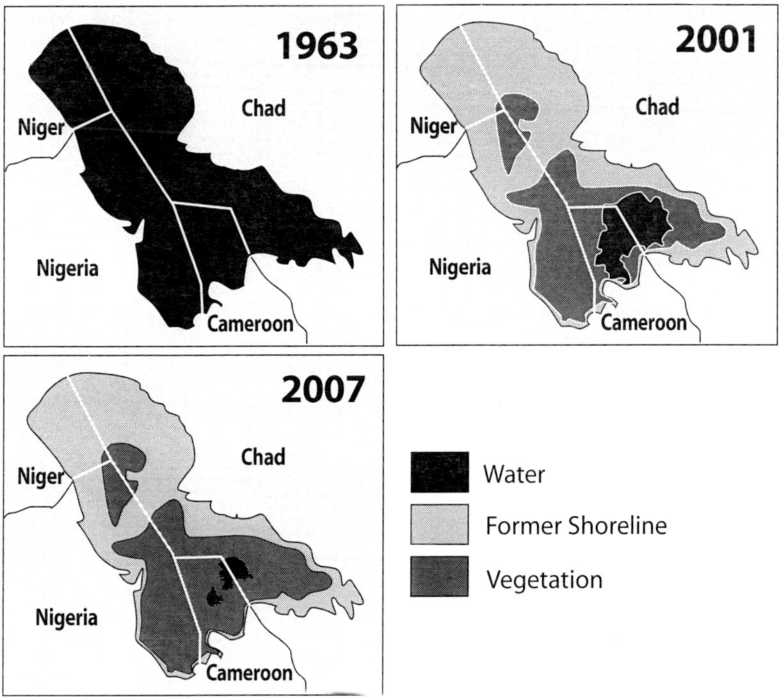

1. A. Describe the change in Lake Chad's water levels over time.
   B. Infer how this change might be currently affecting people living in the surrounding African countries. Use details from the passage to help explain your answer.
2. Predict what will happen to Lake Chad if this trend continues.
3. How might the people living near Lake Chad prepare for the future?
4. African nations are fighting desertification with a project known as the "Great Green Wall." Research this project, and write a digital report including graphics.

Acid Rain

Analyze the illustration of the acid rain cycle and answer the questions.

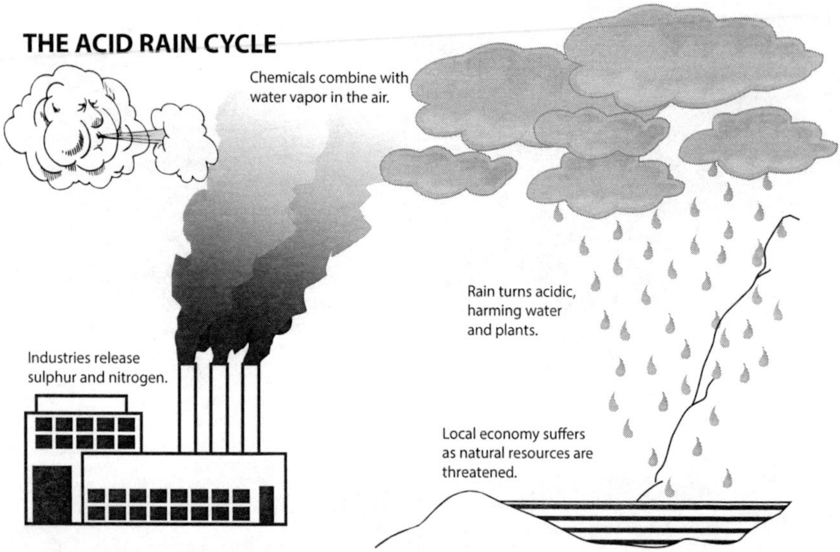

1. How do factories contribute to acid rain?
2. Explain how weather affects acid rain.
3. A. Predict how crops can be affected when acid rain falls.
   B. List three other things in nature that might be affected by acid rain.
   C. Infer how the results of acid rain could affect you in your daily life.
4. A. What actions can businesses take to keep chemicals out of the air and rain?
   B. Explain why businesses might not want to take these actions.
5. Research what is being done to reduce acid rain today. Do you think those suggestions can actually reduce acid rain significantly? Write your opinion in a well-developed paragraph.

A World of Solid Waste

Read the text and answer the questions.

Solid waste is created every day. Unfortunately, the Earth is not getting any bigger. It is becoming harder and harder for us to find places to store the trash we have discarded. Solid waste is becoming a problem worldwide.

Solid waste usually goes by simpler names: garbage or trash. Some examples of solid waste include trash from homes, furniture, batteries, tires, kitchen appliances, paint cans, and aerosol cans. It also includes larger items like cars and debris from construction projects. Items that do not seem very solid, like motor oil and latex paint, are also considered solid waste.

Farms, businesses, mines, and households create trash every day. Even places that try to protect our resources, like facilities that clean our water and air, create solid waste. The trash ends up in dumps, junkyards, and landfills.

Much solid waste is piled up in landfills. As the landfills continue to grow, the soil in and near them becomes unhealthy. This can make it difficult or impossible for plants, animals, and people to live nearby.

One solution to the solid waste problem is to recycle and reuse items. Also, companies that produce goods can use less packaging for their products. If everyone throws out or uses a little less, we can make a big dent in the world's trash problem.

1. A. Define discarded, as it is used in the text.
   B. What is a synonym for debris, as it is used in the text?
2. How does solid waste affect the environment?
3. A. List 3-5 items in your home that will become solid waste.
   B. List 3-5 items in your classroom that will become solid waste.
   C. List 3-5 items you have thrown out this week.
   D. What are some specific steps your family and school can take to generate less waste, as well as reuse and recycle?

4. Divide into groups. Research which countries generate the most solid waste and why. Present your facts graphically and discuss.

Environmental Issues Around the World

Complete the graphic organizer with causes and effects of six major environmental issues.

Cause:

Cause:

Cause:

Cause:

Cause:

Cause:

Effect:

Effect:

Effect:

Effect:

Effect:

Effect:

The Importance of Biodiversity

Read the text and answer the questions.

The Earth is home to millions of species. Some people think there might be over 100 million species sharing the planet! Even if you cannot name every animal and plant on Earth, each species is important.

The variety of life on Earth is known as biodiversity. The diverse animals, plants, and people on the planet perform different functions. All of these functions work together to help keep ecosystems healthy.

For example, some birds eat fruit that contains seeds. They fly away and drop the seeds elsewhere. The seeds take root in the soil, growing into more trees and bushes. Animals and people eat the fruit. As trees grow, they also provide shelter for many kinds of animals, such as birds, squirrels, and insects. Trees are also cut down for timber so people can construct buildings and homes. Without birds to spread seeds, it would be harder for seeds to spread and take root. People, plants, and other animals depend on birds every day.

Animals and plants perform countless other tasks. Some clean the air we breathe, clean the water we drink, provide flood control, or pollinate. Others are used as food or medicine. The role each serves is very important.

Unfortunately, the Earth is losing some of its biodiversity. Animal and plant habitats are being destroyed. Forests are cut town to build cities and towns. Grasslands are turned into farms. Dams change the natural flow of water. Some people hunt certain types of animals until there are few (or none) left. As a result, animals and plants are becoming threatened. Some are facing extinction.

As species are lost, the Earth changes. Without biodiversity, people, animals, and plants will live on a very different planet in the future.

1. A. Explain the concept of biodiversity and why it is important.
   B. Use a dictionary to define ecosystems.
   C. Explain the meaning of extinction, as it is used in the text.
2. Summarize the main idea of the text.
3. Create a fictional situation where biodiversity is at odds with progress. Write a narrative about the situation and how the problem is solved. Present your narrative to the class and discuss.
4. Use online resources to learn how animals and plants help the Earth and how they are threatened. Research the animals and plants below to complete the graphic organizer.

Animal/Plant	Function	Threat
Bees		
Cacti		
Coral reefs		
Tigers		

PROBLEM–SOLUTION–RESULTS

Pollution Solution

Use the graphic organizer to analyze one or more pollution problems. Identify the problem, suggest a possible solution, and describe the results.

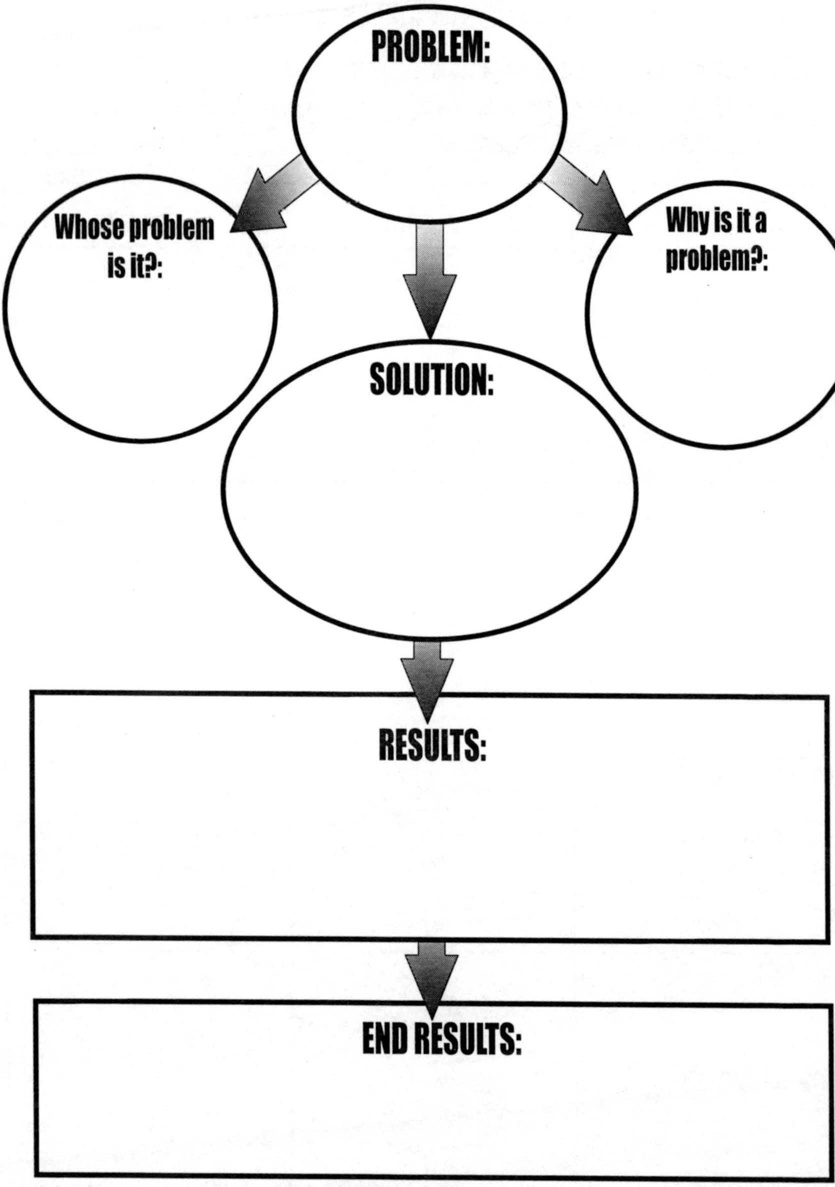

Words About Our World

Rewrite each quotation in your own words. Use the completed chart to answer the questions.

Quotations:	Summarize each quotation:
"In nature, nothing exists alone." — Rachel Carson	
"To be whole. To be complete. Wildness reminds us what it means to be human, what we are connected to rather than what we are separate from." — Terry Tempest Williams	
"Scientists know we must protect species because they are working parts of our life-support system." — Paul Ehrlich	

1. A. Define species, as it is used in the third quotation.
   B. Infer the meaning of the phrase life-support system, as it is used in the third quotation.
2. Who are the speakers? Use online research to write a short biography of each speaker. What do all three speakers have in common? Proofread and edit your work.
3. What is the common theme shared by all three quotations?
4. In your opinion, which quote best describes what is meant by biodiversity? Why?

PRIMARY SOURCE ANALYSIS

Beijing's Air Pollution Problem

These are photographs taken of Beijing, China, in 2005. The first photo shows the smog-filled air of Beijing. The second photo shows the same area after two days of rain. Analyze the photographs and answer the questions.

Courtesy of Bobak/Wikimedia Commons

PART A: Compare and contrast the photographs to answer the questions.

1. What is the main difference between the two photographs?
2. Name one thing you can see in the second photograph that is covered by smog in the first photograph.
3. A. How did the rain affect the air?
   B. Infer why the rain might have had this effect on the air.

PART B: Use the text to identify what is being described.

4. Infer 3-5 things about Beijing, China, based on the two photographs.
5. A. What do you think Beijing's air quality was like 100 years ago?
   B. What do you think Beijing's air quality is like today?
   C. Predict what Beijing's air quality might be like in 10 years.
6. What other types of environmental issues do you think Beijing might have? Cite evidence to support your answer.
7. In your opinion, could the air in your town someday look like Beijing's? Why or why not?

PART C: Make inferences from the text to answer the questions.

8. How are the buildings in the photographs related to the air pollution?
9. A. What could the residents of Beijing do to decrease air pollution?
   B. What could businesses in Beijing do to decrease air pollution?

PART D: Explore the issue further and conduct your own research.

10. Divide into groups. Use online resources to learn why Beijing's air has become so polluted. Present your research to the class and discuss.
11. Imagine you are a child living in Beijing. Create a poster encouraging people to fight air pollution. Share your poster with a partner. Explain why you chose the words and images you did and why you think your poster is effective. Compare and contrast your poster with your partner's.

Oil Pollution and Spills

Oil pollution is an enormous problem in many countries around the world. Analyze the cartoon and answer the questions.

The Real Price of Oil

Courtesy of lenm/Bigstock.com

1. What is the main idea conveyed in this cartoon?
2. How does the caption help convey the cartoon's message?
3. How might the following people react to this cartoon?
   A. a person who owns an oil company
   B. a person who lives on the water
   C. an environmentalist
4. Go online to learn about a country that has suffered a damaging oil spill. Write 2-3 paragraphs about how this country has been affected. Proofread your work. Present your findings to the class.
5. Working in groups, go online to find political cartoons about oil spills. Find 3-5 cartoons that have a similar message. Prepare a computer presentation of the images you collect. Discuss your findings in class.
6. Create your own cartoon about oil pollution. Present your work to the class. Discuss why you chose the images and caption you did.

PRIMARY SOURCE ANALYSIS

Observations of a Child

Read the excerpt from a 1992 speech by 12-year-old Severn Suzuki at the United Nations Earth Summit in Rio de Janeiro, Brazil. Answer the questions.

"In my country, we make so much waste, we buy and throw away, buy and throw away…Even when we have more than enough, we are afraid to lose some of our wealth, afraid to share.

In Canada, we live the privileged life, with plenty of food, water, and shelter—we have watches, bicycles, computers and television sets.

Two days ago here in Brazil, we were shocked when we spent some time with some children living on the streets. And this is what one child told us: 'I wish I was rich and if I were, I would give all the street children food, clothes, medicine, shelter and love and affection.' If a child living on the street who has nothing, is willing to share, why are we who have everything still so greedy?

I can't stop thinking that these children are my age, that it makes a tremendous difference where you are born, that I could be one of those children living in the favellas of Rio; I could be a child starving in Somalia; a victim of war in the Middle East or a beggar in India.

I'm only a child yet I know if all the money spent on war was spent ending poverty and finding environmental answers, what a wonderful place this earth would be!"

1. A. Define privileged as it is used in the text. Find a synonym.
   B. Define favella as it is used in the text.
2. According to her speech, how is Severn's life different from the street children in Brazil? Cite evidence from the text.
3. Infer why the child living in the streets of Brazil wanted to give so much to other street children. What reaction did Severn have to that comment?
4. List several reasons why people's lives are different depending on where they are born.
5. Do you agree or disagree with Severn's statement in the final paragraph? Explain your reasoning.

Greenhouse Gases

Read the text and answer the questions.

The term "greenhouse gases" might not sound very dangerous. However, these gases are a major concern for our planet.

Most greenhouse gases are made by burning fossil fuels to provide energy. For example, fossil fuels are used by cars, trucks, buses, and airplanes. These vehicles burn fuel made from oil, which is a fossil fuel. The creation of electricity also leads to greenhouse gases when power plants burn fuels like coal. Factories also burn fuel for energy. Many of the gases produced by these methods stay in the atmosphere around the Earth.

When sunlight strikes the Earth, some of it turns into heat that is trapped by our atmosphere. The Earth needs the sun's heat, but excess greenhouse gases can trap more of the sun's radiation in the atmosphere than we really need. Many scientists think this can lead to increasing temperatures and climate change.

People and businesses can decrease greenhouse gas creation by using less energy, or by using green sources of energy like solar, wind, or hydroelectric power. Many countries around the world have agreed to take steps to reduce greenhouse gas emissions.

1. A. Use a dictionary to define fossil fuels.
   B. Use a dictionary to define hydroelectric power. What does the prefix hydro mean?
2. List several items your family uses that require fuel to operate.
3. Create a poster or political cartoon encouraging people to save energy. Present your work to the class.
4. Use online resources to learn more about green energy sources. Write 3 paragraphs describing 3 energy sources that you find most interesting. In a final paragraph, describe which energy source you believe is the most effective and practical. Proofread your work. Present your ideas in class and discuss.
5. What is something you can do in your own home to save energy?

Environmental Vocabulary

Use a dictionary and other resources to complete the graphic organizer for each vocabulary word or phrase.

atmosphere	ecosystem	rainforest
climate change	extinction	recycle
deforestation	overpopulation	renewable energy
desertification	pollution	toxic

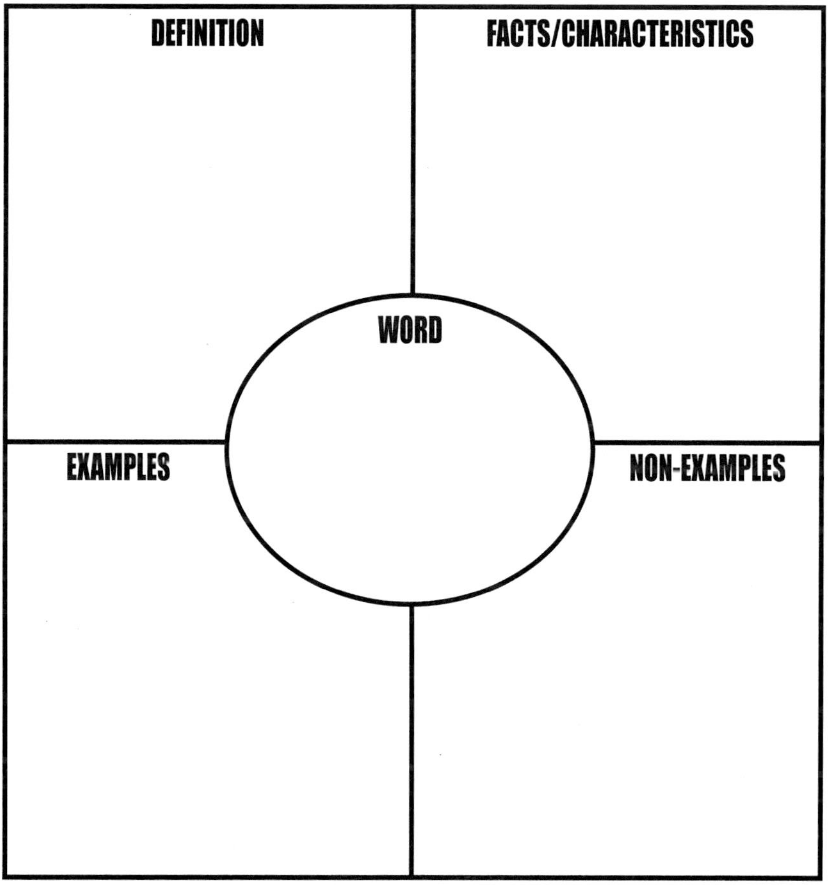

Correlations to Common Core State Standards

For your convenience, correlations are listed page-by-page and for the entire book!

This book is correlated to the Common Core State Standards for English Language Arts grades 3-8, and to Common Core State Standards for Literacy in History, Science, & Technological Subjects grades 6-8.

Correlations are highlighted in gray.

	READING	WRITING	LANGUAGE	SPEAKING & LISTENING
	Includes: RI: Reading Informational Text; RH: Reading History	*Includes:* W: Writing; WHST: Writing History, Science, & Technology	*Includes:* L: Language; LF: Language Foundational Skills	*Includes:* SL: Speaking & Listening
PAGE #	**RI / RH**	**W / WHST**	**L / LF**	**SL**
2	**1** 2 **3** **4** 5 6 7 8 9 **10**	1 **2** 3 **4** 5 **6** **7** 8 **9** **10**	1 2 3 **4** 5 **6**	**1** 2 3 **4** **5** 6
3	**1** 2 3 **4** 5 6 7 **8** 9 **10**	**1** **2** **3** **4** 5 6 7 8 **9** **10**	1 2 3 **4** **5** **6**	1 2 3 4 5 6
4-5	**1** **2** 3 **4** 5 6 **7** 8 **9** **10**	1 **2** **3** **4** **5** 6 **7** 8 **9** **10**	1 2 3 **4** 5 **6**	**1** 2 3 **4** 5 **6**
6	1 2 3 4 **5** 6 **7** 8 9 **10**	1 **2** 3 4 5 6 **7** 8 9 10	1 2 3 4 5 6	1 2 3 4 5 6
7	**1** 2 3 **4** 5 **6** **7** 8 9 **10**	1 **2** **3** **4** 5 6 7 **8** **9** **10**	1 2 3 **4** 5 **6**	1 2 3 4 5 6
8	**1** **2** **3** **4** 5 6 7 8 9 **10**	1 **2** 3 **4** 5 6 7 **8** 9 **10**	1 2 3 **4** **5** **6**	1 2 3 4 5 6
9	**1** 2 3 4 **5** 6 **7** 8 9 **10**	1 **2** 3 **4** 5 **6** **7** 8 9 **10**	1 2 3 4 5 6	1 2 3 4 5 6
10	1 2 **3** 4 **5** 6 **7** 8 9 **10**	**1** **2** 3 **4** 5 6 **7** **8** 9 **10**	1 2 3 4 5 6	1 2 3 4 5 6
11	**1** 2 3 **4** 5 6 7 8 9 **10**	1 **2** 3 **4** 5 6 **7** **8** 9 **10**	1 2 3 **4** 5 **6**	**1** **2** 3 **4** **5** **6**
12-13	**1** **2** **3** 4 **5** 6 **7** 8 9 **10**	1 **2** 3 **4** 5 6 **7** 8 9 **10**	1 2 3 4 5 6	1 2 3 4 5 6
14-15	1 **2** 3 **4** **5** 6 7 8 9 **10**	1 2 **3** **4** 5 6 **7** **8** 9 **10**	1 2 3 **4** 5 **6**	**1** 2 3 **4** 5 **6**
16	1 2 **3** 4 **5** 6 **7** 8 9 **10**	1 2 3 **4** 5 6 **7** **8** 9 10	1 2 3 4 5 6	1 2 3 4 5 6
17	**1** 2 **3** **4** 5 6 **7** 8 **9** **10**	**1** **2** 3 **4** **5** 6 **7** 8 9 **10**	1 2 3 **4** 5 **6**	1 2 3 4 5 6
18-19	1 2 3 4 5 6 **7** 8 **9** **10**	**1** **2** 3 **4** 5 **6** **7** **8** 9 **10**	1 2 3 4 5 **6**	**1** 2 3 **4** **5** **6**
20	**1** **2** **3** **4** 5 6 **7** **8** **9** **10**	1 **2** 3 **4** 5 **6** **7** **8** **9** **10**	1 2 3 4 **5** **6**	**1** 2 3 **4** **5** **6**
21	**1** 2 **3** **4** 5 6 7 **8** 9 **10**	**1** **2** 3 **4** 5 6 7 **8** 9 **10**	1 2 3 **4** **5** **6**	1 2 3 4 5 6
22	**1** 2 3 **4** 5 6 7 8 9 **10**	**1** **2** 3 **4** **5** 6 **7** **8** **9** **10**	1 2 3 **4** 5 **6**	**1** **2** 3 **4** **5** **6**
23	1 2 3 **4** 5 6 7 8 9 **10**	1 2 3 **4** 5 6 7 8 9 10	1 2 3 **4** 5 **6**	1 2 3 4 5 6
COMPLETE BOOK	**1** **2** **3** **4** **5** **6** **7** **8** **9** **10**	**1** **2** **3** **4** **5** **6** **7** **8** **9** **10**	1 2 3 **4** **5** **6**	**1** **2** 3 **4** **5** **6**

For the complete Common Core standard identifier, combine your grade + "." + letter code above + "." + number code above.

In addition to the correlations indicated here, the activities may be adapted or expanded to align to additional standards and to meet the diverse needs of your unique students!